THE LUBITSCH TOUCH

Ernst Lubitch

The Lubitsch Touch

A CRITICAL STUDY

by Herman G. Weinberg

 New York   1968

E. P. DUTTON & CO., INC.

Grateful acknowledgment is made to the following for permission
to reprint copyright material:

S. N. Behrman: Excerpt from his article
"You Can't Release Dante's 'Inferno' in the Summertime"
in *The New York Times Magazine* of July 17, 1966.
Copyright © 1966 by The New York Times Company.
Reprinted by permission.

For Gretchen and Nicola

"Ah, the smell of art—the lovely smell of art!"

—POLLIKOFF in Ben Hecht's
Specter of the Rose.

Acknowledgments

So vital a part of this book is the product of pure research of a kind obtainable only in the far-flung corners of the world that, were it not for the zeal with which friends applied themselves in tracking down even the most minute details, the work in its present form would have been impossible to realize.

In this respect I am indebted most of all to Jay Leyda, who delved into the archives of the Staatliches Filmarchiv der D.D.R. and the Deutsche Kinemathek and brought to light again facts and memorabilia that time had long since consigned to archival darkness.

I am equally indebted to Robert Florey, who drew upon his early experiences with Lubitsch and his own archives of memorabilia, and from whose books about the early Hollywood days I drew to fill in what otherwise would have remained gaps in the full "Lubitsch story."

Heading the list of the film buffs and scholars, the *aficionados*, who also gave generously of their time, their documents, and their enthusiasm, are Andrew McKay and Kirk Bond. And to Cornelia Corson of the Museum of Modern Art Film Department I make a special bow for her invaluable help in making some of the most *recherché* documents of the museum's files available to me. Every film historian should have such a quintet of researchers.

I wish especially to thank Lotte Eisner, that supreme authority on the early German cinema, for answering many questions, and whose writings on this book's subject I invariably consulted. Particularly am I indebted to Samson Raphaelson and Walter Reisch for the interviews they gave me which contain revelations and illuminations never before published and that would, otherwise, have been unobtainable.

Nor must I forget to thank Jean Renoir and René Clair, both of whom responded immediately and with such eloquence to my request for a tribute from them to the master of satirical comedy who would, himself, have been proud to sign such indubitably satiric masterworks as *La Règle de Jeu* and *À Nous la Liberté*.

Grateful acknowledgement is also made to those who so kindly gave me permission to reprint, *in excerpto* or *in extenso*, writings of theirs on Lubitsch or his films that had previously been published, to wit: Seymour Stern, for "So This Is Paris" from *The Greenwich Village Quill*; Condé Nast Publications, for the Jim Tully interview from *Vanity Fair*; Bryher, for "A Note on *Three Women*" by Hanns Sachs from *Close-Up*; *Photoplay Magazine* for Herbert Howe's Berlin interview with Lubitsch; George Pratt of Eastman House for that portion of it reprinted from his valuable book, *Spellbound in Darkness*; Paul Rotha, for "Forbidden Paradise" from his *The Film Till Now*; Dwight Macdonald, for "Trouble in Paradise" from *The Symposium*; The Screen Writers Guild, for "Ernst Lubitsch—A Symposium" from *The Screen Writer*; Penelope Houston, for H. H. Wollenberg's "Lubitsch and Eisenstein" from *Sight & Sound*; *Penguin Film Review* #7 (1948), for Wollenberg's "A Tribute"; Henry Hart, for my own "A Tribute to Lubitsch" from *Films in Review*; *Action!*, The Magazine of the Directors Guild of America, for "A Tribute to Lubitsch 1892–1947"; S. N. Behrman and *The New York Times*, for "Hollywood—'La Grande Époque'" from *The New York Times*; Andrew Sarris, for "Chez Ernst" by Jean-George Auriol from *Cahiers du Cinéma* (English Edition). I wish also to thank those film historians whose works I consulted: Walter S. Bloem's *The Soul of the Moving Picture*, Curt Riess's *Das Gab's Nur Einmal*, Georges Sadoul's *Histoire du Cinéma Mondial, Dictionnaire des Films*, and *Dictionnaire des Cinéastes*, Jean Mitry's *Esthetique et Psychologie du Cinéma* and *Dictionnaire du Cinéma*, Mario Verdone's and Bernard Eisenschitz's monographs on Lubitsch, René Jeanne's and Charles Ford's *Histoire Illustrée du Cinéma*, Vol. 1 (*Le Cinéma Muet*), Ado Kyrou's *Amour-Erotisme et Cinéma*, Éditions Universitaires for their *Dictionnaire du Cinéma*, Siegfried Kracauer's *From Caligari to Hitler*, George A. Huaco's *Sociology of Film Art*, King Vidor's *A Tree Is a Tree*, Heinrich Fraenkel's *Unsterblicher Film*. Nor must I overlook Pem's *Heimweh nach dem Kurfürstendamm*, that many-faceted prism held up to the Berlin of Lubitsch's German period. And I must thank the Museum of Modern Art Film Department, Det Danske Filmmuseum of Copenhagen, and Gerald McDonald for making certain stills available to me, and Paul Falkenberg for his answers to a score of anxious queries.

Also Thomas Robinson of the legal department of Metro-Goldwyn-Mayer, as well as MGM and Loew's, Inc., for authorization to reprint excerpts from the screenplay for *Ninotchka* by Billy Wilder, Charles Brackett, and Walter Reisch, and Dodd, Mead & Co. for permission to reproduce sections of their printed version of it in *The Best Motion Pictures of 1939–40*, edited by Jerry Wald and Richard Macaulay.

Finally there is Nicola Lubitsch, herself, who made certain photos available to me from her private collection that sweetened the whole book.

H.G.W.

Contents

Illustrations

Prologue

It is for the superfluous that we live.
Nothing needs less justification than pleasure.

—BERTHOLD BRECHT

The secret source of humor is not joy but sorrow;
there is no humor in heaven.

—MARK TWAIN

To produce the whole of its effect, the comic
demands something like a momentary anesthesia
of the heart. Its appeal is to the intelligence,
pure and simple.

—HENRI BERGSON

If you want to tell people the truth, you'd better
make them laugh or they'll kill you.

—BERNARD SHAW

A joke is an epitaph on an emotion.

—FRIEDRICH NIETZSCHE

Look for the ridiculous in everything. You will find it.

—JULES RENARD

Life is based on the absurd.

—FYODOR DOSTOEVSKY

A comedian is closer to humanity than a tragedian. He learns not to take himself seriously. A tragedian, thinking always of his noble part, becomes in the end somewhat ignoble. Comedians are much more valuable to the theatre than tragedians. They can do both, and their tragedy, when they do tackle it, has a warmth the tragedian never knows.

—LAURENCE OLIVIER

Comedy offers a more pessimistic world view than tragedy. Comedy deals, after all, with our limitations, not our freedom. It describes our trivial rather than our heroic concerns. But built into the structure of comedy is a reflection of the tragic attitude. Comedy makes "lunacy out of nobility," but the lunacy needs the nobility as a precondition of its own existence, just as a shadow needs an object to produce it.

—H.G.W.

The difference between a lady and a flower girl is not how she behaves, but how she is treated.
—ELIZA DOOLITTLE
in Bernard Shaw's *Pygmalion*

In the films of Lubitsch, women were always treated as ladies. Good manners stood duty as morals.

—H.G.W.

It is not the critic who counts, nor the man who points out how the strong man stumbles—the credit belongs to the man who is actually in the arena.

—MAHATMA GANDHI

There are a thousand ways to point a camera, but really only one.

—ERNST LUBITSCH

Preface

The range of Ernst Lubitsch's art was without parallel on the screen. Comedy, drama, satire, fantasy, tragedy, farce, spectacle—he mastered them all. Yet even such astonishing versatility would not have given his work so wide an appeal had it not been for his *quasi*-Shakespearean concern with people, the multicolored characters who populated and quickened his films. They were a raffish lot, and he delineated them with an acidity that made them as real to us as our closest friends. He subordinated everything to them, frequently even the plots of his films. In a Lubitsch film, the play was not the thing—it was but a device wherewith he could reveal people to us: their petty bickerings, their foibles and weaknesses, vanities, desires, dreams, illusions, in the "human-all-too-human" comedy of life. So it is as a *farceur* that he is best known. Most of the time he was content not to scratch the surface of his characters too deeply but just to show us how thin the veneer of their "respectability" (or "nobility") was. After that, he let them go with a wink or a leer, and we laughed with him, recognizing these all-too-familiar traits in ourselves. It was all good-natured fun, and the world was that much better off for it.

Critics marked his blending of Gallic zest with Attic wit, although it would seem that the culture of Gaul and Hellas were not the wellsprings of his inspiration so much as latter-day Hungary and the Balkans. Lubitsch (a Balkan name) employed a Central European harshness and irony of attack in achieving his effects: it was the repartee of the *mittel-Europa* cafés and clubs, as in the exclusive Budapest club that flourished in the Twenties, with its discreet notice posted in the anteroom: "Members may not bring their mistresses as guests unless they are the wives of other members."

Touché!

"Lubitsch touch!"

THE LUBITSCH TOUCH

The Lubitsch Touch

The Russians have a drink called *kvass*, and at the bottom of the *kvass* is a raisin that adds flavor to the whole. Russian actors used to say, "Find the raisin and the whole bottle is good." Lubitsch always looked for the raisin that would impart flavor to a scene—tang. This special flavor could be said to be like charm in a woman: either she has it or she hasn't, and if she doesn't have it, it doesn't much matter what else she does have. To find the raisin that would enable the audience to savor to the fullest the "taste" of a scene was the quintessence of his method. Did the scene "play" or did it not, was the scene "good" (a favorite expression of his) or was it not? We will return to this many times and in many different ways.

Writing the history of a life, a country, or an art is like taking a long journey in the course of which one passes many wayside stations. Depending on the intellectual curiosity of the traveler, pauses may be made during the itinerary, briefly at some, lingering at others—not digressions but *hommages* paid as at a wayside shrine, for the whole world of art is kin. Thus, even these bypaths off the "main road" have a bearing on the traveler's ultimate destination. They are a part of it. The true traveler encompasses everything he sees along the way.

To understand fully what Lubitsch accomplished one must imagine an American director as having achieved a reputation as the greatest American director, then going to a foreign country like Germany, and soon afterward becoming one of the greatest German directors, as Lubitsch became, soon after his arrival here, one of the greatest American directors. It had never happened before nor is it now, at this late date (and with the dubious course the cinema has now taken), ever likely to happen again. It is a unique case—at least in motion pictures. In the other arts it has happened, as in the case of the American painters Whistler and Mary Cassatt. But not in motion pictures. There is, of course, the example of Alfred Hitchcock, but he did his best work in England and never became an indigenously American director, becoming a hybrid, though a very successful hybrid.

Many are the paths to Parnassus and Lubitsch's journey on his own path was among the most clamorous and exultant. None enjoyed the journey more, save for the single possible exception of Chaplin, nor gave more enjoyment in return.

There were Jews in eighteenth- and nineteenth-century Germany who, despite the already long record of anti-Semitism, managed to achieve the status of *Hofjudentum*—Court Jewry—like the unhappy Süss of Feuchtwanger's historical novel and Mayer Anschel Rothschild. Simon Lubitsch was not one of them. He was a tailor who owned a successful men's clothing shop in Berlin near the Hausvogteiplatzes. To him and his wife a son was born on January 28, 1892, whom they named Ernst, and who was to be their only child. The youth attended the Sophien-Gymnasium where he appeared in school plays, delighting in playing old men's roles to prove that he was a real actor. He also helped out in his father's shop.

At sixteen young Ernst had had enough of school and announced he wanted to become an actor. In his dreams was the theatre, only the theatre. The theatre was a great and glamorous world. The shop was a prosaic little place, the very antithesis of the life he dreamed about. The elder Lubitsch was aghast. "Are you crazy?" he replied. "What will you do in the theatre? That's no serious business. Every day you hear of another theatre manager who has gone bankrupt." He would take Ernst before the store's full-length mirror. "Look," he said. "Look at yourself. And you want to go on the stage? If you were at least handsome—

but with *your* face?" Ernst could not answer. "You'll join the business," Papa Lubitsch concluded. "With me, despite your homely face, you can always earn money." That settled it—at least for the moment. After six month, Simon Lubitsch shook his head sadly. "My son is a real *schlemiehl*. When he hangs up a suit on the rack, five other suits fall down. When he brings a bolt of woolens to show a customer, it unravels and he trips over it, falling on his face." To Ernst he said, "You aren't exactly coordinated, are you, my son?" That wasn't news to the boy. Simon decided to remove this hazard from his shop by making Ernst his bookkeeper.

And then, through friends, young Ernst met Victor Arnold, one of the popular stage comedians of the day, who had already been accepted by the great Max Reinhardt for his theatre. "Well," mused Arnold, "you won't play Romeo, and that's a fact, I'm sorry to say." But Ernst had known that a long time and was weary of hearing it. "Still," Arnold went on, "we can give you a try." Then a double life began for young Ernst. By day he was his father's bookkeeper, and at night he was an actor—in vaudeville, cabarets, music-halls. After a year as a low comedian taking pratfalls between comic sketches in smoke-filled, beer-sodden flea-pits, and studying timing and other niceties of technique with Arnold, he had served his strenuous apprenticeship for the theatre so well that one day Arnold said to him, "Would you like me to introduce you to Reinhardt?" Young Ernst was beside himself with joy. But what if the great Reinhardt took one look at his crooked nose, at his runt-like appearance and disapproved? The next day, at their meeting, Reinhardt recognized something in the ungainly figure before him—he had an instinct for seeing diamonds in the rough, then mining them, polishing them, finally giving them the chance for their talents to flower under his direction, and as a result he had surrounded himself with some of the best actors in Europe: Albert Basserman, Paul Wegener, Emil Jannings, Rudolph Schildkraut, Max Pallenberg, Rudolph Förster, Conrad Veidt, Eugene Klöpfer, Kortner, Moissi, Gründgens, Krauss, Granach, Heinrich George.   *born 1902!*

The year was 1911. Lubitsch was nineteen when he en-

Max Reinhardt in action.

tered the famous Deutsches Theater on the Schumannstrasse where Reinhardt was in command. His first parts were small, to be sure, but sometimes they were fairly respectable parts, and always they were parts in classics or what were to become classics. He played Wagner in *Faust* (Part One) and Famulus in *Faust* (Part Two), the second gravedigger in *Hamlet*, and once even being permitted to undertake a major role, that of the hunchback clown in the pantomime, *Sumurun* (which he was to film a decade later as both the director and star, in the same role). Reinhardt's was a peripatetic theatre, guesting in London, Paris, Vienna. In February of that year, Reinhardt took *Sumurun* to London where a future colleague of Lubitsch's—Alfred Hitchcock—saw him do the clown role at the London Coliseum. (They did not meet, however, until the shooting of *The Loves of Pharaoh* in 1922.) A year later the troupe was again in London, this time with Karl Vollmöller's spectacle, *The Miracle*, during the engagement of which the production was filmed, becoming one of the earliest feature-length motion pictures, although it was, properly, a filmed play rather than a true film.

Reinhardt, himself, didn't think much of the future of the movies, though he was to have a go at it twice in Germany with *Die Insel der Seligen* (The Isle of Happiness) and *Venezianische Liebesnächte* (Venetian Nights of Love). Lubitsch "did" the latter much better in *Trouble in Paradise*. And even Reinhardt's *Midsummer Night's Dream* was far better on the stage in Berlin than it was on the screen in Hollywood. Unquestionably, Reinhardt's forte was the stage, as Lubitsch's was to be the screen. But Lubitsch learned much from him, especially the utilization of masses in large open spaces, as well as the delineation of the small, intimate drama, the *Kammerspiel*.

It is now 1912. Lubitsch is back in Berlin. To augment his meager earnings in the theatre, he worked as an apprentice, property man, assistant, and so forth at the Bioscope film studios there, for motion pictures had already been made for some time in Germany. Though the Berlin theatre was flourishing, the fledgling film industry was still not taken seriously, for it was thought to have no future other than cursory documentation of news events, trick films, the primitive work of Skladanowsky (who had been making films since 1896), slapstick comedies, and the like. But playwrighting, literature, and painting flourished, given impetus by the new art movement called Expressionism, that heightened reality, characterized by its nonobjective use of symbols, purposely stereotyped characters and stylization to give objective expression to inner experience. Wedekind was, perhaps, the archetypical playwright of this movement, as the mystic, Alfred Kubin, was as both novelist and graphic artist, and as Kandinsky, Klee, Feininger, and Franz Marc, among others, were in painting. Indeed, this quartet of painters was part of the nucleus of an offshoot of Expressionism—*Der Blaue Reiter* (The Blue Rider) group—whose headquarters was in Munich. (Marc's *Blue Horses* was to become a well-known symbol of this group.) It was Kubin,[1] however, who perhaps best crystallized the milieu in which Lubitsch entered the world of theatrical fantasy. In his remarkable novel, *Die Andere Seite* (The Other Side), published in 1908, he had evoked the dream city of Perle, a tiny walled kingdom in Central Asia, possibly not too distant from James Hilton's "Lost Horizon," but less sentimental and more allegorical. Four sections divide the city: cheerless, bleak administration buildings where bureaucracy reigns; a luxuriant garden area where the rich reside and disport themselves; the business district, where the middle-class lives; finally, the "French Quarter," with its motley admixture of "Rumanians, Slavs, and Jews." The population included "people of exaggeratedly fine sensibilities . . . in women, hysteria was the most frequent phenomenon . . . the masses also had been selected with an eye to the abnormal or to onesided development: splendid specimens of drunkards, wretches dissatisfied with themselves, political fugitives, blasé characters seeking adventure and old adventurers seek-

[1] It should be recalled that Kubin was the artist whom both Carl Mayer and Hans Janowitz, authors of *The Cabinet of Dr. Caligari*, originally wanted to design the sets for their film, when production on it started in 1919.

ing peace . . . by far the majority of the dreamers were of German birth."

The "Wagnerian" ending of this fantasy city, which was doubtless Berlin in microcosm, foreshadows a film Lubitsch was to make in 1919, *The Oyster Princess*, a satire on *nouveau-riche* Americans. Whereas Lubitsch's millionaire was "the American oyster king," Kubin's is a Chicago meat-packer, and where Lubitsch's "oyster princess" (the hoy-denish daughter of the "oyster king") disrupts a staid old Prussian family of ancient lineage, Kubin's American pro-tagonist disrupts the entire kingdom of Perle by arousing their dormant sense of greed and cynicism.

But it is still 1912, and young Ernst wondered what his future would be. He felt he wasn't progressing fast enough in the theatre; he certainly wasn't earning much. He couldn't live on 100 marks a month. He would like to take a girl out occasionally, he'd like to buy a new suit. Maybe he made a mistake, maybe he should return to his father's shop. There, at least, was security.

Meanwhile the *Kientopp*, what the Germans called their "nickelodeon," was flourishing. From peep shows at fairs to "special attractions" in beer-halls to storefronts hastily converted to approximations of movie theatre facades (with the customers sitting on rows of wooden benches), finally to actual cinema houses, built for that purpose, or at least converted to that purpose, with real seats, a projection booth, and a box office outside in the center of the entrance, so the customers couldn't miss it. It was like this everywhere. A real industry was now burgeoning—not on a very high cul-tural plane, to be sure, but an industry still. People flocked to them, and the need for new films to keep them coming back was crucial to the business. One such entrepreneur (who came from the clothing business, like so many of his Ger-man and American counterparts) was Paul Davidson, a small man with a monocle, who had built over fifty little cinemas in Germany before he decided to become a producer of films to service not only his own chain of theatres but other chains as well, which meant, of course, going into the distribution business.

Heinrich Fraenkel [2] has reminisced over this little Berlin dandy with his ubiquitous monocle ("not without charm, he was," mused Fraenkel) who was given to the same sort of malapropisms later attributed to Samuel Goldwyn, as the time he began a discussion at a board meeting by saying, "Meine Herren, das ist für mich eine *conditio sine Kanone.* . . ." [3] But he *was* the discoverer of both Lubitsch and Pola Negri and later Emil Jannings, and guided all three during his long reign over Union-Film, his producing company ("under Davidson's monocle and Lubitsch's megaphone," as Fraenkel put it), till all three had become world screen personalities.

It is 1913. Lubitsch is approached to enter the movies, not as a handyman, again, but as an actor, a comic. The German screen needed comics. He'd had such experience on the stage, but in the movies? How do you act in the movies? When he was told he'd earn twenty marks *a day*, it was like Clyde Griffiths's first fifty-cent tip as a bellhop, in Dreiser's *An American Tragedy*. Twenty marks *a day*? Done! Lubitsch enters the movies.

For the screen he created a type called "Meyer" or "Moritz," archetypical Jewish names among Germans, in which he was cast as a Jewish comic, a butt of good-natured laughter, like the Cohens and the Kellys and Potash and Perlmutter here of a generation ago, and other ethnic comedy types popularly accepted here like the Amos & Andy Negro, the Chico Marx and Henry Armetta Italian and so forth. Doubtless, though unconsciously, of course, the producers of Lubitsch's German comedies of this *genre* were actuated by the same thing, that indestructible cheerfulness of the Jews, which moved Ernest Renan to say, "When you write of the Jews, make jokes."

The first film was *Meyer auf der Alm* (Meyer on the Alps), directed as far as research can fathom, by one Max Bahr. It can be said to have had the aesthetic of the yodel

---

[2] In *Unsterblicher Film*, Kindler Verlag, Munich, 1956.
[3] This is all but untranslatable. What he's trying to say to the board is, "Gentlemen, a *sine qua non* of the deal is . . ." But the Latin "qua non" becomes "Kanone," the German word for cannon.

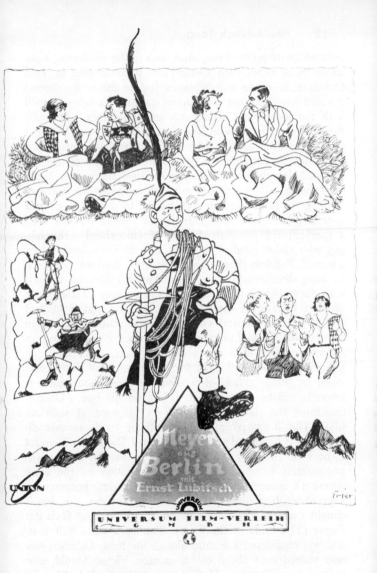

An early poster-ad depicting Lubitsch in one of his popular slap-stick "Meyer" screen roles. (1919)

isolated in its purest form. And who is the producing company? None other than Union-Film, presided over by Paul Davidson, he of the malapropisms, but he also of the shrewd eye and sense of what was happening and, though equipped with the proverbial "little Latin and less Greek," he knew the German bourgeoisie and knew exactly what he was doing. Davidson can be aptly compared with Arthur Mayer, the American entrepreneur who many years later coined the classic, "Nobody ever lost money underestimating the American public." Davidson did not underestimate the German movie-going public and got rich from it by doing the obvious —casting Lubitsch as either the Jewish "Meyer" or "Moritz," a good-natured Bavarian *dummkopf* (blockhead), the fall-guy who makes good at the end. This film was followed by a second, *Fräulein Piccolo* (Miss Piccolo). Bahr was supposed to have directed this one also. Having exhausted himself with these two (which will give you an idea of the range of Herr Bahr), the director then asked his star if he had any ideas for their next comedy. "I was waiting for you to ask me that," said Lubitsch, and proposed a farce about an apprentice clerk in a men's clothing store, who, when he hangs up a suit on a rack, five other suits fall down, and when he brings a bolt of woolens to show a customer, it unravels and he trips over it, falling on his face. "Great!" exclaimed the director. "They'll die laughing at such an idiot! They'll eat it up!" They made it (with another director, as it happened) and it was called *Die Firma Heiratet* (The Firm Marries). So successful was the film that it was immediately followed by another, a variation on the same theme (a country boy who comes to Berlin, becomes an apprentice in a dressmaking concern, marries the boss's daughter and gets half the business). This was *Der Stolz der Firma* (The Pride of the Firm). This opus ran a half hour and was considered a feature film at the time. Lubitsch was now starred even ahead of his mentor, Victor Arnold, also in the cast. Theodore Huff describes this period: "In the first part of Lubitsch's screen career, he acted (and later also directed) a series of short comedies (*lustpiele*), usually laid in a clothing store, and featuring humor of the 'Potash and Perlmutter' type. Lubitsch played a recognizable and representative type—a lively and comic Yiddish clerk who usually won the owner's daughter and half the business. In this series, he became the outstanding German screen comedian, as popular as Max Linder in France, and Harold Lloyd, perhaps even Chaplin, in America, during the same period." [4] Indeed, Chaplin and Lubitsch started their screen careers in the same year, 1914.

One thing should be noted: whereas the Germans accepted and laughed at stock types, like the Jewish comic that Lubitsch played, and were hugely entertained by them, a generation later, whipped into a frenzy by Hitler, they turned against the whole idea of Jewishness in the virulent outbreak of the always dormant anti-Semitism there. This was much like the American public with Chaplin, whom they accepted and laughed at as a comedian, only to turn against him also a generation later when he made *Monsieur Verdoux* and who subsequently became the butt of mass hysteria during the McCarthy period of American history. Chaplin was forced into exile. What would have happened to Lubitsch under the Nazis?

It is July, 1914. A slight flurry had attended that incident at Sarajevo. No one thought anything of it—at least not the general public. The following month, World War I broke out, and the streets of Berlin resounded to the tread of marching feet as mobilization for a two-front war began. Women threw garlands of flowers at the soldiers, toasts of "Nach Paris!" were drunk, and nothing could have been duckier. . . .

But film production, even in the countries at war, went on. Everyone thought it would blow over in a few weeks, at most a few months. It was business as usual. Besides, the Allied blockade of Germany cut off the supply of films from abroad, which provided the stimulus for developing a film industry at home. The philosophy of the time (if "philosophy" is the word for it) was that of the heady attitude in the lyric from *Die Fledermaus:*

[4] *An Index to the Films of Ernst Lubitsch* (British Film Institute), January, 1947.

Glücklich ist
Wer vergisst
Was doch nicht zu ändern ist.[5]

Despite the success of *Der Stolz der Firma*, Lubitsch's career came to a halt. No one could write any more scripts for the character he had invented. They had run out of ideas. "If I wanted to continue," Lubitsch said, "I'd have to write my own parts. With a friend, the actor Erich Schonfelder, I wrote a series of comedies, one reel each, for Union-Film, to whom I sold them as author-star-director. They were getting a bargain—three for the price of one. That's how I became a director. If my career as an actor had not stopped so suddenly at that time, I wonder if I would ever have become a director."

Lubitsch's next film was thus his first effort as a director, *Fräulein Seifenschaum* (Miss Soapsuds), which he wrote and also starred in. The heroine was a lady barber (because of the war there was an actual shortage of male barbers in Germany), and when her clients got fresh with her she would let them have a mess of lather in the face. That's all there was to the plot. The repetitions of this single gag didn't faze the audience; they all but died laughing each time. During its filming, Lubitsch asked Davidson for six-and-a-half marks extra so he could buy a secondhand top hat from a coachman so that one of the lady barber's clients would be nattily accoutered in a top hat when he got a splotch of lather in his mush. Lubitsch justified the extra expense by telling Davidson it would be more hilarious that way. Years later, riding the crest of his success in Hollywood, he would invariably ask his scenarists during the writing of a scene, "Is it hilahrious? It must be hilahrious!" [6] Before he got through with them (he invariably collaborated on all his scripts), it was.

He made a total of seven slapstick comedies that year. In 1915, while the German army on the Western front was locked in a death grip with the French army in the arma-

---

[5] "Happy is he who forgets what cannot be changed."
[6] This is an approximation of how Lubitsch pronounced the word.

Lubitsch (left) sometimes alternated his *"dumkopf"*-Meyer roles with "soigné" characterizations as a "man-about-town," as in *Shoe Salon Pinkus* (1916), his first directorial collaboration with scenarist Hans Kräly, with whom he was to do so many memorable films.

geddon at Verdun, he made four. By now he was directing most of his own films. In 1916, he made six. In 1917, he made four more. But for a long time, now, he hadn't really been happy. He had entered the world of the theatre to play Shakespeare, Schiller, Kleist, and Goethe. Now he was just a clown, and not even in the theatre. The only consolation was that he was earning money, a thousand marks a month. He thought he'd start his own producing company, which would at least give him status. He worked hard at it, invested everything, but it didn't go, and soon he was broke again. But out of it all, out of even being a *bajazzo*, he learned many things: he learned how to refine his technique, as both actor and director, and above all, he learned about life. At twenty-four, disillusioned but not bitter, he was on the threshold of that special quality in his art that was to make him world famous as a director—he had come to recognize the dramatic virtue of irony.

He went back to Davidson. Now he was directing all his own comedies and, sometimes, still starring (or playing secondary roles) in them. Nights he appeared at the Apollo Theater in Berlin in topical skits and singing popular songs in close harmony. After the show, he'd go to his *Stammtisch* at Mutter Maentz's, a café hangout for theatre and film folk near the Kurfürstendamm, where the deeply carved hieroglyphic of his Hebraic face with its crooked nose and twinkling eyes (which Ben Hecht was to find tragic years later), made him a cherished person among his old cronies, whom he would regale till dawn with his wit and *echt*-Berlin humor. Like Pascin, who used to sit at Paris cafés with friends and amuse them by drawing quick, acidulous sketches of what various women passing by looked like under their clothes, Lubitsch would likewise amuse his friends by "casting" them, or other habitués of the place, as crooks, blackmailers, and the like for hypothetical scenarios. How they laughed, and how unerringly true his casting was!

His subsequent reputation as a great joker is rooted in this period. It can even be said to mark the beginning of what was to become world famous as "the Lubitsch touch." This sharp-edged kidding and roguish horseplay was typical of Lubitsch wherever he happened to be. For instance, he took huge amusement—he who was so gentle with his players as a director—in roaring at his actresses whenever visitors were permitted on the set "to see how a big director worked."

There was a Polish actress in Berlin, Apollina Chalupec, who had Hungarian ancestors and some gypsy blood too. Reinhardt had seen her dance in Warsaw in the pantomime, *Sumurun*, was struck by her temperament, and brought her to Berlin to appear in his own production of that show. Davidson saw her in it, was highly impressed, and was introduced to her by Reinhardt. He broached the subject of her appearing in films. She had previously appeared in but one film, *Liebe und Leidenschaft* (Love and Passion), an autobiographical scenario she wrote at seventeen and directed herself. It was such a disaster that it bankrupted its producer. Davidson's instinct was better than her performance in that film (released as *Slave of Sin*), and he next approached Lubitsch to do a serious film with her, an idea Lubitsch immediately rejected, saying that the public would never accept him in a serious role. "Not as an actor, as the director," said Davidson. "Nothing doing," answered Lubitsch. "Once the public sees the name 'Lubitsch' outside a theatre they expect a comedy. It's not for me." Davidson then slyly called Apollina. "Sorry," he said. "I had just the perfect director for you but he refuses." "He *what??*" she hurled back, incredulously. "Who dares refuse to direct Pola Negri?" "Who's Pola Negri?" asked Davidson. "Me!" she answered. "It's my new name, like it?" "Great," said Davidson. "What's the name of that director who has the gall to reject me?" "Ernst Lubitsch," said Davidson, convinced he had played his trump card.

She was indeed a very persuasive woman. Reinhardt was right about her temperament. She and Lubitsch made the film, *Vendetta*, says Curt Riess, not exactly an artistic triumph but a commercial success. Above all, it established Negri on the German screen. She knew she had Lubitsch to thank for that. Davidson, seeing the possibility of a new genre of film for Lubitsch—the serious drama—decided on an immediate follow-up, *Die Augen der Mummie Ma* (The Eyes of the Mummy Ma), about an Egyptian religious fanatic who pursues a woman, who has attracted him, to the ends of the earth and eventually destroys her. Very lurid it was, very "Egyptian-exotic," but it had elements of authentic tragedy on the theme of obsessive love. Again Lubitsch resisted at first, finally succumbing to Davidson's blandishments. Emil Jannings played the wild-eyed, dark-skinned Egyptian, and Negri was the unhappy object of his passion. It was the first screen work the German press took seriously.

The war was over. Devastated by a crushing defeat, the streets of Berlin swarmed with beggars, prostitutes, and war-maimed soldiers. On the heels of skyrocketing inflation, black-marketeering was rife. Cold, hungry, and miserable, the

once proud and arrogant city lay prostrate after four years
of carnage. Yet in this miasma the arts flourished: the com-
passionate art of Käthe Kollwicz, Max Beckmann, and Heinrich Zille, the bitter art of Georg Grosz and Otto Dix, the
nihilism of Dada, the frenzy of Expressionism.[7] Profiteers
flourished, making merry nightly in the *lokals* to the blaring
of American *Neger Jazz*, guzzling black-market champagne
at astronomical prices, and flocking to *Die Fledermaus* to
revel in its hedonistic songs that neither wars nor the back-
wash of wars could stop:

> They say that if you drink up,
> Your span of life will shrink up;
> I'll gladly pay the Piper,
> If Heidsick is the Piper . . .

Johann Strauss's Eternal Spring . . .

"Cocaine? Naked girls? Morphine dancers?" Every dead-
fall, lean-to, alley, corner, shadow, place of assignation, or
maison de rendezvous had its denizens who offered "sur-
cease" from too much or too little or just from the con-
fusion of what to do with the intoxication of the war's end.
Postwar Berlin was the cocaine center of Europe, and often,
for the desperate, the cocaine turned out to be either synthetic or just potato meal or even ground chalk, simulating
the magical white "snow." A characteristic joke of the time
told of a man left so bereft by the war that he decided to
hang himself. He bought a rope, but since it was synthetic,
it broke and he fell harmlessly to the floor. Taking this as
a sign from heaven that he should live, he went into a café
for some coffee. But since the coffee, too, was synthetic, it
made him ill and he died.

Also, pros't, mein Lieber!

So they drank up and then went to esoteric clubs and
cabarets (Berlin had the most degenerate dives in Europe,

---

[7] Erich Pommer had a prosaic explanation for German film Expressionism, e.g., as a way of competing with Hollywood with
something new. But in all the other arts the movement was rooted
in the trenches at Verdun and elsewhere. Piscator described this,
for instance, as the beginning of his Epic Theatre, precursor of the
Theatre of Brecht.

from the most deluxe to such baneful swamps as would have astonished Dante)—dives like "The White Mouse" on the Jägerstrasse where they showed pornographic and semi-pornographic films to a clientele that could purchase black domino masks from the cloakroom attendant which they wore during these seances so they wouldn't be "recognized." *Sittenfilme* (morality films) they were called, to give them a pseudo-scientific aura.

But the arts flourished and were even in ferment . . . new expressions were being formed; the old way of doing things had outlived its usefulness—in literature, music, painting, the drama . . .[8]

And the motion pictures . . .

Come hell or high water, as they say, the public had to be entertained, and motion pictures were the entertainment of the masses. During the day there were street fights, hunger riots, and revolutionary outbreaks among the sailors (six weeks after the Armistice the German fleet mutinied, followed by Bolshevik uprisings in Kiel and Hamburg), workmen, fishermen, and the unemployed—all invariably beaten down by the police in bloody riots; in the daytime the Spartacists, emulating their ancient Roman forebears, the slaves under Spartacus, rose up against the Social Democrats of the Weimar Republic under Ebert and were massacred together with their leaders, the indomitable Rosa Luxembourg and Karl Liebknecht. But at night everybody flocked to the movies, at least those who couldn't afford seats for *Die Fledermaus* or the classical theatre of Reinhardt. What matter that ex-General Ludendorff, considered by most to be one of Germany's arch war criminals, somehow was still around (the Kaiser had long since fled to Holland) demanding that the big Ufa studios be the instrument to piece together again the *Kaiserreich*—like Humpty-Dumpty after the great fall—by producing propaganda films to strengthen the people's morale at home and to sell Germany and the German ethos abroad? The half of Ufa owned by the

[8] For a vividly detailed account of this ferment, and how the German film was affected by it, read George Huaco's *The Sociology of Film Art* (Basic Books), 1965.

government was bought back by private interests; and now the Deutsche Bank owned the majority of stock of the great studio complex. Four days later the Minister of Finance washed his hands of the whole matter and declared that the government would have nothing more to do with Ufa.

So much the better. People flocked to the movies to forget their miseries—good; Davidson, and his fellow producers would give them films to help them forget. Besides, impoverished by the war, the country's first bid to rebuild her economy was to revitalize her export market to earn dollars and pounds sterling abroad, to earn hard currency that still had value, and to compete with Hollywood's film industry, now that the war had virtually wiped out the French film industry.

That some of these postwar films happened to be good was, at least at first, only incidental (and almost beside the point), since from its inception the cinema never pretended to be an art—that developed through the stubborn will of scattered artists who happened to be working in the medium. And in this connection, an observation made by an American critic many years later, is interesting: "It is curious," wrote Otis Ferguson, "that at a time when the movies were struggling to attain some sort of form, and no one was sure or even cared much that anything worthwhile would ever come out of them, there were those who knew that they wanted to do just that."

By what prescience?

Anyway, Lubitsch was one of them. Méliès and Feuillade in France were two others in 1918, Guazzoni and Pastrone in Italy, Seastrom and Stiller in Sweden, Protozanov, Meyerhold, Vertov, and Kuleshov in Russia—and, of course, Chaplin, Griffith, and Mack Sennett in America. They were the first film notables. This was the hierarchy of the film world when Lubitsch embarked on the direction of *Carmen*. It had not been easy for Davidson to broach the subject to him. Besides, hadn't it already been filmed ten times (by actual count)? The Bizet–Mérimée work was even then a hardy perennial of the stage, screen, and opera. You "couldn't miss" with *Carmen*. "Besides," said Davidson to his star

director, "what a role for Negri," recalling her raven hair,
flashing eyes, and seductive smile that could turn a saint
from his vows.

"Are you starting up with that temperamental Polish
witch again?" stormed Lubitsch. "*Nee, nee, ausgeschlossen*—
that's not for Papa Simon's son!"

Finally he declared he'd listen to the proposal but only
for the length of five cigars—not one puff longer.

After the third cigar (it had already become part of his
physiognomy, that ubiquitous cigar), he spoke his first word,
"Carmen . . ."—as if savoring all that the word implied.
This was followed by two minutes of heavy silence. In two
minutes more he was soon in a heated discussion with his
scenarist, Hans Kräly, as to how the role should be characterized. With this film, Lubitsch's first big personal success
internationally, he really put the German cinema on the
map. It was the first distinctive German film, and was voted
the best German film of 1918. Three years later it was
shown in America (as *Gypsy Blood*) and was also a hit there
with both the critics and the public. Three years before, in
1915, De Mille had also made *Carmen*, as his first bid for
international fame, starring Geraldine Farrar and Lou Tellegen in the Carmen–Don José roles (played by Negri and
Harry Leidtke in Lubitsch's film). Under the title of *Das
Weib und der Hampelmann* (Woman and Puppet) it was
mercilessly derided in Berlin. Farrar, perhaps because of
tender memories of her great romance with the German
Crown Prince, was tolerated, but Lou Tellegen was torn
apart.[9]

After *Carmen*, Pola Negri was hailed as "Germany's foremost screen actress." Years later she said that she owed it
all to Lubitsch, since the film was made under heart-breaking
difficulties with pitifully little resources at an excruciatingly
unhappy time for Berliners, at a time when it was an
achievement just to survive, let alone to achieve distinctive
work in the arts. Lubitsch told the story in flashback, as
Mérimée had (the "frame" scenes of a gypsy encampment

[9] Chaplin's *Burlesque on Carmen*, also made in 1915, was much
better.

ABOVE: Lubitsch's first international screen hit, *Carmen* (1918), with Pola Negri and Harry Liedtke (as Don José), in which Negri was not the glamorous gipsy siren of Bizet's opera but the low-down earthy slattern of Mérimée's original. BELOW: Lubitsch's next hit and his first satirical feature was *The Oyster Princess* (1919). (Julius Falkenstein, left, and Ossi Oswalda, as the hoydenish "princess," right.)

at night were hand tinted, an innovation at the time). The sets were highly evocative of nineteenth-century Seville, the streets and corners of the Spanish town being cleverly conjured up with the barest means. Realistically dirty gypsy hovels, wild craggy *sierras* through which the smugglers passed, the seething waterfront at Gibraltar (especially striking in its composition): it was all there, done on the Ufa backlot at Neu Babelsberg (The New City of Babel—an apt name for a film studio location that brought the four corners of the earth to this one place). The close-up was used most tellingly, as was the moving camera (also still an innovation at that early date).

"The war had shocked all Europe into rebellion," wrote Maria-Ley Piscator in her book *The Piscator Experiment*— "not only political, but ethical, social, and esthetic." The Russians didn't even wait for the war to end before they had their own upheaval during the October days of 1917. The young Eisenstein was then at the Eastern front where he did propaganda on agit-trains. When the war ended for Russia, he went to the factories where he staged plays of social protest in their actual settings or on the stage of the Proletcult Theatre, as in his staging of Pletnyov's production of Jack London's *The Mexican* for which he designed the constructivist [10] settings. He was yet to make his first film, though Vertov and Tissé had been turning out *Kino Eye* and *Kino Pravda*, newsreel compilations documenting the new Soviet world. "The 'Kinodrama' is opium for the people," wrote Vertov in *Lef & Novy Lef*. "The 'Kinodrama' and Religion are deadly weapons in the hands of the capitalists. The scenario is a tale thought up by literary people. Down with the bourgeois tales—the scenario! Hurrah for life as it is!"

Eisenstein, as noted, was yet to do his first film, a 200-meter parody of Vertov's *Kino Eye* (the camera as all-seeing eye), which he was to make for his staging of Ostrovsky's

[10] Constructivism was the Soviet art movement born of the general postwar ferment whose positivism challenged the despair of German Expressionism. Its founders were Malevitch, El Lissitsky, Naum Gabo, and Pevsner.

Enough Simplicity in Every Wise Man, a frothy comedy-satire. Eisenstein (like Lubitsch) was always the great kidder, right from the start. Griffith, who lacked the vital element of humor, had shown his dour reaction to the war that year with *Hearts of the World*, and Chaplin revealed his reaction in the corrosively humorous *Shoulder Arms*. Stroheim made an auspicious debut as author-actor-director with *Blind Husbands*.

1918 was, indeed, quite a year for the fledgling cinema. And Lubitsch? He had turned out another batch of comedies to keep his franchise in this *genre*. Then came a major comedy, a satire called *The Oyster Princess* (1919), about a "dollar princess" (*vide* Leo Fall's popular operetta of that name) and her millionaire father, the American "oyster king," who invade an old aristocratic Prussian family in an attempt to buy a title for the daughter by a fortuitous marriage. All Europe was gaga about things American, for America was where the machine had triumphed, making possible undreamed-of luxuries; anything American was the best and most sophisticated, anything was possible in America, there being no caste system; besides, didn't America prove how rich and powerful she was with her youthful strength (Europe was old and tired), by winning the war for the Allies in a few months? But all this made America a juicy subject for satire, too, and this was the *raison d'être* of the film. Nor did Lubitsch spare the blue-blooded Prussian aristocrats. They had the same "exaggeratedly fine sensibilities" of the upper classes of Alfred Kubin's "mythical" city of Perle, and were given to the same outbursts of hysteria. The title role was played by Ossi Oswalda, a gamine type, "the Mary Pickford of Germany," as she was popularly known. Thus, consciously or not, he was obeying one of the first laws of dramaturgy. You do not set up a straw man and then knock him down. You must be able to take as well as give, to have the capacity to laugh at one's self before laughing at others. In this way characters become lifelike and believable. Aristophanes knew it, and every great comic master and many great masters of tragedy knew it. It is the leavening in the bread of the art of dramaturgy. And when dramaturgy became cinematography, this prime law remained unchanged, as it will always remain unchanged.

The Oyster Princess was a summing up of everything Lubitsch had learned about the art of comedy. It foreshadowed the method he was to use to such scintillating effect in Hollywood. Even when much later he kidded the Russians and their "brave new world" in *Ninotchka*, he gave the Russians lines just as good and incisive as he gave their French seducers. In *The Oyster Princess* we find details of its satire that have since become known as "the Lubitsch touch." In its broadest sense, this meant going from the general to the particular, suddenly condensing into one swift, deft moment the crystallization of a scene or even the entire theme. The close-up, of course, played an important part in this (now far more advanced than that historic early close-up of Mae Marsh's nervous hands in the trial scene of Griffith's *Intolerance* three years before) by magnifying a detail whose virtue was its laconic wit. "Your goal?" asked Alfred Kerr,[11] many years later apropos the art of dramaturgy, and answered: "The briefer!" This idea was new to the cinema and Lubitsch was certainly its earliest practitioner. Spontaneously (perhaps even unconsciously at first) he had arrived at the idea of utilizing the power of the metaphor by suddenly compressing the quintessence of his subject in a sly *comment*—a visual comment, naturally—that said it all. For this, one had to have a subtle sense of humor, where comedy was concerned, and a definite *Weltanschauung*, or world view, a point of view, an attitude. Not only does the director isolate a moment of his *mise-en-scène* for emphasis, he also makes a personal statement at the same time. That Lubitsch had chosen comedy (and slapstick, at that) as his initial *forte* was, of course, part of it. There is a moment in every day in which we are all ridiculous. Or the contretemps of a moment is ridiculous. No one sees this more quickly or more sharply than the comedian, or the writer or director of comedy. So ingrained is this marvelous sense of the ridiculous in the true dramaturgist, whatever his own *Weltanschauung* may be (and, in truth, whatever his medium),

[11] A noted Berlin drama critic of the Twenties.

that we find sardonic glints similar to "Lubitsch touches" even in the somber works of Sternberg, Stroheim, Eisenstein, and Pudovkin, to name a high-echelon quartet that comes first to mind.[12]

And what was the "Lubitsch touch," *au fond*, but the raisin at the bottom of a bottle of *kvass*? It permeated his whole work, once he had found it, not just individual scenes. And there were discernible types of "Lubitsch touches": the "Freudian slip," or unconscious action (Pauline Frederick playing with Lew Cody's tie in *Three Women*); the conscious action (Ronald Colman as Lord Darlington in *Lady Windermere's Fan* moving Mrs. Erlynne's letter closer to Lord Windermere, who blindly reaches for it behind his back to keep it unseen by Lady Windermere); the metaphorical action, where Maurice Chevalier in *The Smiling Lieutenant* tries to amuse the prim princess (Miriam Hopkins) by playing checkers and, being bored by it as she is, suddenly throws the checkerboard on the bed—to continue "playing" there; the symbolic action, where Marie Prevost contemptuously flings off the scarf that Monte Blue had solicitously placed about her shoulders to protect her from the chill night air in the garden, for she is trembling with warmth for him, not from the night air's chill, in *The Marriage Circle*; the Freudian dream in which the action is depersonalized, as in the episode of Monte Blue's nightmare of the cane that taunts him, in *So This Is Paris*; the sound track that makes expressive whispered dialogue we do not hear, such as the brief snatch of *sotto voce* Oriental coochdance music while Herbert Marshall describes the delights of Constantinople into Edward Everett Horton's ear, in *Trouble in Paradise*; or the sound track used in roguish counterpoint

---

[12] Others certainly were Murnau, Pabst, Vidor, Buñuel, and Renoir—through whose work, like the quartet previously named, mordant humor flashes like heat-lightning. Such masters of *sangfroid* as René Clair and Preston Sturges certainly owed much to Lubitsch (and Chaplin). Before them, that veritable pleiades of Lubitsch disciples, Malcolm St. Clair, H. d'Abbadie d'Arrast, Monta Bell, the early Lewis Milestone, Richard Rosson, Roy del Ruth (in *Wolf's Clothing*) and Erle Kenton (in *Other Women's Husbands*), showed that they had learned their Lubitsch lesson well.

to the image, as when the garbage collector in his gondola pushes off for his next collection 'neath a romantic Venetian moon and suddenly bursts into heartfelt song with "*O sole mio . . .!*"—also in that endless epiphany of delights, *Trouble in Paradise*. These are just a few instances, of course, but they show what varied forms the Lubitsch touch could take. One quality all had in common, however (with the exception of the example cited from *Three Women*, which is strictly psychoanalytical), was mockery, always in its salutary sense, never its impertinent one (he had too much sensibility for that); anti-sentimental, to be sure, because nothing made Lubitsch laugh more than the "merry-go-round" men and women play in the "sex game," though he did have sentiment, which is a different thing.

The year is now 1919. Fritz Lang has emerged as a director, as has Murnau. In America Griffith has enchanted filmgoers and the critics with *Broken Blossoms*, while in the newly established U.S.S.R. Lenin has nationalized the film industry, proclaiming on September 19th of that year that the cinema was the art most vital to the new Soviet nation, and a state school for cinematography was established.

Lubitsch, with the success of *The Oyster Princess* behind him, next tried a serious film called *Rausch* (Intoxication), from Strindberg's *There Are Crimes and Crimes*, starring Asta Nielsen. Little is known of it, but Strindberg was a long way from *Meyer auf der Alm* and its yodel humor.

And then came *Madame Dubarry* . . .

At a time when Germany was still smarting from her defeat by the Allies, the suggestion of making a film dealing with French history, which the producers hoped would be shown and received in France, as, indeed, everywhere in the world market, was thought a ridiculous idea by the backers. Besides, for a full-scale spectacle like that, money was needed, and lots of it, and lots of *matériel*, and things were still bad: there was no coal to heat the studios, little electricity, everyone was hungry. What a time to make what Davidson said would be "the greatest film of all time!" Negri, of course, was to play Dubarry and Lubitsch would be the director. Eduard von Winterstein was to be Louis XV.

But Emil Jannings had obtained a copy of the script and felt the role was for him. He had made a reputation of sorts under Reinhardt at the Deutsches Theater, but thus far had made little mark on the screen. Lubitsch shook his head at the idea. "You're a good actor, Emil," he said, "but a king you're not. A king is an aristocrat, understand? Look at yourself—you don't look like an aristocrat." "I am an actor!" declared Jannings, "and if I don't play this part, I'm through with films! If I can't play parts that I don't look like, then I shouldn't even be on the stage—I chose the wrong profession!" "But Monsieur Dubarry is a good part, too," said Lubitsch. "And you'll play more good parts for me in the future." "I play the king or I'll never play for you again!" exclaimed Jannings, flushed and shaken. "Don't be a *dummkopf*, the role's not for you," insisted Lubitsch. "Try me," pleaded Jannings, "let me do a short scene and if you don't like it you can give it to anyone you want." Lubitsch, remembering how Victor Arnold once gave him "a try" when he desperately wanted it, agreed. Jannings, ecstatic, made up for the part: powdered wig, lorgnette, satin breeches and velvet coat, ruffled shirt, delicate lace emerging from his sleeves, a jeweled decoration at his throat and another jeweled starburst at his lower left side, silver buckles on his slippers, gleaming white silk hose, elaborate rings on the fingers of both hands—in short, the works. Best of all was the way he carried himself perfectly as *le Bien-Aimé*. Despite his bulk (anyway, Louis XV *was* corpulent) he comported himself with elegance, grace, and distinction, bringing his lorgnette up to an eye to give one of the pretty court ladies a meaningful "once-over," accompanied by a smile that promised a rosy future for her, nodding slightly to a favored courtier or "old flame"—in short, the perfect picture of a decadent monarch, sure of himself and enjoying his high station as the king and, behind the king, a man, and an all-too-human being.

In the darkened projection room, only Lubitsch and Jannings are present. They are viewing the rushes of Janning's test scene. The director is silent. Jannings sees only the glow of his cigar. Lubitsch hasn't said a word. The test is over, the lights go up. "All right," says Jannings, who can't stand the suspense any longer. "If you don't like it, say so. . . ." Lubitsch removes the cigar. "*Quatsch!* What do you mean, if I don't like it? The part is yours, naturally. I was just thinking about rewriting the script to make the part of Louis XV bigger. And I've also been thinking what you and I should do together next." (Winterstein got the part of Monsieur Dubarry.)

When Lubitsch asked for 250 extras, the front office thought he had suddenly lost his mind. He would bankrupt the studio. Davidson backed him up. "He can have 350—as many as he wants!" Before he was through, Lubitsch had engaged over 2000 extras. Joe May also filled his screen with milling extras for his "monumental" films (*Veritas Vincit, The Indian Tombstone, The Mistress of the World*) and so had the Italians in their operatic spectacles, *Cabiria, Quo Vadis, The Last Days of Pompeii*, and the like, but they remained just milling extras. With Lubitsch a scene with 250 extras became a scene with 250 human beings. Having observed Reinhardt exploding a stage with life in *Oedipus Rex* or *Wallenstein*, he remembered how you imbue the individuals of a crowd with passion. His people of Paris were really hungry, they really wanted to tear down the Bastille and free its innocent victims from the system that had brought them to hunger and desperation. Even the defenders of the king were men with a deep loyalty to their monarch and thus would die to save him if necessary. His sets evoked the Paris of the *ancien régime*: the streets and byways, the parks and gardens, the grim Bastille, and the rococo elegance of Versailles. How did Lubitsch accomplish all this with the paltry means at his disposal?

On September 18, 1919, *Madame Dubarry* had its world première at Ufa's flagship theatre, the luxurious Ufa-Palast Am Zoo, a 2000-seat house second to none in Paris, London, or New York—built less than a year after the war's disastrous end. A specially written musical score accompanied the film, played by a full symphony orchestra. The film ran for two hours and fifteen minutes including an intermission. At its conclusion, the enthusiasm of the audience broke like a

ABOVE: Then came the epochal *Madame Dubarry*. Here the Comtesse Dubarry is presented at court and meets her next conquest, Louis XV. Emil Jannings and Pola Negri starred. (1919) BELOW: The next stage in the heady rise of the erstwhile *midinette*, as mistress of the king. She will end on the guillotine. (*Madame Dubarry*.)

storm—for Lubitsch, for Negri, for Jannings. The press was as enthusiastic, save for the Leftist press. They accused the film of betraying the French Revolution, saying that the revolution was made to appear the result of a private matter between Louis XV and his mistress, La Dubarry. In any case, Lubitsch's purpose was not to show the spiritual antecedents of the French Revolution, as in Beaumarchais's *The Marriage of Figaro* or in the social tracts of Jean-Jacques Rousseau, but to tell the story of the little *midinette* who became the mistress of Louis XV at a time of great social ferment, and how forces that she knew nothing about eventually destroyed her.

The film, a milestone in the artistic development of the screen, ran for three months to packed houses at the Ufa-Palast Am Zoo, followed by engagements at the Ufa chain of theatres throughout Germany, then on to Vienna, Zurich, Paris, London, and finally to New York. In New York, where Wagner's operas still had to be sung in English because anti-German feeling still ran high at the war's end, the film, under the title *Passion*, was advertised as "a European spectacle" with Pola Negri, "the famous Continental star." Lubitsch's and Jannings's names didn't even appear on the film. Not the slightest indication was given that the picture had anything to do with Germans or Germany, on the screen or in the press. First National, which bought the film for only $40,000 for the U.S. after it had been rejected by every other American company, was fearful of the anti-German boycott and determined to protect its investment by hoodwinking the American public. They were glad to be hoodwinked, as it happened, for *Passion* was a rousing success not only at the immense Capitol Theatre, New York's own counterpart to the Ufa-Palast Am Zoo, but all over the U.S. When the true origin of *Passion* finally became known, sophisticated New York took it in its stride, but in Los Angeles some alarmed film people and organizations like the American Legion made a *shtunk* and tried to force it off the screen, as they did with *The Cabinet of Dr. Caligari*, that black flower of postwar German Expressionism made the same year.

It is symptomatic of the hysteria of the time that even so staid a journal as *The New York Times* said in its issue of December 12, 1920: "The origin of *Passion* is to be excused because its star is a Pole and its subject matter is French."

A year later, when passions cooled down, somewhat, over *Passion*, the *Times* reported (January 30, 1921): "The apparently Teutonic Lubitsch must have worked in Paris or under French influence at some time because he is not 'heavy.'"

With *Madame Dubarry*, Lubitsch became the great "humanizer" of history on the screen. And what if he used history as a background for boudoir intrigue? In an era when history was being debunked (*vide* the several works of Lytton Strachey in this *genre*), these films were regarded as legitimate "humanizers" of history. Who will say with authority to what degree Napoleon's love life (not to mention his digestive problems) did not instigate decisions that were subsequently thrashed out on the battlefield? *Madame Dubarry* was also the first film to depict the French Revolution. Griffith's *Orphans of the Storm* came out three years later.

What mattered was that screen history was being made. The acting in *Madame Dubarry* was excellent even in the smallest parts, as in the subtle playing by Reinhold Schünzel as the crafty Choiseul. The use of the masked screen and vignettes betokened a cinematic literacy—film "punctuation"—that made many other films of the time appear analphabetic by comparison. Always excepting Griffith, there was nothing in America to match Lubitsch, and Hollywood was worried. Alongside the historical films of Lubitsch, most American films look standardized and rigid. "If you can't beat the enemy, join him" was an old maxim that never was more apropos. Soon Hollywood was to begin enticing these now internationally famous names to its own studios to pump new life-blood into the American film industry.

But that time had not yet come. It is still 1919 and Alfred Hugenberg, chief financial backer of Ufa, encouraged by the success of *Madame Dubarry*, and an avid nationalist, saw in the decadent French court of Louis XV, as delineated in the film, subtle anti-French propaganda. "Good. Let's show up those decadent French! And why not those decadent English?" Why not, indeed? So they found another highly colored subject which would "show up" the Tudors, the very soul of British royal lineage, as deriving from a lascivious king, a "bluebeard" who chopped off his wives' heads every time he saw another pretty face. That would be Henry VIII, of course, and the film was *Anna Boleyn*. But one ex-enemy they steered clear of—America—(*The Oyster Princess* had been made before, without the benefit of Herr Hugenberg's ministrations, not to say his marks). Germany might have to borrow money from America and you don't antagonize a possible creditor, he might not like it. As it turned out, Ufa *did* have to borrow heavily from Paramount and MGM some years later (1926) to keep afloat, so that Ufa became Par-Ufa-Met.

Three major works were to precede *Anna Boleyn*, however, on the Lubitsch agenda. (Of course Lubitsch was to do *Anna Boleyn*. After *Madame Dubarry*, who else?) Before the year's end, *Die Puppe* (The Doll) came out, a fantasy inspired by themes from E. T. A. Hoffmann, from which Offenbach had also drawn for his *Tales of Hoffmann*. Set principally in a doll-maker's *boutique* (a mechanical doll is brought to life and marries the doll-maker's apprentice), utilizing all manner of camera tricks including the split screen, superimposition, high-speed photography, multiple exposures (there is one shot of twelve images of mouths in a single frame), the film was full of droll effects. It is inventive even before the film proper starts by showing Lubitsch, himself, putting together a miniature set (which turns out to be the opening scene with which the film begins)—perhaps the only such opening device in screen annals. Here, too, was "the Lubitsch touch" at work, side by side with the old slapstick of his apprentice days. Amusing, also, were the anticlerical barbs directed at a group of hedonistic monks in a monastery who somehow become involved in the zany proceedings.

From the epic sweep of *Madame Dubarry* to the delicate

fantasy of *Die Puppe* and then to the broad burlesque of
Kölhiesel's Töchter (Kölhiesel's Daughters) Lubitsch proved
by his range that his versatility was second to none in the
film world. A low peasant comedy set in Bavaria (the Bava-
rians are the Neapolitans of Germany)—the scene of his
debut in *Meyer in the Alps*—he wrote *Kölhiesel* together
with Hans Kräly, who by this time was working on all his
scripts and was to follow him to Hollywood—it provided
the very popular new star, Henny Porten, with her most
famous role. Here she played two roles, the pretty Gretl
and homely Liesl, both daughters of the farmer, Kölhiesel.
Jannings (after his success as the debonair Louis XV in *Dubarry*) was wittily cast by Lubitsch as a dull, stupid farmhand, and oafish beer-seller. And he was as good and true in
this part as in the royal role. Jannings was right, he *was* an
actor in the best sense. Subsequently, *Kölhiesel* was remade
as a sound film, again with Henny Porten, due to the great
popularity of the silent version. It was never shown in the
U.S., probably because the humor was considered strictly
local.[13]

Then came Lubitsch's last short film, *Romeo und Julia
im Schnee* (Romeo and Juliet in the Snow), a provincial
farce set in the mountains in which the Montagues and
Capulets are Bavarian peasants.

Lubitsch from now on will only make features, for the
most part big-scale productions.

He was ready now for something he had been waiting a
long time to do. He had played under Reinhardt in the
ballet-pantomime, *Sumurun*, and now he would "do a Reinhardt": he would film it himself and replay his part of
the hunchback clown who hopelessly loves his troupe's
dancer (which Negri would play again). The challenge of
evoking the Arabian Nights on the screen was irresistible.
Lubitsch was doing a screen Arabian Nights for the first time,
as he had already done so many other things on the screen

---

[13] In one of the earliest books on film aesthetics, Walter S. Bloem
in *The Soul of the Moving Pictures* (1924) singles out the performances of Henny Porten in *Kölhiesel's Töchter* and Ossi Oswalda
in *Die Puppe* as examples of what good screen acting should be.

Lubitsch as the hunchback clown in *Sumurun* (1920), hopelessly enamored of the dancer in his troupe who falls victim to an old sheik, who buys her for his harem and kills her out of jealousy. Notable for Lubitsch's performance.

for the first time. And who could play this *pagliaccio* better than he; who understood the heartbreak of this homely little hunchback clown, who adored the beauteous dancer, Yannaia, better than he did? He enjoyed playing the part, he let himself go, even doing things he'd never tolerate from his other players. How he rolled his eyes, how he wrung his hands, how he agonized, how he suffered! He confessed to Pola Negri during the shooting that deep down he always wanted to be a successful actor. Directing was interesting, of course, but acting—ah, that was something else! Should Negri tell him how he was hamming it up as the hunchback? Should anyone tell him? None dared.

The première in 1920, again at the Ufa-Palast Am Zoo, ended in an ovation. Negri and Harry Liedtke, in the two principal roles, took curtain call after curtain call but the house was shouting, "Lubitsch! Lubitsch!" "Go out," said Negri, "they want you." "That's silly," said Lubitsch. "I haven't any such intention . . . didn't you see how bad I was in it? Why didn't you tell me?" "Lubitsch! Lubitsch!" cried the house. And when he finally appeared between Negri and Liedtke before the curtain, the applause doubled, tripled into a deafening thunderstorm, but Lubitsch vowed to himself that never again would he act on the screen. The reviews were great, and when the performances were singled out, Lubitsch was included in the praise for his touching playing of the hunchback clown. Years later, Josef von Sternberg, who had intensely disliked Jannings's performance in Lubitsch's *The Patriot*, praised that of Lubitsch in *Sumurun*, calling it "wonderful." Like all true artists, Lubitsch had taken a risk, with the salutary results that only those who "play for the highest stakes" can know.

Again Lubitsch had shown his inventiveness. For the opening he had the domes of mosques and minarets rising from behind a confluence of hills, a city rising from the desert, toward which a caravan was wending its way. But it was a *trompe-l'oeil*, a camera trick to deceive the eye into thinking it was seeing a real city when, in fact, the domes and minarets were miniatures just a few feet high. Wegener, who that year had produced and played the title role in *The Golem*, stalked, a sinister figure as the tyrannical sheik, through the harem beauties and droll eunuchs of his palace, while to balance the plot's melodrama there was considerable slapstick humor centering around the twin servants of a merchant of the bazaars. Negri was seductive as the dancer and Lubitsch superb as the hunchback clown who, after the death of his beloved at the hands of the jealous sheik, must continue to cavort and laugh to amuse the crowd.

In a sense, *Carmen, The Oyster Princess, Madame Dubarry, The Doll, Kölhiesel's Daughters,* and *Sumurun* were "escapist" pictures, but that's what the public wanted. They did not want to be reminded on the screen of their own miseries. When Piscator established his Proletarian Theatre, the proletarians didn't flock there, they flocked to the farces, fantasies, and highly colored spectacles made by Lubitsch.

And, since financier Hugenberg thought he was "getting even" with France in *Madame Dubarry* by showing up the decadent court of her Bourbon progenitors, he decided to show up the decadent court of the Tudor progenitors of another ex-enemy, England, by backing a film on the rascally Henry VIII. And so *Anna Boleyn* (1920) (called *Deception* in the U.S.) was made with Lubitsch again at the helm, Jannings as the king, and Henny Porten as Boleyn. Although money and *matériel* were still scarce, and inflation, now at its peak, had reduced the populace to desperation, it was "business as usual" in the film studios. On the Tempelhof lot arose Windsor Castle, Hampton Court, the Tower of London, and Westminster Abbey, under the meticulous supervision of the architects, Poelzig and Kurt Richter, against which the pomp and pageantry of that royal era were de-

Aud Egede Nissen, as Jane Seymour, and Emil Jannings as Henry VIII, in a scene from *Deception* (*Anna Boleyn*). A decade before the Korda–Laughton version, Lubitsch and Jannings had already set the prototype for the lusty "King Hal" *sans* the gratuitous facetiousness of the later film. (1920)

picted with intermittently deft touches that made real human beings of the historical figures. Jannings as Henry VIII—a lusty though brutal monarch, a gourmand and ruthless cavalier with the ladies of the court, a swine who was withal a shrewd diplomat—was right out of Holbein's portrait. Henny Porten made a touching Anne Boleyn, though whitewashed. Theodore Huff reminds us in his Lubitsch *Index* that "she deliberately schemed to replace her mistress, the queen, and was probably more than a little guilty of the adulterous charges brought against her by Henry after he had wed her." However, as Huff goes on to say, "the picture as a whole was more historically accurate than the 1933 Laughton version which pictured Henry as a likeable and amusing fellow, pursuing bobbed-haired girls through the 'moderne' settings." *Selah!*

Lubitsch took care of part of the unemployment problem for a while by employing up to 5000 extras for the film, and it now superseded *Madame Dubarry* as "the biggest film of all time."

Again the mask and vignette were employed for emphasis or nuance, such as the framing of the Archbishop of Canterbury in a mask shaped like a Gothic arch. There was an excellent scene of a *fête champêtre*, as well as the striking opening scene of the below-deck quarters of a vessel bringing Anne to England, and a most vivid, harrowing scene of the execution of Anne by the black-hooded headsman in the Tower. "*Lubitsch kann alles!*" (Lubitsch can do everything!) was the byword of the day. Whatever the *milieu*, he knew exactly where he was and how to depict it in the most expressive way.

There followed next a virulent antimilitaristic satire, as a momentary relief from the spectacles—*Die Bergkatze* (1921) (The Mountain Cat)—starring Negri (as the "mountain cat" or "wildcat") in a role as the temperamental daughter of a brigand chief having it out with the local gendarmerie. The *décor* and costumes, in the Expressionistic manner (Lubitsch's only venture into this *genre* of design) were a parody of the Balkan *milieu*—Montenegro, perhaps—a satire not only on militarism and Balkan splendor, but on East

Pola Negri as "the wild mountain girl" in *Die Bergkatze*, an anti-militarist satire notable for its fantastic sets and "never-never-land" costumes of Ernst Stern and Emil Hasler, and its broad burlesque. Five blundering brigands in it, Pepo, Zorfano, Masillio, Tripo, and Dafko, were certainly forerunners of the Marx Brothers. (1921)

European manners also. Its irony was lost on the public, however, even in Germany, and because of this, because of its ridicule of militarism, and because of its highly stylized acting (not to mention the bizarre sets) and grotesque humor, it was never shown in the U.S.

Lubitsch had enjoyed his exotic "breather" and was now ready to tackle a spectacle again. It is 1921, and the German cinema is producing works that will become historic: Buchowetzki's *Danton*, Jessner and Leni's *Backstairs*, Lang's *Der Müde Tod* (*Destiny* in the U.S.), Lupu Pick's *Shattered*; and Lubitsch is about to crown his spectacles with *Das Weib des Pharao* (*The Loves of Pharaoh* in the U.S.).

The ancient Egypt of the pharaohs was now evoked on the Ufa lot, with its vast palace interiors, its pyramids and sphinxes, its temples, its desert wastes and oases, the pharaohs' ancestor, the mighty Nile, the superstition-and-priest-ridden "kingdom of the dead." To Jannings, naturally, went the role of yet another king, the cruel yet pathetic Pharaoh Amenes. Since Negri was not available, the part of Theonis, the beautiful slave girl over whom the pharaoh and the King of Ethiopia wage a bloody war, only for both of them to lose her to her true love, Ramphis, went to a Viennese stage actress from the Lessing Theatre, another Reinhardt pupil, Dagny Servaes—her first and last screen role.

Das Weib des Pharao was produced on a scale vast even for Lubitsch and ranked in scope with the biggest spectacles of the time—*Cabiria, Intolerance, Theodora, The Thief of Bagdad, Ben Hur.* By this time, too, the German film equaled Hollywood in brilliance of photographic technique (and, with *The Last Laugh, Variety, Faust,* and *Metropolis,* was soon to surpass it by far). The acting, especially that of Jannings as the pharaoh and Wegener as the King of Ethiopia, was exemplary. Only Dagny Servaes as the heroine lacked something. Certainly she had not the sparkle and depth of

A scene from *The Loves of Pharaoh* (*Das Weib des Pharao*) with the strength and barbaric splendor of the Fritz Lang of *Siegfried,* but made over a year and a half earlier. (1922)

feeling Negri always gave her playing. Despite its "monumental" aspect as a spectacle, the film was illumined with the keenest psychological direction.

It was another triumph for Lubitsch. By now he was ready to make his first visit to the United States. Sufficient fanfare had preceded him there. They would certainly know who he was. Besides, Ufa asked him to take a print of the *Pharaoh* film with him to show the American movie moguls. Also he wanted to see America for himself and study American production methods. He had plunged into film-making so enthusiastically it appeared that he had all but invented the medium for himself.

On December 24, 1921, Lubitsch arrived in New York with a print of *The Loves of Pharaoh* (it had already been bought by Paramount and retitled that). On March 3, 1922, the film opened, with *The New York Times* calling it "a magnificent production and stirring testimony to the genius of Ernst Lubitsch."

While in New York, he attended the première of Griffith's *Orphans of the Storm* to see how the master had handled the French Revolution in comparison to his own in *Madame Dubarry*. He was also copiously interviewed. In his reported opinion Chaplin was still the greatest (this before he had seen *A Woman of Paris*, which was to have such a stunning effect on him); he liked *Broken Blossoms* and Lillian Gish in *Orphans of the Storm*, but especially *Broken Blossoms*, which went over very big in Germany. "Griffith is a great director, and it is this picture which decided me to visit America and study your methods. Another film I liked very much was *Forbidden Fruit*." This was a minor work of De Mille's; it was the attention given to detail in it which fascinated Lubitsch. He also liked Harold Lloyd, he said, Mary Pickford, and Douglas Fairbanks. "They are all very popular in Germany." *Foolish Wives*, which had just come out, he called a masterpiece, but he felt its story was inadequate to Stroheim's talents. Then, in summing up, he said, "The American moviegoing public has the mind of a 12-year-old child: it must have life as it isn't. That's the only handicap of the American screen; you have everything else." *The*

Moving Picture World in its issue of January 7, 1922, still referred to him as having been born in Poland; the anti-German feeling after World War I died hard. He spoke sparingly of the *Pharaoh* film, saying he preferred that the interviewer see it and judge for himself. A few bare statistics emerged: it took two months to build the sets and ten months to shoot. The film employed an aggregate of 126,000 extras, cost only $75,000 to produce (it would have cost a million here). Lubitsch shot 90,000 feet of film, which he reduced to approximately 9500 feet in the incredibly short period of ten days because, as he said, he shot with the cutting already in mind and recorded the cuts, scene by scene, as he shot them.

In June of that year, Lubitsch was back in Berlin, already embarked on a new film with Negri. "As an antidote to the

A sketch by Ernst Stern for a set in *Die Flamme* evoking the café night life of *fin-de-siècle* Montmartre. Set designing for the screen reached its peak of expressiveness in the German silent cinema. (1922)

Pola Negri as the cocotte Yvette (as incisively drawn as Maupassant's "Yvette") and Alfred Abel in *Die Flamme*, Lubitsch's own *Woman of Paris* before he had seen Chaplin's epochal excursion into screen subtlety. Pictorially, the composition of this scene could have been signed by Manet.

big historical frescoes," he said, "I feel the necessity to do a *Kammerspiel* film." This was the small, intimate type of film—the screen equivalent of chamber music. It was *Die Flamme* (1922) (The Flame), a *comédie des moeurs*, about a *demimondaine* who cannot adapt to a bourgeois life.

Set in the *fin-de-siècle* Paris of Degas, in Montparnasse, it told of a *cocotte* who meets a composer, falls genuinely in love and marries him. But she loses him because she cannot, despite all her efforts and suffering, become a meaningful part of his life, and throws herself from the window of their home in despair. The gaslit Paris of the period was delicately evoked in the quasi-Impressionist sets of Ernst Stern; Negri's playing was full of youthful ardor and girlish charm, despite her role as a *pensionnaire* in a brothel (this was no taffy harlot of Hollywood); and Lubitsch's direction was studded with gem-like touches that were subsequently to make this characteristic of his style world famous. Siegfried Kracauer recalls one "in which the cocotte prepared her brothel room for the composer's first visit by shifting the furniture so that the room suddenly looked as respectable as he then believed her to be." And I recall another where the husband is being called for by a crony of his, for a night of carousing, and Negri pleads with him not to go. The husband's cynical friend nudges his foot, indicating he should pay no attention to her, whereupon the wife, who has noticed the callous hint, bends down and wipes the "dirty spot" off her husband's shoe. Of such exquisite miniatures was the fabric of this somber tale woven. Released as *Montmartre* by Paramount in the U.S., the film was marred by a happy ending substituted for the original and logically tragic one, and was otherwise so severely mutilated in the re-editing as to negate Lubitsch's intentions almost completely. It was also the last film both Negri and Lubitsch made together in Germany.

II

In the earthquake to come, it is to be hoped that I won't allow bitterness to quench my cigar's glow.
—BERTOLT BRECHT

In October, 1922, Lubitsch left for his second trip to America, as a result of an invitation from Mary Pickford, then "America's sweetheart," and its most popular feminine screen star. She wanted "the greatest director in Europe" to guide her in her next picture. Leaving from Bremerhaven, Lubitsch's "team" consisted of Sven Gade, the Danish director and scene designer, Erich Locke, as assistant, Heinrich (Henry) Blanke, as personal secretary and first assistant, and Andrew Marton. Papa Simon was there to see his son off, tearful at his departure for a *terra incognita* of Indians, pumas, and serpents.

Los Angeles, 1922 . . .

At the turn of the century it was not much more than a cow pasture in whose center some sort of a town was beginning to rise. By the early Twenties it had taken really exotic form, suddenly "sprouting" palm trees, which were not indigenous but imported from the Hawaiian Islands, and in the middle of which began to rise pseudo-Riviera white-and-pink stucco villas and sophisticated adaptations of early California Spanish missions, *orangeries, haciendas, palazzi, pavillons,* and *pergolas*—not to mention the ubiquitous swimming pools which went with every style of architecture or pseudo-architecture. For the rich, which certainly included the movie colony, it was *la dolce vita* incarnate, a tropical climate in which the sun shone almost every day (good for film-making) and a weekly paycheck *(sans* income tax) that almost made Indian rajahs look like bums surviving on handouts by comparison.

At the film lots or in the *sierras* on the outskirts of the city, Westerns were being made full blast—"pictures about horses," as Ben Hecht was later to characterize them, "for horses." While at the Mack Sennett studios the Keystone Kops and, at the nearby beaches, the Keystone bathing beauties were cavorting, the former on rooftops and careening dizzily through the streets, the latter on the rocks:

> By the sea, by the sea,
> By the beautiful sea . . .

. . . from among whose undulating ranks Lubitsch will soon choose a fetching *demoiselle,* a pretty witch named Marie Prevost (of French-Canadian extraction), whom he will rescue from these shenanigans and cast in her first "straight" role, as the flighty wife in his epochal *The Marriage Circle.* On the studio stages, the hothouse era of Cecil B. De Mille is in full orchidaceous bloom with its opulent sets and "daring" sexual implications (sometimes paralleled by Biblical morality fables as if the screen were a perpetual Sunday school or church pulpit). For a decade, from 1914 to 1924, De Mille ruled supreme; then came *The Marriage Circle,* which swept away the bric-a-brac, flounces, and furbelows of De Mille's fancy interiors and turned his "clothes horses," as the over-dressed female stars like Gloria Swanson were facetiously called, into delicious and recognizably human morsels of femininity. But between De Mille and the Lubitsch of *The Marriage Circle* there took place an event

Lubitsch in Hollywood, December 1922, still in his Berlin "director's outfit," here admiring the tie of Robert Florey, liaison for Douglas Fairbanks and Mary Pickford, for whom Lubitsch was "imported" to direct a film with her.

which De Mille did not understand, but which Lubitsch did
—Chaplin's A Woman of Paris.

But it is still the age of innocence, when the "Chinese"
heroine of a film (East Is West) could be called Ming Toy
and nobody batted an eye.

Pola Negri followed Lubitsch to Hollywood—the foreign
"invasion" had begun, though it was never a real invasion,
for the European contingent had been invited one by one,
nay, lured to come here. Thus on the heels of each other soon
appeared Emil Jannings, Conrad Veidt, Erich Pommer,
Alexander Korda, Paul Leni, Lothar Mendes, Lya de Putti,
Karl Freund, Lajos Biro, F. W. Murnau, E. A. Dupont, Ludwig Berger, Camilla Horn, and many others—stars, directors,
cameramen, and scene designers, leaving Ufa all but bereft of
many of its best talents.

When Lubitsch rejected the script of Dorothy Vernon of
Haddon Hall, a sentimental and banal romance set in Queen
Elizabeth's court, offered him by Miss Pickford as their first
picture together (he said it nauseated him), he countered
with one he'd brought along from Germany against such a
contingency: Faust (Part One) in which she would play
Marguerite to Lars Hanson's Faust. When she in turn rejected Faust, Lubitsch, prepared even for this emergency,
suggested Rosita, to which she agreed. In it she would play
a sort of female François Villon.

Meanwhile, Pola Negri was busy filming lurid melodramas
like Bella Donna and The Cheat under George Fitzmaurice
and found herself ideal "copy" for the publicity department
of her studio (Paramount), being compared to the volcanic
Mt. Etna, and being allegedly involved with Gloria Swanson
in a fight over the studio's cats (Negri wanted them out).
She was also reputed to be the sultry object of Chaplin's
affections in a highly publicized "romance," and he was
followed by Rudolph Valentino.

While the studio blurbs were treating a public avid for
such things with the belly dance of advertising for Negri
like "a tiger woman with a strange slow smile and world-old
lure in her heavy-lidded eyes—mysterious, fascinating, an
enigma," or "all fire and passion that speaks of the perfumed

Douglas Fairbanks and Lubitsch watch Mary Pickford rehearse a
song as an itinerant street singer who lampoons the king, and who,
overhearing her, and being a gay dog, sets her up as his mistress.
Unlike the unlucky *midinette* of *Madame Dubarry*, she survives the
royal blandishments with her true love. (*Rosita*, 1923.)

Orient, of smoldering passions and hidden storms," amid
wild-eyed tales of temperamental outbursts, tears, and hys-
terics, Lubitsch was already embarked on *Rosita*, in which
Miss Pickford played a street singer of Toledo, Spain,
during the Empire period of the nineteenth century, who
becomes involved in court intrigues as a result of a song she
sings lampooning the king. It was derived from a minor
French play, *Don Caesar de Bazan*. There were temperamental outbursts at the Pickford studios, also, between director and star. A contemporary journalist noted, "What
with Ernst Lubitsch tearing up scenarios and pulling down

sets at the Pickford studio and Pola wrecking the morale and general properties at Paramount, it looks as though the 'German Menace' will ruin Hollywood yet."

But Lubitsch liked Pickford and was very patient with her. He also was smitten with Hollywood, writing back to Germany that it was a "Film Paradise." And he got along very well with the press except in one area. They had wanted him to say that he wasn't German, but Polish or even Rumanian, but he wouldn't. "If they won't accept me as a German, I'll go back to Germany." What Lubitsch liked especially about Hollywood was the lack of a caste system: unknowns were given a chance to become stars overnight, a thing impossible in Europe (particularly Germany) where to become a star meant a long and tortuous apprenticeship. Shooting on *Rosita* commenced March 5, 1923, ending May 31—three months of hell for director and star.

Though good friends, personally, Pickford and Lubitsch fought throughout the production, with Pickford's "team" attacking Lubitsch's, and vice versa. In the melee, the cameraman, Charles Rosher, quit, "to avoid being hit by the flying crockery"—as one wag put it. Pickford would storm off the set, exclaiming: "Doors! He's a director of doors! Nothing interests him but doors!" As for Lubitsch, when the last scene had been shot, he was convinced his brief American career was finished. What came out of all the rumpus, as far as Miss Pickford was concerned, was not a Pickford film but a Lubitsch film. She returned to a director who "understood" her: Marshall (Mickey) Neilan, for whom she had made *Daddy Long Legs* and other such childish effusions and had him guide her through her *idée fixe*, *Dorothy Vernon of Haddon Hall*, today mercifully forgotten.

On September 14, 1923, *Rosita* premièred at the Lyric Theatre in New York, and the reviews were unanimously enthusiastic. "Nothing more charming than Mary Pickford's new picture, *Rosita*, has been seen on the screen for some time," wrote *The New York Times*, ". . . It is exquisite." "That distinguished and lovely film . . ." was how *Vanity Fair* referred to it.

The scenes of Pickford singing:

ABOVE: Lubitsch in action. (*Rosita.*) BELOW: Mary Pickford as *Rosita*. Through the eyes of Lubitsch she had real charm.

> I know a king, a royal rake,
> Who rakes in all his subjects make . . .

charmed everyone, as did, indeed, her whole performance, in which she played her first adult role. And the *Times* also reported, scarcely a month later, that the film was enjoying "a fabulous success."

No, Lubitsch's American career wasn't finished, it had just begun with an auspicious debut, to say the least.

And then he saw Chaplin's *A Woman of Paris*. . . .

It premièred at the George M. Cohan Theatre in New York, October 1, 1923. The picture opened with a foreword about men and women being not more than human. "They err only in blindness. The foolish condemn their mistakes— the wise pity them."

Chaplin had made it to reward his long-time leading lady, Edna Purviance, with her first straight role as dramatic actress

A superb set for *Rosita* by the Dane Sven Gade, of an old fortress turned into a prison, shows how well Lubitsch had learned his lesson in *mise-en-scène* from Reinhardt. One can almost hear the echoes of treading feet and clanking irons in this vast vaulted interior.

in a serious role. He, himself, did not play in it (appearing just momentarily in a bit part).

It's effect was electric: an important segment of film direction in America from that day onward was no longer the same. Soon it was being bruited around the film capitals of Europe that the American cinema with two films, *Foolish Wives* and *A Woman of Paris*, had come of age. Certainly, these two were the most sophisticated motion pictures made up to that time.

Chaplin in his autobiography says, "It was the first film to articulate irony and psychology." This is only partly true, for Lubitsch had already expressed both qualities in Germany, especially in *The Oyster Princess, Die Bergkatze*, and *Die Flamme*, and Stroheim had, in his sardonic *Foolish Wives*, done likewise. But to the extent that it was *A Woman of Paris* that caused a furore for delineating these aspects of screen dramaturgy, rather than its several predecessors, it may be said to have been the first film to exert a strong influence in this direction. Just as three years later, the question heard everywhere was, "Have you seen *Potemkin?*" so it was in the fall and winter of 1923: "Have you seen *A Woman of Paris?*" Because if you hadn't, you hadn't seen what the screen could really do.

The story was simple enough. Marie St. Clair and her sweetheart, Jean Millet, decide to leave the oppressive French provincial town in which they live and go to Paris. They agree to meet at the railway station and leave together, but Jean's father is suddenly taken ill and Marie, thinking Jean has changed his mind when he doesn't come, leaves without him. In Paris she becomes the mistress of the rich Pierre Revel. One day she encounters Jean and his mother, who, after the father's death, are now also living in Paris, where Jean intends to pursue his career as a painter. Old memories stir in both Jean and Marie, and she informs Revel that she's leaving him to get respectably married. But when she overhears an argument between Jean's mother and her son about the advisability of marrying a kept woman, Marie returns disillusioned to Revel. Jean kills himself in despair, and his mother, bitter with the thought of revenge ("that blind justice," as a title says), seeks out Marie to kill her, too, but touched by Marie's real grief over the death of Jean, she relents. The two leave Paris for the country, where they will live together. One day, Marie is sitting in the back of a hay wagon jogging along a road, when from the opposite direction passes a chauffeur-driven Rolls Royce in which are Pierre Revel and a friend. "By the way," asks the friend, "whatever became of Marie St. Clair?" Revel shrugs his shoulders. Marie and Pierre pass without seeing each other.

That ending was the one for America. For Europe, Chaplin had a harsher ending. Marie, philosophical about Jean's suicide, returns to Revel.

In the hands of almost any other director, such a story would have made a "nothing" picture, though no native American director would have dared the "European" ending. In the hands of Chaplin, even with the "American" ending, it was a revelation.

From the arrival of the train at the station, indicated only by the passing lights of the train windows across the facade of the station (the first time this now-familiar device was ever done) to Revel's opening of a dresser-drawer in Marie's apartment to take out a pocket handkerchief, and in which we see some of Revel's collars, thus laconically stating the relationship between them; from a breakfast scene in Revel's apartment between him and his friend during which they facetiously discuss Revel's women, including Marie, and, finally, Revel says, "Call her up," to which his crony smilingly replies, "Which one?" to Marie contemptuously flinging her pearl necklace, a gift from Revel, out the window when he taunts her about marriage and the poverty she must be prepared to endure with her painter sweetheart, and she suddenly rushes out in a panic, to Revel's laughter, to retrieve it when she notices a tramp in the street about to pick it up. Throughout the film, with almost no let-up, there are these highly expressive "touches." Thus there is a "Chaplin touch" in *A Woman of Paris* (and before that, in a score of his brilliantly articulated comedies) as fine and expressive as the famous "Lubitsch touch."

A Woman of Paris was without rhetoric, without fustian.

OPPOSITE: The film that changed the whole course of motion-picture direction in Hollywood and had an incalculable effect on the subsequent work of Lubitsch—Chaplin's *A Woman of Paris*, starring Edna Purviance and Adolphe Menjou. (1923) ABOVE: A rare moment—Lubitsch meets his idol, Chaplin, and extolls the latter's *A Woman of Paris* as a milestone in screen dramaturgy. (1923)

Chaplin resisted wallowing in the sentimentality such a quasi-"soap opera" story would have afforded others. A simple title, "Time brings many changes," covers the entire transition from Marie's mounting the train steps at the little provincial railway station and our next view of her as the toy of the wealthy Paris playboy, Pierre Revel. The imagination of the audience fills in the intervening time lapse. And, of course, there are wonderful details, minute in themselves, such as the one so expressive of the contrariness of life when Marie visits Jean in his Paris studio, and he offers her a cup of tea together with a napkin that has a big hole in it, but which he has folded in such a way as to cover up the hole. Marie unfolds the napkin while talking to him, placing it on her knee and, of course, sets down the cup of tea right over the hole. Or, when Jean visits Marie's apartment and they are interrupted by the arrival of Revel, there's no big scene of recrimination. Revel merely offers the young man a piece of chocolate. The adjective "cool," so popularly used today in its slang connotation, was already descriptive, *sans* a label, of the method by which Chaplin achieved forty-five years ago many of the best effects of his film.

"This film lives," said *The New York Times*, "and the more directors emulate Mr. Chaplin the better will it be for the producing of motion pictures."

To Eisenstein, *A Woman of Paris* was the most remarkable production of the motion pictures up to that time. He found it to be highly significant in its power to stimulate.

And so, Lubitsch, completely enraptured with the psychological subtleties, and with this economy of statement—the almost clinical detachment with which Chaplin made out of a little story a landmark film—followed the dictum of Emerson: "The best proof of artistic reverence is emulation."

Although making no attempt to recapture the gray melancholy of Chaplin's incisive film, he learned from it how to utilize in the domain of comedy the allusive art of nuances and subtle indications. In *The Marriage Circle* (1924) Lubitsch subtracted irrelevancies from the field of vision, as Chaplin had done, and presented his characters in the light of clear day. Whereas Chaplin had made a drama with glints of comedy, Lubitsch now made a comedy with glints of drama.

The setting was Vienna because Vienna was the city of aristocrats (dramatically speaking, Berlin belonged to the bourgeoisie) and, of course, the play from which it derived was Viennese. Only aristocrats had time for frivolity. And the means to indulge in it. But in one important respect he broke with a tradition of the European drama. Ashley Dukes, in his introduction to Schnitzler's *caprice viennoise* called *Anatole*, describes the world of Schnitzler as one devised for men "and, in effect, although unconsciously, was contemptuous of women." Chaplin of course, had long since held to this tradition (one has only to recall the timid character embodied by Edna Purviance in the numerous comedies he made with her and even the passive role she played as "destiny's plaything," without a will of her own, in *A Woman of Paris*). Where Lubitsch departed from Chaplin, breaking with this tradition, was in his American work beginning with *The Mar-*

Another milestone—the signing of Lubitsch by Harry and Jack Warner to a five-picture contract that resulted in five masterpieces—*The Marriage Circle, Three Women, Kiss Me Again, Lady Windermere's Fan,* and *So This Is Paris.* (1924)

riage Circle and in the galaxy of his films that immediately followed—*Three Women, Forbidden Paradise, Kiss Me Again, Lady Windermere's Fan,* and *So This Is Paris*—in which the woman is dominant, *she* is the sexual aggressor (until *The Love Parade* when Lubitsch finally sums up all this female dominance and makes a wry comment on it).

In his American work, right from the start, beginning with *Rosita* (isn't *she* the aggressor also?), Lubitsch recognized sex, which is to say, the tradition of erotic sensibility, as the first delightful fact of life, to be treated sportively, frivolously, like Fragonard and Boucher did, or with tenderness, as Watteau did, as the occasion dictated. Although this was primarily a French tradition (*vide* the theatre of Labiche, Marivaux, Feydeau, Meilhac, Halévy, Sardou, de Najac) it became also an American tradition, especially in the sex comedies made by Lubitsch in Hollywood. Note that in Europe, where sex was taken as a matter of course, Lubitsch was very decorous and serious about the subject. But in America, with its taboos and repressions, its surface puritanism, he became facetious on the subject and decided to make American audiences laugh at something they took so seriously. Actually, there were two American fetishes he satirized—sex and money. Like those Restoration wits and gallants, Congreve *et al.*, Lubitsch was almost as obsessed with money as he was of sex, as a fact of life.

One fact is that films like his American sex comedies would never have been made in Europe—they were possible only with the "ooh-la-la" attitude toward sex in America—nor would they have been made by Lubitsch had he remained in Europe. He would have had little reason to make them. Indeed, this kind of film was not made by anyone else there after his departure. In short, the filmed "sex comedy" began as a distinctly American institution. (Of course later on, much later on, it was to be taken up abroad, for a while in pre-Hitler Germany, but particularly in France and postwar Italy. Ado Kyrou mentions the pre-Hitler "l'esprit berlinois," and we have only to recall the effervescences of such heady concoctions as Ludwig Berger's A *Waltz Dream*, Erick Charell's *The Congress Dances*, Willi Forst's *Maskerade*, Walter Reisch's *Episode*, Geza von Bolvary's *Two Hearts in ¾ Time*, *The Merry Wives of Vienna*, *The Theft of the Mona Lisa*, and the Reinhold Schuenzel–Franz Doelle *Amphitryon* (French version, not the German original), to realize how much they had learned from the "American" Lubitsch, for they all possessed a lightness and verve astonishing for the usually heavy German film. France came out with Marcel Pagnol's *The Baker's Wife*, not to mention René Clair's works of pure joy and, of course, Sacha Guitry, "France's own Lubitsch." In Italy there were De Sica and Blasetti, among others; unforgettable is the pure gold of the former's *Gold of Naples*, particularly the "pizza" sequence, which is "pure Lubitsch."

America was obsessed with sex—the stringent censorship here proved it Freud had observed that the more the attraction, the greater the inhibition, and obsessions lend themselves to comedy as well as drama. Very well: Lubitsch would

Lubitsch at work on *The Marriage Circle*. Gone are the clothes that looked like they were designed by Krupp. Attired in Hollywood tropics, still chewing his ubiquitous cigar, the director now embarks on a work of the most delicate irony. (1924)

make sex comedies, set in Vienna or Paris or even mythical kingdoms, where you could "get away with it." To Americans, foreigners were decadent—America, itself, must remain pure. In contrast to women seduced in *Foolish Wives* or kept in *A Woman of Paris*, he would show *woman* as the seducer, and sex would be depicted as not more than a pleasant pastime. Whereas Chaplin in *A Woman of Paris* had cast Adolphe Menjou as the rich playboy [14] (Americans associated Menjou's sleekly elegant clothes with "villainy"; the American screen hero at that time was usually very simply or even raggedly dressed, such as the characterizations of Richard Barthelmess and Charles Ray), Lubitsch would cast Menjou as just an average husband with a frivolous and even faithless wife. Surely America would understand that. America did and laughed, blushingly, with him.

The plot of *The Marriage Circle* can be summed up in a line by Alexander Dumas: "The chains of matrimony are so heavy that it takes two to carry them, sometimes three." As a matter of fact, the plot of most of Lubitsch's American films could be summed up in that witty line "Be friends, be lovers, be what you will," warned Count Almaviva, "But as for being husband and wife—good God in Heaven!" A marriage that is floundering gets tangled up with one that is ecstatic, and when the various husbands and wives become unscrambled, including a "fifth wheel on the cart,"—a bachelor on the loose who becomes involved with both ménages—everyone is mated with his heart's desire or is willing to settle for an approximation of that state of bliss. That's all. But what Lubitsch (and his scenarist-in-irony, Paul Bern) did with it is a marvel. Remembered over the years as much as the delicious "touches" of this merry-go-round is the film's gentleness, its sense of good breeding and good manners: a vanished world of roses, kisses and embraces, of whispers and sighs, of a woman's shadowed arm encased in georgette beckoning across a moonlit garden, a scarf of *crêpe-de-chine* scudding across the grass in the night breeze, charming people patting each other reassuringly on the cheek, on the arm, on the shoulders, wherever one can be patted reassuringly, a close-up of an envelope received in the mail addressed to the *Hoch-*

[14] This was Menjou's first role as a suave man of the world.

For a first miracle, he rescues Marie Prevost from Mack Sennett slapsticks and Monte Blue from red Indian and other "bruiser" roles and casts them as the most sauve of sophisticated worldlings. For the second miracle, he introduces a new theme for Hollywood—woman as the sexual aggressor. This was a characteristically European attitude and, if anything, anti-American. (*The Marriage Circle*.)

wohlgeborene Frau Mizzi Stock (The Honorable Mme. Mizzi Stock), and hand-kissing all over the place. I mention this so it should not be overlooked that in the midst of the delicate irony, the sarcasm, and even the harshness of some of the observations, a *milieu* was being presented in which these charming people lived that was an ideal world in microcosm, an untroubled world (did such a thing ever really exist?).

With the success of *The Marriage Circle* behind him, Lubitsch now reveled in the intoxication of work in this artificial paradise—those wonderful early days in Hollywood that still remain so marvelously fresh in the memory of all who shared in that pioneering work. It was as Kay Boyle wrote of another *milieu* at that same happy time:

> Of days spread like peacock tails,
> Of days worn savagely like parrot feathers . . .

In the light malice of *The Marriage Circle* he had found a *genre* that he felt would serve him well. What matter if it substituted for the *echt-Wienerisch* patois of Nestroy [15] the Hollywood patois of its nimble scenarist, Paul Bern, or its director, the already "Americanized" Lubitsch? Their Americanese was still "spoken" with a Continental accent, giving their "speech" a European savor and piquancy that charmed audiences both in America and Europe.

What would he do next?

The plot of *Three Women* (1924) was as old as the hills: a mother (a rich widow) and daughter are unknowingly in love with the same man, a worthless fellow who deserves neither. He plays one against the other, playing up to the mother for her money and to the nubile daughter to add her to his "harem" as well as for the fortune she will inherit on marrying, until he gets his comeuppance. Out of this dross, Lubitsch spun pure gold.

Whereas *The Marriage Circle* was a frolicsome roundelay on the theme of sex, *Three Women* is an agitated piece on the dual theme of sex and money. In fugal counterpoint is limned the threnody of that saddest of aches, that of encroaching age. The film opens brutally with the mother weighing herself on a sheer white bathroom scale in mercilessly sharp photography against a clinically black background, as if to isolate this anxious moment in each day's routine, and she becomes bitter at what the scale tells her. She reads a letter from her daughter away at school: ". . . in a few days I'll be eighteen . . ." and, incredulous, rereads the line. She examines her face pitilessly in a mirror; later she will so light a room before a rendezvous with her scamp-lover as to flatter that face and dissipate the ravages of time. In all this Lubitsch is no longer kidding; now he is in dead earnest. And he overlooks nothing. When the daughter's room is shown at the college dormitory, a picture of her mother is framed on the mantlepiece. It is placed at one end,

[15] Johann Nestroy, a nineteenth-century Viennese playwright of light comedy.

He next takes Pauline Frederick, who had wallowed in lachrymose "Madame X" roles, and Lew Cody, a stock "cad type" in all studio casting files, developing his new theme but tingeing it with the saddest of edges—the inexorable encroachment of advancing age on youthful desires. (*Three Women*, 1924.)

because at the other end is also a picture of her father, who plays no role in the story, but it is natural for *his* picture to be there, too. A dozen other good directors would not have given him a thought.

We have described elsewhere the "Freudian slip" action of the mother playing with the tie of her would-be paramour, in the analysis by Dr. Hans Sachs. And of all the ways Lubitsch could have introduced the third woman of the title, the mistress of this rascally "lady-killer," Lubitsch introduces her as the most feline of the three, stalking like a female panther back and forth in her cage, as she stalks back and forth in her boudoir, whose exoticism is like a gilded cage. Even his introduction of the mother is characteristic, for she slides down a chute during a charity ball right into the arms of the man she will give the "glad eye" for no other reason than he was there and, *grace à dieu*, younger than she is. "Do you realize," one of his anxious creditors tells him (he owes everybody) during the *fête*, "you just held three million dollars in your arms?" That does it. When he smiles at her, it is her jewels he is smiling at. And how delicious to see them pat each other reassuringly in a later scene. How Lubitsch doted on having his characters pat each other reassuringly! And when this rake comes to his mistress's apartment, he goes straight to a closet and takes out dress clothes to change into—an echo of *A Woman of Paris*. Humorous touches are studded throughout, as when the portly creditor with a penchant for sweets feigns to be asleep during a "business meeting" our roué is having with the mother (he wants to "invest" her money for her), and the entire trayful of sweets is gone by the time his nap is over. And there is the archetypical Lubitsch touch when, after the double-dealing cad has just met the daughter (now living with her mother), he leaves their house, turns to wave *au revoir* with his hat to the mother, watching him from the window, then, with the camera gliding up another story, notices the daughter also watching him from *her* window, whereupon he raises his hat a trifle higher for her benefit.

Lubitsch had by now become a sort of "cinema William Morris," a self-confident zealot whose faith and energies gave him a stature his professional colleagues began to marvel at and the surface luster of whose style they were soon to imitate, though, as Mike Nichols was to observe a generation later, "If you're any good, you go on from there." Though his sharp psychological perception was his single most outstanding accomplishment, the ever present danger facing all dramaturgists—theatrical or cinematic—was fatuity, to be shunned at all costs; he was ever aware that because he was Lubitsch he was, to paraphrase Henry James, "under a special obligation to be amusing." The worst he could say of a scene in a screenplay submitted to him was that it was "dull . . . oh so dull." If it was dull it was fatuous. If it was intended as a humorous scene it has to be "hilahrious . . . Is it hilahrious? . . . It must be hilahrious!" Lubitsch's concern was to fill his comedies with those "secrets" to which Mr. Nichols referred in an interview at Brandeis University recently: "Any good movie is filled with secrets. If a director doesn't leave anything unsaid, it's a lousy picture. If a picture is good, it's mysterious, with things left unsaid." In a Lubitsch film, the audience had to contribute to the full realization of the work, to fill in the implications, often even to supply the "tag line," the meaning of a quick or even a slow fadeout (like a clever stage "blackout" in a revue). Does not Gaston Monescu in *Trouble in Paradise* say to the rich widow, Marianne, of a love letter she has received from one of her wooers, a bumptious ex-Major: "*Not* the Major . . . I don't mind his grammatical mistakes. I'll overlook his bad punctuation." Then with a sad smile, "but the letter has no mystery, no bouquet. . . ." The films of Lubitsch had this mystery, this bouquet. When the camera in *The Marriage Circle* glides down from the happily married Florence Vidor ecstatically singing Grieg's "Ich Liebe Dich," her husband's favorite song, to the unhappily married Marie Prevost, accompanying her at the piano and on the make for Monte Blue, Florence's husband who is standing by, the mischievously ironical smile Prevost gives Monte Blue, and on which Lubitsch holds his camera to a slow fadeout, would have made even Balzac and Maupassant smile, let alone what it would have done to those two satyrs, Anatole France and Remy de Gourmont. What the whole film is about is contained in that malicious smile.

With Lubitsch and Negri both in Hollywood and both now established on the American screen, it was inevitable that they should do a picture together again, as in "the good old days" in Germany. It was *Forbidden Paradise* (1924), a tale of frail queens and frail women, remotely derived from a play, *The Czarina*, by two ebullient Hungarians, Lajos Biro and Melchior Lengyel, and even more remotely based on certain "colorful" incidents in the highly colored life of Catherine II ("the Great") of Imperial Russia. Negri made a very regal queen who was at the same time a very feline woman; Menjou was purest sarcasm as her cynical chamberlain, all too aware of her frailty where men were concerned; Pauline Starke was the most virginal of ladies-in-waiting to

the czarina; Rod La Rocque was the most handsome and
stalwart of Her Majesty's lieutenants, affianced to the virginal lady-in-wating, *bien entendu.* Reams have been written
about the "touches" in this one: the goldfish that darts suddenly across a moonlit pool, beside which sit the young
lovers, their kiss blurred in the pool's reflection by the impulsive movement of the tiny creature; the officers' revolt
against the czarina put down in three quick film shots: the
general's hand moving to his sword, the chamberlain's hand
pulling out a checkbook, the general's hand loosening from
his sword with an "in that case" gesture; the lieutenant bursting in upon his queen with the news of the revolt, panting
and disheveled, but loyalty to her personified, and her silent
awe of his zeal (not to mention his handsomeness), her but-
toning up an opened buttonhole on his tunic followed by his
proudly expanded chest which pops the button right off his

So as to work with Pola Negri again, he makes his next film for
Paramount, to whom she is contracted. They test her makeup for
a scene in *Forbidden Paradise,* a satire on the frailty of queens—
and women. Five years ago these two had made film history with
Madame Dubarry. Would they again? They did. (1924) The seduc-

tive queen, aching for love, meets her match in a handsome, stalwart lieutenant, devoted to his betrothed, her virginal lady-in-waiting. Negri as the all-too-womanly queen—scorned. The new theme, of woman as aggressor, is now played on a ruthless battle-field—the boudoir. (*Forbidden Paradise.*)

uniform; the queen's attempt to kiss him but, being so much shorter than he, slyly moves a small stool nearby with her foot so she may be able to reach him; the medal that the lieutenant receives, being the queen's new favorite, which is duplicated on the chests of all the rest of the officers who once also enjoyed that distinction; finally, the French ambassador, who has been waiting all this time to be received, now that the queen has been forbidden her paradise with the lieutenant (because he loves only his fiancée) is received and emerges afterwards with a medal, too, as the chamberlain and he exchange smiles, the ambassador a shy one, the chamberlain an all-too-knowing one.

She cannot have the dashing Lt. Alexis so she will have to settle for the coxcomb French Ambassador, come to present his credentials. Her chamberlain (Adolphe Menjou) shows her his photograph. "Not bad . . . not good . . . but not bad!" She primps to receive him. "Ah, frailty!" thinks the cynical chamberlain, "Thy name is indeed woman!" (*Forbidden Paradise.*)

As much a part of the general air of mockery which permeated the film were the pseudo-Byzantine sets, neo-Loew's baroque, vast and polished to a fare-thee-well, and the amusing anachronisms—if one *insisted* that Catherine II flourished in the eighteenth century—such as the czarina's very Twenties-bobbed hair, the Panhard (or was it a Lancia or Hispano-Suiza?) open motor car, a flashlight, wrist-watch, a handy checkbook to mollify a crisis, and the like. Verily, the Catherine of Lubitsch was a queen for all seasons, as she was also the eternal woman; so-called anachronisms merely underscored this. Richard Watts, Jr. who, with the late John S. Cohen of *The New York Sun* and Ted Shane of *The New*

Yorker, formed a triumvirate who were among the most enthusiastic appreciators of Lubitsch in those early days, called the film, "The most delightful of photoplay comedies, the finest work of all concerned with it."

With each new picture he seemed to be outdoing himself. How long could even *he* keep it up?

Josef von Sternberg was to note in his autobiography [16] years later, "In *The Marriage Circle* and other works, this famous director contrived a kind of innuendo that became known as 'the Lubitsch touch.' The basic theory behind this often amusing contrivance was that, no matter what happened, one would always have a twinkle in the eye and never lose his *sang-froid.*" It was thus that by maintaining his aplomb, despite his satiric irreverence to established shibboleths held sacred by great masses of people, and by the suppleness of his handling of even the most risqué scenes—in short, by "keeping his cool," in today's parlance—he avoided any contretemps with the censors or the film industry's own Production Code. He was, in fact, a censor's delight. Only once in Germany were scenes of his censored—some gamey details in *Sumurun*—and only once in Hollywood, in *Heaven Can Wait,* where one scene was censored by Darryl Zanuck in the script. For the rest, nary a cut was ever made; Lubitsch was too sly for the censors and outwitted them at their own game.

If any further proof were needed, *Kiss Me Again* (1925) supplied it. Adapted from an old boulevard farce by Victorien Sardou and Emile de Najac (George Jean Nathan coined a verb, "to sardou," to describe the invariable goings-on in these Gallic shenanigans that convulsed Paris audiences at the century's turn: "Unbeknownst to her, Armand plans to *sardou* her in the *chambre separée* that night."), this spurt of froth was called *Divorçons* (Let's Get Divorced). It was a big success on the stage in Paris in 1880 and also in New York two years later. Marie Prevost, in the play's original role of Cyprienne, the wife seeking the divorce, was essaying a role previously played by no less than Réjane and Duse! André Maurois once said, "Americans don't like to talk about emotions, they prefer physical love, what goes on behind the bed-

---

[16] *Fun in a Chinese Laundry* (Macmillan), 1965.

room door. For the French it is what *precedes* the bedroom door that counts. 'Every beginning is lovely' is a saying that fits the case perfectly."

What precedes the bedroom door is the stuff of what now became Lubitsch's most "hilahrious" satire on the human animal to date. The curious thing about *Kiss Me Again* is that few seem to have seen it. It is almost always passed over and never discussed by film historians.[17] And yet it may well be Lubitsch's most dazzling work. It is that most exuberant example of *lebensbejahend*, that saying "yes" to life, its complete affirmation. Robert Flaherty once told me that next to Dovzhenko's *Earth*, it was his favorite film. How's that for a range in taste?

"A champagne picture in a beery movie world," extolled *The New Yorker* at the time. "*The Marriage Circle* still stands as the best adventure of the films into intelligent comedy. *Kiss Me Again* is even better." Couldn't he keep it up, though? But let Ted Shane, a former film critic of this magazine, describe it as he did in a notable dithyramb of the period:

As far as we are concerned there is only one (1) authority, in this world at least, on Sex (you may have heard of the thing—it has to do with species propagation, marriage, love, alimony, hearthstone worship and other such trivia) and his name is Ernst Lubitsch. The esteemed Herr specializes in the more social side of the biological manifestations in the human animal, doing so in what we might term (might we, please?) unglamorous, unillusioned fashion. In more fluent words, the estimable Nordic (of the Teuton branch) recognizes the human animal under sophisticated sex circumstances as an ignoble concoction of surly humors, strange and endless vain conceits, silly shifting appetites, and inconsiderate, selfish, cruel, and illogical desires, but holds them entirely blameless for being as human as that all the while. In fact, he laughs at them.

All of which lecture in the Seldes manner is not meant to preju-

[17] This is similar to the total oblivion into which the perfectly charming silent screen comedies of H. d'Abbadie d'Arrast have fallen. D'Arrast was one of the most brilliant disciples of Chaplin (for whom he worked as assistant on *A Woman of Paris*) and of Lubitsch. His films include *Serenade*, *A Gentleman of Paris*, *Service for Ladies*, and *The Magnificent Flirt*. All were exquisite.

dice you against the man, but to let you know that the Attila of Hollywood has done another sex masterpiece in *Kiss Me Again*. It is Continental high comedy done in the Central European manner with Germanic harshness and irony of attack. It is as far from America as Mr. Lubitsch is above the sophistication of Mr. Will H. Hays.

It goes like this: Mr. Monte Blue is married to Miss Marie Prevost and she is unsettled under the yoke. So she naturally leans toward the sveltitude of Mr. John Roche with his bushy coiffure and tapering, pianistic fingers, both of which are necessary implements to his love making. Thereupon ensues an old-fashioned and ordinary triangle jumbling, out of which Mr. Blue emerges with his lady.

But in the meantime, Mr. Lubitsch has held the hands of his actors, shown them how to bicker, quarrel, heckle, peck, pick at each other, and vie for the upper hand in the ever shifting love situation. As a result we have startling pantomime and a hilarious picture.

(It was Mr. Shane, incidentally, who once suggested that Lubitsch do Maupassant's *Yvette*.)

Rhapsodizing about a performance of Sir Laurence Olivier's National Theatre Company in Jacques Charon's staging of Georges Feydeau's wacky farce, *A Flea in Her Ear*, at Expo 67 last year, Clive Barnes in *The New York Times* spoke of "the gust of each delicately measured laugh (which) builds up into a whirlwind of carefully controlled hilarity . . . The story does not matter. Bedrooms, boudoirs, and salons, doors opening and closing, infidelities, promises of infidelities, hopes of infidelity, misunderstandings of infidelity, the wronged husbands, the clever wife, the ardent lover, the fool, the rogue—but this carousel of honestly adroit cliché is of no importance. These are toy marionettes who have to do nothing but make us laugh, and not wonder why we are laughing. Feydeau's jokes spurt out, his plots whirl around, and the audience, gloriously unthinking, unfeeling, dives head-first into a sea of merriment. Style here is everything. . . ." And he goes on to discuss the difficulty Anglo-Saxon actors have in catching the elusive frivolity of the French boulevard-farce style. He sums up by declaring that the company performs with the ease of friends and the insight of surgeons.

One thinks of an equivalent French film, René Clair's *The Italian Straw Hat*, after a similar rowdy farce by Labiche and Michel, and which so felicitously fits Mr. Barnes's impression of the Feydeau opus. Clair preserved under theatrical amber the bourgeois Paris of the 1890's with the same vertiginous daffiness and with the same hilarious results. But for witty Frenchmen to write and direct witty French farces comes as naturally as breathing. What about a German working with an American cast, not trained players at all, at least not to the degree of virtuosity attained by the Messrs. Charon, Olivier, and Clair? Under those parlous circumstances, for Lubitsch to tackle this kind of French farce (because the goings-on in *Kiss Me Again* apply perfectly to what Clive Barnes said about the Feydeau bash) requires dexterity of the most nimble and quick-witted sort. "It is rare enough to find a photoplay director who can treat of sex in a detached and lightly humorous manner," commented Richard Watts, in *Theatre Magazine*. "It is perhaps even rarer to find one who can show the interplay of character by ironical and satirical pantomime. In *Kiss Me Again*, Lubitsch has accomplished both feats. The result is just about the finest of all photoplay high comedies. The appeal of the picture is almost entirely an intellectual one. There is no attempt to tug at your heartstrings. Every effort is aimed at the intelligence."

Just a few of its felicities: a cinematic one in which a sudden rainshower is indicated without calling for a flood of water but in the most evanescent way imaginable; the "grounds for divorce" scene; the final peroration. Let us take the last two: in the first, Monte Blue, his wife, Marie Prevost, and her new boyfriend, John Roche, are in the wife's lawyer's office to get a divorce. It's the wife who wants the divorce, as she has suddenly become enamored of the pianistic prowess (among other things) of the svelte John Roche, with his good looks and wavy hair. The lawyer explains there must be grounds for the divorce. As there are no grounds save the whim of the wife, the lawyer (Willard Louis) suggests inventing one. "Hit her in front of the witnesses here," he says. "I'm a witness, my secretary" (vi-

Back to Warners for *Kiss Me Again*, perhaps the most exquisite light screen comedy ever made on the subject of *l'amour*. The delicious scene where Monte Blue must give his wife (Marie Prevost) grounds for divorce by striking her while her lawyer (Willard Louis) and her lover (John Roche) are present as witnesses. (1925)

vaciously played by Clara Bow) "is another and, of course, him—" indicating the wife's anxious boy friend. Monte, willing to oblige, raises his arm to strike her. She interrupts with, "Yes hit me! I always knew you'd do it some day, you brute!" This, of course, is the wrong thing for her to say; it unnerves Monte. "Try it again," says the lawyer and then, turning to the wife, "And you keep quiet." Monte tries again, pulls his arm all the way back to let fly with a hefty smack, but can't do it, and drops his arm in despair. Marie smiles. "We're not getting anywhere," admonishes the lawyer. "Again!" And the wife, knowing full well that since her hubby has really nothing against her and is, under any circumstances and for whatever reason, incapable of striking her (being, for that matter, a gentleman incapable of striking *any* woman), watches his third attempt. "Go on!" shouts the lawyer, impatiently, "Give her a real whack!" "Yeah," says the wife, "Give me a real whack—*I dare you!*" Whereupon the lawyer turns to her with, "I thought I told you to keep quiet!" Monte gives up. They all give up. And the wife? She has a triumphant smile. She wanted the divorce, or thought she did, but she likes this revelation better. Finally, wife and hubby are reunited during a touching *tête-à-tête* in their bedroom. The flowery pianist pays his usual evening call on his inamorata, unaware that the husband is in the house. While awaiting her, he sits down at the piano and begins to negotiate some very fancy arpeggios over the keyboard, *sforzando*. Enter the husband in his pajamas. He goes over to the pianist, who looks at him agape. "Softer," urges the husband to the ardent musical fellow, gesturing with his hands as a conductor does who wishes to draw a *pianissimo* from the orchestra. "*Softer . . .*" Whereupon hubby with a beatific smile at the pianist, and a farewell wave of the arm, leaps gaily toward the bedroom.

What a year 1925 was, not only for Lubitsch but for everyone! Two of the year's ten best films were by him (*Kiss Me Again* and *Lady Windermere's Fan*), and the others included Chaplin's *The Gold Rush*, King Vidor's *The Big Parade*, Stroheim's *The Merry Widow*, Murnau's *The Last Laugh*, James Cruze's *Beggar on Horseback*, Sternberg's *The Salvation Hunters*, Tod Browning's *The Unholy Three*, and Fritz Lang's *Siegfried*. Other films still to be seen that year included *Forbidden Paradise*, Griffith's *America*, Fairbanks's *The Thief of Bagdad*, Buster Keaton's *The Navigator* and *Sherlock, Jr.*, and Harold Lloyd's *The Freshman*. From Germany came Leni's *Waxworks*, and from France, René Clair's *Paris Qui Dort* and *Entr'acte*, and Feyder's *Faces of Children*. And next year would come Eisenstein's *Potemkin*, Flaherty's *Moana*, the Capra–Langdon *The Strong Man*, Murnau's *Tartuffe* and *Faust*, Lang's *Metropolis*, Pabst's *Secrets of a Soul* and *Street of Sorrow*, Lotte Reiniger's *Adventures of Prince Achmed*, Stiller's *Hotel Imperial*, Renoir's *Nana*, Pudovkin's *Mother*, Taritch's *Ivan the Terrible*, Room's *Bed and Sofa*.

This was the summit of the "Golden Age" of the silent

When he can't do it, wifey realizes that maybe hubby must really love her, as he confesses he most truly does, in a tender reunion scene in their bedroom, while the lover is displaying his pianistic prowess in the living room, unaware of the husband's return to the ménage. "Softer," says the husband to the lover, before he leaps back to the bedroom in his pajamas with a triumphant grin. "A champagne picture in a beery movie world," extolled *The New Yorker*. (*Kiss Me Again*.)

cinema. Never again were there to be two such resplendent years in all screen annals as 1925–26.

His method was simple, direct, patient. He didn't believe in many rehearsals, feeling they tired the actor and robbed him of his spontaneity. If a scene *had* to be done over several times, he never lost his patience or courtesy. When under a nervous strain, during a break for the changing of the lights or a new camera setup, he would pace back and forth, usually behind a piece of scenery, his arms behind him, the ubiquitous cigar clenched unlit between his teeth. Sitting on a small camp chair, he would lean forward in his intensity, his hands gripping the arms. The more intense he was, the more he leaned forward. And his face would mirror all the emotions of the players, male or female. Sometimes he would jump up and show an actor how to do a scene, taking the role himself, even if it was a girl's. To show Pauline Stark, during *Forbidden Paradise*, how she should react in a scene, he suddenly became a shy young girl. He acted all the parts, if necessary, even those of the secondary roles, to make sure every player knew what he was after. With the camera and lighting crew, the grips, with the whole technical *équipe*, he was extremely popular. Yet he was most exacting and not at all easy to please.

Some directors liked to improvise—not he. It must all be down in the scenario, everything thought and worked out. Nothing was left to chance. With some directors scenes were not always filmed in their chronological order. But Lubitsch could not work this way. How could one do a scene at the middle or the end of a film without having carefully mapped out every detail that went before? Each scene had to "grow" out of the preceding one; a film was a series of propulsions or combustions, like an engine which keeps a vehicle going. He would try whenever possible for a scene to "play" without the necessity of subtitles in the silent days. The less titles the better, he said. He said the ideal picture would have no titles at all. (Vide, *The Last Laugh*.) "We are still borrowing from the stage or the novel," he maintained. "Some day we will discover the true motion-picture style." Then: "I believe in realism—actors should act the way people do in real life. It can be a light film, a comedy, if you like, but it should still be real. In that way the audience will believe what it is seeing. . . . My chief worry is always the story. It's harder to decide on the story than it is to direct. I like American pictures, they speak clearly. I think *A Woman of Paris* is a marvelous production. I like it because I feel that an intelligent man speaks to me, and nobody's intelligence is insulted in that picture. The treatment is wonderful. . . . I also don't believe in fancy clothes, nor in sweet, 'nice' acting, which is unreal. I want to touch the emotions of people—they know what is real and what is not.

My players also use as little makeup as possible, only what is necessary for the lights. . . . I believe that, in the future, stories will be written directly for the screen, as they should be. . . . As far as I can, I try to keep the action going without tiring my players. I think over my medium shot when I am making my long shot. And I am ready for what I want when it comes to a close-up. I don't want to get the actors fatigued, and only when it appears absolutely necessary do I go over a scene several times. You can lose the feeling when you do." [18]

The next film was, in a way, a mad stunt. He would film Oscar Wilde's play *Lady Windermere's Fan* without using a single Wildean epigram. What would that lover of paradoxes, Mr. Wilde, himself, have thought of *such* a paradox? Wrote Ted Shane in *The New Yorker* after the film opened in 1925:

Oscar Wilde will have no cause to turn over in his grave. Der Herr Lubitsch has done magnificently, if somewhat Germanically, by the Gifted Magpie of the perfumed sayings.

He has attempted and succeeded in transfilming a Wilde without use of a single tinseled Wildean epigram from the play, rather trusting to his own great sense of cinematic wit and the dramatic. The result is a Wilde of wondrous characterization and situation, well interspersed with pictorial wit, acted by the usual splendid hand-held lubitschean actors. Perhaps the vigilant German may seem to have stressed the surface tragedy of the fine play to the apparent sacrifice of the brilliant and eternal fragrant epigrams, but this can hardly be considered a grievous fault and may be mended by a judicious insertion of a line from the play at this point and that in the subtitles. For Wilde is there—in picture terms it is true—but still essentially the Wilde of the gorgeously unreal puppets, of the amorous *bon vivant* Lord Darlington, of the supersentimental harlot-motherly Mrs. Erlynne, of the fourth dimensionally virtuous and slightly thick Lady Windermere (virtuous to the *n*th point of virtue as are all the Wilde heroines), of the gossipy, over-lusting clubman type (constituting the Wildean villain), of the chilly, screechingly clever British drawing rooms, of the

[18] Condensed from Harry Carr: "How Great Directors Work," in *Motion Picture* magazine, May, 1925.

Lubitsch retrieves the fan dropped by Lady Windermere (May McAvoy) in the garden scene with Lord Darlington (Ronald Colman). Curiously, the set designers for Lubitsch's five Warner films are not identified, and yet the designer of this beautiful formal garden certainly merits credit. (*Lady Windermere's Fan*, 1925.)

scandal, of the backbiting, of the painfully correct serving men, of the high odor of British clowning manners, of paradoxical this and of sentimental that, and of cheek tonguing thus and thus.

Again, Lubitsch had enchanted with the light malice of his observation and by the visual transportation of the brittle, artificial world of Wilde, turned the Wildean persiflage into the most perspicacious observation. Could he *still* keep it up, that is, outdo himself with *every* new picture? "It's the sixth consecutive bull's-eye by that efficient marksman, Ernst Lubitsch," said *The New Yorker*. "It comes closer to perfection than any production of the year, with the inevitable exception of *The Last Laugh*." (That was the year that included *Kiss Me Again*.) Especially singled out was the charm with which the Royal Ascot race meeting was depicted. And Georges Sadoul, dean of film historians, years later called it "Lubitsch's best silent film, (full of) incisive details, discreet touches, nuances of gestures, where behavior betrays the character and discloses the sentiments of the personages. With Lubitsch a new art carried on the subtleties of Marivaux and the comedy of manners made its debut on the screen." Edmund Wilson, surely no movie fan, rhapsodized about it at the time (as he had previously rhapsodized about *Kiss Me Again*), pointing out even its physical beauty.

He has clothed it in such beautiful photography and directed it with so much resourcefulness that he has turned out a very attractive film. The silver and gray London streets, the white-gowned or black-morning-coated figures, standing in high-ceilinged rooms or looking out of long-curtained windows, are in his most distinguished manner; and his theatrical ingenuity, his great knack of shooting commonplace incidents from inobvious and revelatory angles are as effective as ever.

This tailor's son from lower middle-class Berlin showed the elegance of the "high world" of London's Mayfair with the flair of one to the manner born. No "blue blood" from Eton, Oxford, Cambridge, or Harrow, could have done it: this near-miraculous transliteration, not only from one medium to another, but with the self-imposed handicap, out of sheer bravado (and artistic integrity, not wishing to lean on Wilde for support). No English attempt at filming Wilde was ever as successful. *The Importance of Being Earnest* (1952), filmed many years later, even with Gielgud, Redgrave, and Joan Greenwood in the cast, and with the benefit of Wilde's dialogue, never quickened to life. An attempt was made in America to remake *Lady Windermere's Fan*, this time as a sound film with the benefit of Wilde's dialogue. The picture was *The Fan* (1949), directed (if that's the word) by Otto Preminger, and the result was a disaster.

Although Lubitsch resisted borrowing from Wilde, he occasionally substituted a title (there were very few) of his own which was in the Wildean spirit. The opening title read: "Lady Windermere was facing a grave problem—how to seat her guests at dinner." Immediately the tone is set. Or, "The relations between a man and a woman can be told by the way he presses her doorbell." There is not a moment of waste footage, everything that is shown counts. The effect, when this roguish comedy-drama is over, is that of having seen a witty play, though not a word of dialogue has been spoken. Only once have I seen a comparable *tour-de-force*, and this in a brief scene only between those two protean players, Marguerite Moreno and Louis Jouvet. It is in the French film *Le Revenant*, where Moreno, greeting the return of Jouvet who has been away a long time, brings him "up-to-date" on events in a soliloquy during which Jouvet merely smiles in reply, with all the many kinds of smiles possible. When she finishes, Moreno says in admiration, "The years haven't changed you—you're just as witty as ever." And so superbly is this scene played, we are convinced that we have, indeed, been listening to a witty conversation, when, in truth, Jouvet has not said a single word.

Before leaving *Lady Windermere's Fan*, let us pay tribute to the beautiful playing of Irene Rich as the *déclassée* Mrs. Erlynne. When one remembers how utterly banal she was in films under other directors, and then sees her in this role, one realizes what *real* direction can do. For the first and last time in her career she was second to no actress on the American stage or screen. Edmund Wilson relates that when she

"Stately portals, tall yew hedges . . ." (Hofmannsthal: Prelude to Schnitzler's *Anatole*.) Mystery of the garden . . . mother and daughter in confrontation . . . Mrs. Erlynne (Irene Rich) and Lady Windermere (May McAvoy) . . . maternal anxiety vs. youthful brazenness. . . . "Lord Windermere is looking for you," says Mrs. Erlynne. "I'm sure he has not missed me," replies Lady Windermere, "You've entertained him so well." Lubitsch always liked formal gardens, they served him well . . . for the breeze that stirs up Marie Prevost's scarf vis-á-vis Monte Blue in *The Marriage Circle* . . . the goldfish's sudden darting across a pool that shatters the lovers' kiss in the moonlight's reflection in *Forbidden Paradise*. . . . The heart-to-heart talk between the incognito mother and her daughter, away from the gossiping tongues of Mayfair in the brilliantly lit house beyond the terrace in *Lady Windermere's Fan*.

made a personal appearance with the film, she didn't look anything at all like she did in *Lady Windermere's Fan*. One had to take the management's word for it, it appears, that this was indeed Irene Rich. As Sternberg was to note years later, there are no bad actors or actresses, there are only bad directors. But she could take direction (as Sternberg said of Dietrich) when there *was* a director.

Mordaunt Hall, then motion-picture critic for *The New York Times*, tells of being called by Harry Warner, president of Warner Brothers, for whom Lubitsch had made four films by now: *The Marriage Circle, Three Women, Kiss Me Again,* and *Lady Windermere's Fan*. Would Mr. Hall please come to see Mr. Warner on a matter of the utmost urgency? Once there, the movie executive began to complain. "Mr. Hall, you are taking the bread and butter out of my mouth," he lamented. "You like Ernst Lubitsch's pictures, but they don't make any money. You pan our pictures that pay." Mr. Hall says he rose from his seat and left without a word.

The next Lubitsch picture was a box-office hit. It was released by the canny Warner Brothers under the hotsy-totsy title of *So This Is Paris* (1926). Not only did Mr. Hall like it, but the moviegoers loved it. Harry Warner must have been very surprised!

Years later, in a facetious book in pure Hollywoodese, *My First Hundred Years in Hollywood*, Jack Warner recounts being in Vienna in 1926 seated at dinner next to a countess who said:

"What do you do, monsieur?"

"My name is Jack Warner," I said. "I make movies. You know— John Barrymore, people like that."

"I never heard of him," she said.

"Well . . . you've heard of Ernst Lubitsch, the great German director. He works for me."

"I don't know him."

With some desperation, I tried again. "Have you ever seen Rin-Tin-Tin?"

"Ah-h-h!" she exclaimed. "Ring-Ting-Ting, I know him!"

From that moment on, the name of Jack Warner meant something in Vienna.

The first "Lubitsch touch" may well have been devised by Sir Thomas Malory in the fifteenth century in his *Morte d'Arthur* when he related the tale of how King Mark, Iseult's husband, found her and Tristan sleeping together with the gallant knight's sword placed between them. King Mark removed Tristan's sword and substituted his own, leaving the couple to discover this comment when they awakened. A most appropriate gesture when we consider the sexual symbol of the sword.

Lubitsch did an amusing variation of this in *So This Is Paris*, with a cane. Same symbol.

"The most uproarious of his farces," extolled Richard Watts in *The New York Herald Tribune*. "The most hilarious of his works, the funniest comedy imaginable . . . adult and magnificent satirical farce." "It is Lubitsch at his merriest, at his wittiest," remarked John S. Cohen in *The New York Sun*. "A riot of fun . . . hilarious . . . the best thing Lubitsch has done," exclaimed Palmer Smith in the *Telegram*. And so it went. Lubitsch had outdone himself again. Wrote John S. Cohen in *The New York Sun*:

No attraction in New York is half so gay and heady as *So This Is Paris*, Ernst Lubitsch's latest film comedy, which was exhibited to spontaneous applause at the Cameo last night under the benevolent auspices of the International Film Arts Guild. It commences an indefinite stay at popular prices today, and, if the joy with which the first audience welcomed it is any box-office guide, the photoplay should run merrily along at the Cameo for a mere matter of some six months or so. It is Lubitsch at his merriest, his wittiest. We all know, of course, that Lubitsch is one of the two most skillful cinema directors in the world. We should know, in addition, that he is, perhaps, the finest wit in all the length and breadth of celluloid land. It is safe to estimate that the wit in *So This Is Paris*, his new satiric comedy at the Cameo, is 95 per cent Lubitschean. The remaining five per cent may be credited to the clever Hans Kräly, the author of the scenario. Let us then remain cognizant of the fact that—as a mind—Lubitsch belongs in the varying classes that include Carroll, Wilde, Congreve.

Richard Watts, too, in *The New York Herald Tribune* made no attempt to restrain himself. Since this wonderful genre of film has today completely disappeared from the

The inebriated Dr. Giraud (Monte Blue) is surprised to learn that he has been flirting with his own wife (Patsy Ruth Miller), a drollery made possible in that age of innocence by the simple removal of her domino mask. We are too "knowing" today to equate the state of husbandhood with fatuity, but in the process of acquiring this "knowingness" we have lost something. Did not Wedekind, a decade before, make us believe in his story, "The Inoculation," that a man could bare the nude body of his mistress lying on his bed, keeping only her face covered, before the gloating eyes of his mistress's husband, his best friend, without the husband recognizing his wife? That night the husband even brags about the beauty of his friend's mistress to his wife. "She was magnificent, my dear," he says at dinner. "You could never hope to compete with her." (*So This Is Paris*, 1926.)

screen, we too feel impelled to extoll fervently this magnificent slyness, this wit as tart as pickled lime with which Lubitsch could dress up such a daffy plot of two amorous couples who get entangled willy-nilly and make of it a glittering affair. He alone could tread consistently, harmlessly, among the treacherous shoals of sex, but the actual sexiness was as cool as the passion life of a dandelion.

The fine scorn that Herr Ernst Lubitsch has for the institution of sex deserves at least rapturous contemplation. All the rest of the world, as I need hardly add, is violently excited over the significance of the sex urge. Psychoanalysts dissect it, reformers assail it, and the younger generation, of all ages, rejoices in it—but all of them in their several ways take it with infernal seriousness.

Meanwhile, the brilliant German sits back calmly and laughs contemptuously at the antics it causes. In all of his American pictures—save, of course, Mary Pickford's *Rosita*—he has scoffed quietly at the comical idiots its manifestations make of us. Now, in his latest picture *So This Is Paris*, he ends his reticence on the subject and begins to laugh out loud.

The film opens showing the corner of a living room into which a pretty, frightened odalisque rushes, followed by her master with bared knife and determined countenance. He raises the knife, she cries out, he brings it down on her, she expires, and he looks appalled at his terrible deed. Slowly the camera glides to the left and we see an old, grizzled accompanist at the piano, playing the music for this pantomime in rehearsal. A male "nautch" dancer, stripped to the waist, in turban and pantaloons, now begins (we see a close-up of the piano score) "The Dance of Sorrow," with fluttering hands and expressionless face, followed by the familiar oriental "sarabande," in which one palm stretches forward as the other goes backward, derived from countless Egyptian wall paintings by way of countless "Oriental" dancers and from the dreamy illustrations on packs of Rameses and Egyptian Deities cigarettes. The mocking tone is set. From then on the film becomes a hilarious shambles before Lubitsch is willing to let go, and the last shot is perhaps the loudest laugh ever in a Lubitsch film. In between are a thousand felicities of which I shall cite only three particularly high points. Suzanne, the wife of Dr. Giraud, who lives opposite the "nautch" dancer and his wife, sees him from her window apparently nude (because he's stripped to the waist), and, shocked, orders her husband to go over and complain. Dr. Giraud dutifully grabs his cane to thrash the brazen fellow, but when he gets there he finds that the dancer's wife is an old flame of his, Georgette Lalle. They have a jolly reunion, after which the husband returns, forgetting his cane, but assures his wife that he broke the stick over the shameless fellow's noggin. But Monsieur Lalle (the dancer) has noticed the doctor's pretty wife from *his* window, and decides to return the cane as an excuse to visit *her*. When Suzanne sees that the cane is whole, she stalks to the bedroom where Dr. Giraud "exhausted" from his fray with the dancer (as he said) is taking a nap, and she flings the cane contemptuously on the couch beside him. She returns to Lalle. Dr. Giraud awakens, sees the cane, and wonders how it got there. Back now to Suzanne and Lalle. He is flattering her voluptuousness in a desperate effort to woo her as quickly as possible. Shy and embarrassed, she tells him he'd better leave since her husband is in the next room— but suddenly she remembers the cane. Dr. Giraud, hearing her coming, jumps back on the couch again, face to the wall, as if still asleep. Suzanne opens the door stealthily, retrieves the cane, gives it back to Lalle, and finally persuades the ardent Romeo to leave. Dr. Giraud turns from the wall and looks for the cane. It is gone. Again he is puzzled, this time as to how it disappeared, and why. Now truly exhausted, he falls asleep, and has a nightmare. From out of a corner of the screen the cane is pointed toward him like a billiard cue. It taunts him with the same trial thrusts a billiard player essays before he sends the white ball clicking to score a point. At this moment the cane, all by itself, thrusts itself "home" to score *its* point, right down his gullet—which wakes him up with a start. I think this would have made the dour old Dr. Freud, himself, smile. Another high point: the impressionistic Charleston Ball sequence, which shows that when Lubitsch wanted to, he could set ablaze visual

ABOVE: Lilyan Tashman, as Georgette Lalle, his old flame, and Dr. Giraud (Monte Blue) enter the Charleston contest at a New Year's Eve ball. (*So This Is Paris.*) BELOW: Mme. Lalle and Dr. Giraud win the Charleston contest—their prize a basket of champagne. Here Lubitsch rehearses the role of the master of ceremonies announcing the winners. (*So This Is Paris.*)

fireworks to match the most *avant-garde* cinema virtuosi. Amid the razzle-dazzle of this intoxicating scene is a close-up of the dancers' frenzied feet doing the Charleston, shot with the camera on the floor, in which the swift kaleidoscopic blacks and whites recalls for a moment the dynamic abstractions of play of light in Moholy-Nagy's *Lichtspiel* (Lightplay) and *Schwarz-Weiss* (Black-White) Again: when Suzanne, hearing over the radio that her husband (who did not go to serve a week's sentence in jail for bawling out a police officer) has just won the Charleston contest with Georgette Lalle, she goes after him in a huff. She arrives just as he is about to leave, squiffed to the gills. Not recognizing his wife (she is wearing a domino mask) he starts to flirt with her. He winks—but cannot reopen his eye. The eyelid is stuck—naturally, after all that champagne! After a panicky moment, the eyelid becomes unstuck. He grins with relief. But his wife, furious, now takes him by the arm to lead him home, while he smiles not only in surprise but also in high anticipation of the delights this sinuous little creature doubtless has in store for him!

By this time, everyone was "going Lubitsch," or so it seemed. "Lubitschean, sophisticated comedy, full of marital complications, petty jealousies, and humors of the married but otherwise unemployed," as John S. Cohen, Jr. put it. Richard Rosson's *Don't Tell Your Wife*, Roy Del Ruth's *Wolf's Clothing*, Lewis Milestone's *The Cave Man*, Erle Kenton's *Other Women's Husbands*, and Malcolm St. Clair's *The Grand Duchess and the Waiter* were archetypical. Indeed, one critic of the era, Ted Shane of *The New Yorker*, invented a special style to cope with these films, as seen in the following excerpts from his reviews of the latter two works:

The Grand Duchess and the Waiter is recommended without breath of reservation. Refashioned from a turgid, Froggy affair which sped in and out of the great Metropolis sometime during the season's theatrical debacle, it has been alchemized into pure, fine-worked platinum and has been set with a flashing jewel to boot. To keep right on shouting, it is become as graceful as milady's waving fan and as radiantly playful as a light breeze. It is become suave, polished comedy, creamy to the taste and soothing to the seat of comfort.

No plot is written over the face of its effete nonsense. Which, since the world is sick of plots, criticism and the term "sex appeal" is everything in its favor. It takes the formless form of a twinkling mass of colored lights, flashing with the charm of Adolphe Menjou, Florence Vidor, involuted through a wealth of delightful high comedy clowning. The oldest semifarcical undercurrent is employed: that of juxtaposing a slick, tophatted, humorous dandy who masquerades as a superior waiter, with a high and mighty lady whom he desires. He merely woos till all goes woosey for her. Then the end.

The acting is all highlights. Mr. Menjou has never been more downright ingratiating and smooth. Nor has Miss Vidor ever been lovelier or more truly inspired. The surrounding personages are gifted, too, carrying on their support with as much restraint and finesse as their leaders.

But the greatest lump of laurel to Mr. Malcolm St. Clair. His promise as a director is crystallized in this latest comedy-potion. He stands top of the list of native directorial genius and riff-raff (bless its motley ranks). He is our homegrown Lubitsch.

A previous work from this charmer was *Are Parents People*, in which Betty Bronson made so delicious a debut and in which André de Beranger (the Monsieur Lalle of *So This Is Paris*) made so hilarious a debut. It was also the initial effort of St. Clair as a director of silken comedy. Before that, he had been making those dog epics with Rin-Tin-Tin that Lubitsch found going on at Warner's when he signed with them. As you can see, the influence Lubitsch had on him was considerable.

Then there is the case of another director, Erle Kenton, whose sole claim to fame is that he, too, was once mesmerized by the art of "the Lubitsch touch," as witness:

Despite its title, *Other Women's Husbands* is delectable enough movie pie. An almost sophisticated narration of marital pastimes, it flavors of subtlety, wittiness and cleverness by virtue of its being absolute imitation of the style and manner of the Sultan of Satire, Herr Lubitsch. Step by step of its semi-charming way, the hand and prop of the grand maestro is evident. There is his emphasized pantomime, his genial kidding of his characters, his sofa stuff, his

finely arranged backgrounds, his typical witty gags and folderols of
direction. There is not, however, his highly economized story-telling.
This synthetic gem fails to attain the high polish the maestro would
have given it by being too flatly told, slow in getting to its point
and pretty shallow at the end.

Of course, the producing end of the thing is plagiarism on the
face of it, but since the honorable Lubitsch is an employee of the
Warner Brothers (the Shuberts of Hollywood), and the Warners
are responsible for *Other Women's Husbands*, it might all be said
to be, in a manner of speaking, in the family. No one need run to
court for literary swiping, as the lady Sophocles, Anne Nichols, is
doing because of *The Cohens and the Kellys*. Moreover, we had
rather see imitation Lubitsch a hundred times than a genuine D. W.
Griffith once.

"*Old Heidelberg* (subsequently called *The Student Prince*,
1927) is something new for me," said Lubitsch in New York
on the eve of sailing for Germany to shoot exteriors in the

The "German colony" of Hollywood celebrating the betrothal of
Vilma Banky and Rod La Rocque. L. to R.—the first Mrs. Lubitsch,
Hans Kräly, Mrs. Erich Pommer, Emil Jannings, Vilma Banky, Rod
La Rocque, Mrs. Emil Jannings, Victor Varconi (standing), Lu-
bitsch, Mrs. Victor Varconi, Mrs. Abraham Lehr, and Erich
Pommer. (1927)

old university town for his next film. "I got tired of frothy French farce comedies—and maybe the public is tired of them too." [19]

Robert E. Sherwood describes him then as "an extremely short, dark, thickset man, with ponderous shoulders and huge, twinkling eyes. In appearance he resembles a combination of Napoleon and Punchinello; in character he combines the best features of each. He is dominant, aggressive, emphatic and decisive—thereby bearing out his Napoleonic exterior. His kinship to the little figurehead on the jester's bauble is evident in the nimble alertness of his wit, the indefatigable irreverence in his attitude toward all the musty traditions, all the trammeling fetiches of his profession. He has no use for hokum, splurge and exaggerated bunk and he says so to everyone (his employers included). He still speaks with a musical comedy German accent, but it doesn't seem to bother him to any great extent. He is supremely voluble and forges confidently ahead through the intricacies of an alien language, without regard for the obstacles of speech which continually confront him."

When asked what opportunities this old chestnut about a student prince in love with a barmaid presented for the characteristic Lubitsch originality, he smiled, "Well, for one thing, there won't be any duels in it." "What?" exclaimed his interviewer in surprise, "A picture about old Heidelberg without student duels?" "That's right," said Lubitsch. "Who wants to compete with Douglas Fairbanks when it comes to duels?"

What was the director of *The Marriage Circle* and *Lady Windermere's Fan* going to make out of the beery sentimentality of this weepy favorite? Lubitsch's production company (MGM) had the answer to that. Hadn't Stroheim, two years before, turned the same trick with *The Merry Widow* with felicitous box-office results? Both were successful stage operettas, both had bittersweet librettos, both had

---

[19] Of course, two years later he was back at the old stand with another frothy French farce comedy, of which his public seemingly never tired, but this time the mixture had a new ingredient—sound. (*The Love Parade*.)

catchy music that was world renowned, and each director had an individual style which, when wedded to these elements, almost insured a fresh approach and a popular success. MGM proved it was right both times.

"In *The Student Prince*," Lubitsch told an interviewer, "I tried for simplicity. It's a tender, romantic story, and I treated it that way."

"Then it won't be anything like *Forbidden Paradise*, say."

"Not in the least! There I was above my characters, looking down on them, laughing at them. Here I'm on the same level with them, I'm one of them."

"A startlingly beautiful piece of cinema art," wrote Donald Thompson in *The Telegram*. "A thousand and one delightful touches on the part of the remarkable Mr. Lubitsch serve to make *The Student Prince* a joy," beamed Wilella Waldorf in the *New York Post*. "There never was a sweeter Kathi nor a more lovable old codger than the prince's tutor as played by Jean Hersholt," extolled George Gerhard in another journal. "But superimposed upon the stellar work of these two is the direction of Ernst Lubitsch, that German wizard of the screen. . . . In almost every sequence one could sit back and marvel at his artistic touch, his manner of raising humdrum scenes to the point of imaginative flights." "Mr. Lubitsch, whose *The Marriage Circle* is the finest and richest comedy yet put into the films, has done with *The Student Prince* exactly as was right and as was expected of him," said Quinn Martin in *The World*. Finally, from the Abou ben Adam of film critics of the time, Richard Watts in *The New York Herald Tribune*, "It captures the mood of tragic, sentimental love, of separated true lovers, and of a nostalgia for lost youth that is highly moving. . . . The director has made his work so shrewd a fusing of sentiment and highbred comedy that the picture does for wistful romance what Stroheim's *The Merry Widow* did for that of a more earthy type. . . . I predict it will be a considerable success."

Watts was right. The picture was a hit. The following year, 1928, Stroheim told the same kind of story, of an ill-starred love between a prince and a commoner, in the somber *Wedding March*, and the year after, 1929, Sternberg told it again, in the equally somber *The Case of Lena Smith*. All ended unhappily, but only *The Student Prince* ended happily for its financial backers.

One recalls the light satirical edge of the scenes of royal pomp and panoply as *The Student Prince* opens, which made one secretly pleased that Lubitsch wasn't giving up his franchise in this area even for a sentimental operetta. And when Kätchen, the innkeeper's daughter and barmaid, bounces on the bed to show Prince Karl Heinrich how good the springs are, and the shy young prince blushes at what she innocently appears to be doing, we knew then that the director of *Kiss Me Again* and *So This Is Paris* was still there, "cloven-hoof" and all, for all the "love's old sweet song" of the scenario. But the picture is basically charged with sentiment, as a true love story should be, and in this respect has an affinity with the unhappiness of Stroheim's *The Wedding March* (Part Two), as when the prince's return to the capital, after his romance with Kätchen and during his father's (the king's) illness, is accompanied by bleak rain, while in the now desolate Heidelberg fallen autumn leaves swirl in a wind as the lonely Kätchen stares from her window. The prince's return to the empty beer garden, now bereft of laughter and song, and his last meeting with Kätchen in the field, once a carpet of daisies during their short-lived summer romance, now withered and sere with autumn's chill—all this has an almost tactile feeling. And there is the final scene of the lovelorn prince and his princess (whom we never see—another Lubitsch touch, for she is nothing to him) in their nuptial carriage—a marriage that is just another entry in the Almanach de Gotha and nothing more.

Just as Lubitsch had a reunion with Pola Negri in the U.S. and made the memorable *Forbidden Paradise* with her, it was inevitable that he and Emil Jannings should get together, since they were now also both here, for another of *their* memorable pictures together. The result was *The Patriot* (1928), from Alfred Neumann's dramatization of his

ABOVE: Norma Shearer as Kätchen, the barmaid, in *The Student Prince*, that old war-horse about "the good old days" at the University of Heidelberg. *Kitsch* made palatable by the sensibility of Lubitsch for the opportunity here offered for archetypical operetta sentiment and bittersweet romance—a vanished world, vanished as if it had never existed. (1927) BELOW: Lubitsch with his pet scenarist, Hans Kräly, going over the script of *The Patriot* before the start of actual shooting. (1928)

novel about the mad Czar Paul I of Russia and how his best friend, Count Pahlen, had to have him killed "for the good of the state." This is what makes Pahlen the "patriot" of the title. Lewis Stone played Pahlen very well, indeed, and Jannings was magnificent as the czar: a pathetic, friendless, imbecilic monster, cruel and childish, murderous, lecherous, but, most of all, stark, raving mad—something of an anticlimax for the lubricious Catherine the Great, whose idiot son he was. Yet the czar was still a human being, and there were moments when, between his outbursts of loutishness, he was genuinely touching in his despair, as Jannings played him, especially toward the end when he realizes there is a plot to assassinate him, and he runs through the vast palace halls crying for Pahlen to save him. For Jannings the part was a "field day," and he made the most of it, and that "most" was as good as either star or director had ever done in their historic spectacles together.

"A mighty picture," raved *The New York Times*. "Jannings outshines even his performances in *Variety* and *The Last Laugh* as the mad czar. . . . This motion picture is a credit to the screen." "Not the least of Jannings' feats," wrote Richard Watts in *The New York Herald Tribune*, "was his ability to make Paul at the same time a homicidal maniac, a boorish clown and a pitiful, moving human being. . . . Though the picture is essentially a tragedy, Ernst Lubitsch, who directed, has made, at least half of it, that sort of sly, brilliant sex comedy that mocks the czar's amorousness without ever obtruding on the tragic mood of the drama. . . . The prankish Lubitsch, whose chief directorial joy it is to be ironically facetious in his attitude toward screen amorousness, has, as it happens, made these scenes with the supposedly ponderous Jannings the latter's finest." The messianic Benjamin DeCasseres, in an ode surely not matched since Pindar, delivered himself of such a "trumpet voluntary" heralding the picture's grandeur that one must constrain oneself in quoting from it lest one be accused of resorting to the most shameless hyperbole. *"The Patriot* is the greatest motion picture ever made; it is the *Hamlet* of the screen—and Emil Jannings is the greatest actor in the world. As for Lubitsch, it is his greatest masterpiece of direction. With *The Patriot* he ranks easily with Max Reinhardt and Gordon Craig!"

Nine bullseyes in a row, and each in turn acclaimed as having outdone the others. It stands as a record unparalleled in screen annals.

Again the ubiquitous "Lubitsch touch" was evident, as much a part of a Lubitsch picture as the equally ubiquitous cigar was a part of his physiognomy. For instance: the crazy monarch is putting his guard through their paces. "Squads right, squads left, one, two, one. . . ." Suddenly he loses interest and rushes off, leaving the troops with one foot upraised. Pahlen is recounting an amusing sexual escapade with his mistress to regale the czar, who is lappng it up in high glee. Suddenly the glee turns to panting concupiscence,

"Lights! Camera! Action!" Lubitsch on the set at Paramount ready for a scene for *The Patriot*. (1928)

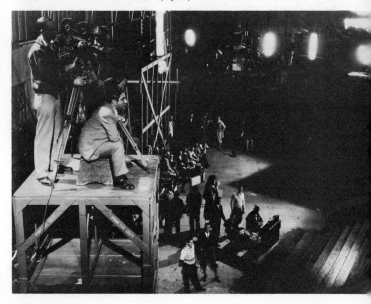

Lewis Stone as Count Pahlen, the czar's confidant and closest friend, and Emil Jannings as the nutty Czar Paul I. Pahlen is telling the czar a risqué anecdote about his mistress. (*The Patriot.*)

and the czar rushes off to his own mistress, slamming the door behind him. The camera holds on the door. A moment later, the door opens slightly, and we see the czar's arm holding her pet pekinese by the scruff of the neck as he drops it to the floor, momentarily exiling it from the room. Fadeout on the bewildered pooch. (That dog gets exiled quite a bit throughout the course of the film, until finally the czar, in exasperation, throws him out the window.) Another time, the czar, having been playfully slapped on the cheek several times by his coquettish mistress, suddenly wakes to the importance of his position and socks the lady in the jaw with considerable violence, sending her tumbling over the floor. Or still another time: when he is inspecting his platoon of guards in the palace, he suddenly stops before one of them, leers at him, approaches and pokes his finger in the man's face, rams his thumb into his mouth, then belabors him with his whip—all on a sudden whim. (It is this soldier who is later called on by Count Pahlen to strangle the czar when the ruler subsequently takes refuge on his throne, all else having failed him.) Another time the czar, at dinner, has moved his chair close to the beauteous Countess Ostermann. He fawns on her, hopeful of some reciprocal glance. In the midst of his ardent wooing of the now terrified countess, and with no transition, it occurs to him he is too far from his plate, so he slides his chair back to its proper place and begins ravenously to eat. Or when furiously involved with important state papers, he suddenly throws them all up in the air and begins very seriously to rearrange several insignificant *objets d'art* on his desk. Or he will suddenly become lonesome, running through the palace corridors crying out for his only friend—Pahlen, who will be his murderer. "It is the tragic point of the drama," as Richard Watts pointed out, "that Pahlen, a ruthless plotter, a traitor to the king who loved and trusted him, a betrayer of his sweetheart, is at the same time a gallant patriot, who was willing to sacrifice not only his life, but his honor, in the interests of his country. At the end, his victim slain, his people freed, and a new emperor on the throne, he seats himself in a room in his home, where he can hear the tumult of the triumphant mob about him, and dies at the hand of the very man who had killed the czar, as the nearby church bells proclaim a new ruler of Russia."

Even the death of the czar has its own "touch." Failing to find Pahlen, the frightened czar hides behind a curtain. His assassin enters the room looking for him. Alas, the curtain is too short—there are the czar's feet sticking out at the bottom. And despite all that has gone before, this isn't funny—this is a touch to bring tears to the eyes.

That was Lubitsch.

There is a bit of fluff by Alfred de Musset (described by him as "a proverb in one act") called *A Door Should Be Either Open or Shut*, consisting of a dialogue between a

ABOVE: The anecdote so inflames the concupiscence of the czar that he rushes immediately to his own mistress to duplicate the anecdote for himself. Vera Voronina as Mlle. Lapoukhine, the delectable mistress. (*The Patriot*.) RIGHT: A moment of horseplay on the set between the star and director of *The Patriot*.

bachelor count on the make and a married marquise. The only action consists in the lady suddenly leaving or just as suddenly deciding to come back, which is to say, the opening and closing of the door. Nor must we overlook Georges Feydeau's riot of ribaldry, *A Flea in Her Ear*, whose physical action consists almost entirely of people running in and out of doors—this time for *three acts*. Labiche and Michel in *An Italian Straw Hat* (so devastatingly transported to the screen by René Clair) relied equally on doors for the principal action. And so it went with the boulevard *farceurs* in the gaslit Paris of Offenbach and Degas.

So the idea of using doors as a comic device was old stuff on the stage. But on the screen it was something new, and its greatest exponent was Lubitsch. We have mentioned Mary Pickford's exasperation with him "as a director of doors" during the shooting of *Rosita*, and have delineated his use of this device in *The Patriot*. In *The Marriage Circle*, when Monte Blue leaves Marie Prevost in a huff, to emphasize the finality of his leaving her, Lubitsch has him go out of door after door after door, until he is finally in the street, glad to be out of that trap. In *Passion*, Mme. Dubarry opens a door in Louis XV's palace that is not a door at all, but a secret panel that opens into the king's bedroom. In *Lady Windermere's Fan*, the exit of Lady Windermere through one door of Lord Darlington's apartment and the entrance of Mrs. Erlynne through another forms the dramatic climax of the film. We have already described the opening and closing of the bedroom door in Dr. Giraud's apartment (the episode with the cane appearing and disappearing) in *So This Is Paris*. There is also the quarrel between the young married woman and her lover (Maurice Chevalier) at the beginning of *The Love Parade*, first heard through the closed door of her bedroom, then continued as the door opens and they both come in, the woman holding a lady's flouncy garter in her hand, which she has apparently found in his pocket, and is jealously demanding to know whose it is. "Yours!" he smiles. "Mine?" she exclaims, lifting up her skirt to show the garters on her two shapely legs. In *Monte Carlo*, while Jack Buchanan is massaging Jeanette

MacDonald's scalp and face to relieve her nervous tension, her initial objections gradually change to sighs of "oohs" and "ahs" and accompanying exclamations of pleasure at the soothing effect, whereupon Lubitsch cuts suddenly to Zasu Pitts, her maid, listening in awe at the door to what must be going on inside. Again in *The Love Parade*, after a quarrel between Chevalier as the prince consort and Jeanette MacDonald as the queen, when he is placed practically under "house arrest," there's a knock on the door. Chevalier, still angry, goes to open it. "Any old clothes?" asks a bearded old-clothes man. "No!" shouts Chevalier, about to shut the door abruptly. "Those clothes aren't going to fit you when you get out of here," remonstrates the old fellow. The door bangs shut on him. There is the closed door at the beginning of *Trouble in Paradise*, before which stand two young women jabbering away excitedly in Italian in a Venetian hotel corridor because the occupant has not answered their ring (the occupant has been knocked unconscious by a burglar), the episode that starts the whole plot rolling. Even in Lubitsch's brief section in *If I Had a Million*, the director builds his suspense by having Charles Laughton go through a series of doors, each of increasing executive importance before he goes through the ultimate and most prestigious one to deliver his devastating (and now famous) razz to his boss. The dramatic crux of *Angel* is a door through which Herbert Marshall, as the husband doubtful of his wife's fidelity, must or must not go, a decision which will either win or lose his wife's (Marlene Dietrich's) affection. And, of course, there are the doors of the deluxe Parisian hotel in *Ninotchka* behind which is the suite occupied by the raffish trio from Moscow representing the Soviet Trade Commission. They've been told that if you ring three times a maid comes in, a pretty *French* maid. They try it and, sure enough, a pretty young maid comes, knocks on the door, and goes in. The camera stays focused on the door. Exclamations of approval are heard through the door. A moment later she comes out, delighted, and returns with two more maids like her. They all enter and this time the hilarity from behind the door is tripled.

Douglas Fairbanks, Jr., who co-starred in *That Lady in Ermine*, quotes Lubitsch as saying, even at that late date, that "doors were as important as the actors." Lubitsch had many levels of this kind of wacky humor, told just as laconically, as often as not emanating from a perfectly "dead pan" when a comic touch was desired.

Trying to explain it to an interviewer, he said: "It's the king in his bedroom with his suspenders hanging; [20] it's the gondolier hauling garbage on a moonlit night in Venice, singing romantically despite his gondola full of garbage; it's the husband bidding his wife a tearful *au revoir* as he sees her off on a journey, then rushing madly to the nearest telephone booth to call up his inamorata. It's based on the theory that at least twice a day the most dignified human being is ridiculous."

A psychiatrist defined it as having "the subtle ingredients of irony, pathos, bitterness and laughter—all in one hypo shot. It is more often sarcasm, felt rather than seen, or it springs out of an impossible situation which might easily degrade a hero or disqualify a genius."

Actually, it belongs in the realm of psychoanalysis.

On another occasion Lubitsch said of it: "If I knew what it was, I mean, if I became conscious of it, I might not have done it." Then: "Can I help it if people read hidden meanings into my work?" And he laughed. As we have said, he was a great kidder.

III

Film is the language of images, and images don't speak.
—PIRANDELLO

From the very beginning, attempts had been made to synchronize motion pictures with sound. Edison filmed opera stars and behind the screen played cylindrical recordings of

[20] Stroheim once told me what he regarded as the difference between Lubitsch and himself. "Lubitsch shows you the king on his throne, then follows this with the king in his bedroom. I show you the king in his bedroom, first, so you'll know what he is when you see him on his throne."

ABOVE: Lubitsch had a method of playing the piano all his own. Here he takes time off on the set of *The Patriot* for a solo jam session. BELOW: He played the cello, too. The fingering and bow arm accurate. He "picked it up" by himself, as he did the piano.

the arias they were shown singing on film. But this and more elaborate effects never really caught on. In 1924 D. W. Griffith declared the sound film was technically impossible and saw no future for it, anyway, as "it would ruin the magic of the silent film." He believed in effective music scores for films and, indeed, collaborated on the score for *The Birth of a Nation*. (Later he was to try his hand at making sound films when they were a fact, but his heart wasn't in it.)

By 1928 the photoelectric cell had been invented, thus making it possible not only to record the musical score for a film in synchronization with the action on a soundtrack accompanying the film images, but also to record the voices of the actors and, indeed, all sound effects. So movies began to talk. Warner Brothers, those canny pioneers, paved the way with *The Jazz Singer*, from the Samson Raphaelson stage hit, and starring Al Jolson.

Long before sound, Stroheim had lamented its absence and, when it came, prepared a dialogue version of his *Blind Husbands*, which remained an unrealized project.[21] Carl Dreyer, whose *The Passion of Joan of Arc* had stunned everyone the year *The Patriot* came out, said that if he had been able to use sound when he started, he would have preferred to record the voices of Joan and her inquisitors. James Cruze, whose *The Covered Wagon*, *Hollywood*, and *Beggar on Horseback* were among the brighter lights of the Hollywood *aurora borealis*, disliked talking films, though later he made several, including *The Great Gabbo* and *David Harum* —not on a plane with his best silent work. Monta Bell, yet another Lubitsch and Chaplin disciple, also disliked them. So did René Clair, who then proceeded to make three smash-hit sound films in a row to contradict his censure— *Sous les Toits de Paris*, *Le Million*, and *À Nous la Liberté*. King Vidor with *Hallelujah*, Rouben Mamoulian with *Applause*, and Sternberg with *The Blue Angel* and then *Morocco* —all proved that the best elements of the silent and sound film could be fused into a perfect, homogeneous whole, with none of "dat ol' black magic" of the silent film lost in the

[21] His first talking film, *Walking Down Broadway*, was scrapped by its ornery producer and remade by another director.

transition. Murnau, alas, did not live to try his hand with sound, and it is one of the real tragedies of the screen that this was not to be vouchsafed us. Another German director, Lupu Pick, felt so desolate about what had happened to his beloved medium, the silent film, that he committed suicide. Eisenstein, Alexandrov, and Dovzhenko in the U.S.S.R., however, issued a manifesto proclaiming the new age of the sound film and setting down its aesthetic principles. (A partial realization of them can be seen in *Alexander Nevsky*, *Romance Sentimentale*, and *Ivan*.) Pudovkin's *The Deserter* was a very experimental first sound film, as was Walter Ruttmann's *Melody of the World* and Fritz Lang's *M*. Some made the transition from silence to sound gracefully, others did not. Meanwhile, in Paris there was organized a "League of Silence," composed of critics, directors, and producers, who were opposed to talking films. And in Berlin as late as 1954, during the film festival there, Thomas Mann stated, "If I may say so, I find it sad that the silent film had to be supplanted by the sound film. The development of the silent film had really reached a high degree of expressiveness."

Chaplin, of course, held out longer than anyone, deriding sound in the opening scene of *City Lights* (1931), singing a gibberish ditty five years later in *Modern Times* (1936) (a triple accomplishment, for he was being both satirical and creative in the truest sense by inventing a parody French *lingua franca* à la James Joyce, and, of course, being very funny in the process), and not till a decade later, in 1940, did he make his first talking film, *The Great Dictator*.

And Lubitsch? In 1923 he was highly doubtful of both sound and color, which he said could lead to the most disastrous aesthetic results. Curiously, what interested him then were the possibilities of the stereoptican (three-dimensional) film. But he, too, when sound was an established fact, not only dived right in, but also hailed it as a medium superior in its possibilities to the silent film. He didn't miss a beat in the transition.

André Malraux has called the art of painting and sculpture "the voices of silence," and, indeed, the art of the silent

Lubitsch at work. A close-up for *Eternal Love*. The director is lying prone behind the light on the wooden structure. The audience will see the finger of the girl pointed directly at them (the camera). (1929)

film by 1929, when the floodgates of the sound film opened, had reached a very high degree of expressiveness which now would be inundated. But even he would have had to admit that *The Love Parade* (1929), Lubitsch's first sound film, was one of the felicitous justifications of the new medium.

Having become the "Reinhardt of the silent screen," in both the spectacle and the *Kammerspiel* film, Lubitsch would now have to become its Offenbach. Wasn't Offenbach, the son of a German-Jewish cantor, the very quintessence of the Parisian spirit in the Second Empire of Louis Napoleon? Wasn't the world's greatest can-can, the one in Offenbach's *Orpheus in Hades*, as French as "La Marseillaise"? So why shouldn't the German Lubitsch do a typical French operetta, an all-out buffoonery on the order of *Gaieté Parisienne* and, yes, *Orpheus in Hades?* There was no good reason why, so he did.

Two magnums of champagne in the foreground, one on each side of the screen, point at a line of revue girls kicking their legs up to this tune:

—which Lupino Lane, as Maurice Chevalier's valet, with his upturned nose like one of Molière's lackeys, takes up in a reprise with a flouncy lyric about setting a table for two for a midnight rendezvous.

This was the first song heard in a Lubitsch film. It was to be the forerunner of many more, all catchy and bouncy, done in the true operetta style. Just as he inspired his writers, he inspired his composers, pleading for a "Lubitsch song" and invariably getting it. And when even another director was inspired by Lubitsch, as Mamoulian undeniably was in *Love Me Tonight* (also with Chevalier), the songs in it, especially "Mimi," were typical "Lubitsch songs."

Ernst Vajda, co-scenarist with Guy Bolton of *The Love Parade*, told of Lubitsch's concern with the appearance of his actresses. He would even don an actress's clothes to show her how she should look and walk in them. Jeanette Mac-Donald's wardrobe was always most carefully supervised by him. He was allergic to zippers so Jeanette had to be buttoned into her costumes.

He would come to Vajda's house to work on scripts [22] because Vajda's cook was better than his own. He'd come in the morning and after a few hours concentrated work they'd break for lunch, following which he would sit at the piano and regale himself for an hour or so to relax before resuming

[22] They did four films together.

work. He played by ear, since he couldn't read a note, but would play difficult things that he picked up (like Liszt's "Liebestraum"), and was really a fairly good piano player.

He had always liked American stage musicals, especially minstrel shows, so it was natural for him to make his first sound film a musical one. Besides, there were "movie-esque" stories that could be realized only with music, like *The Love Parade*, which is about a queen and her bored prince consort who finally revolts and manages a happy end for himself and his no-longer-so-imperious bride, a sort of musical *Taming of the Shrew*.

Now, with sound, dialogue became not just a matter of repartee but in the phrase of John Simon, "as in Wilde, repartee plus style." And, indeed, the wit of the dialogue in *The Love Parade* crackled like a whole arsenal of mocking catherine-wheels interspersed with the most ardent romanticism. Even when the words spilled over into song, or were catapulted into a song, the song's words came not as a break in the action, but as its climax. "Lupino Lane's opening song snapped the picture off as if it had been flung out by a rubber-band," observed Kenneth White. "Chevalier's singing of 'Nobody's Using It Now' seemed the only end to a series of exasperations. (And) when a song, like 'Paris, Please Stay the Same,' came in the middle of an episode, Lubitsch did not let it die out but multiplied its effects in a comic mood to carry the farce that much farther." In short, he achieved a greater fluidity with this first screen musical than the stage musical itself had achieved up to that time, and it is not until the theatrical presentation of *My Fair Lady* a generation later that we find its match on the stage in quite the same way.

"In his comedies," remarked the critic, Kenneth White,[23] "his camera flies from playful attention to detail up to the individuals whose manners they expose, and back again; his camera moves constantly to obtain speed, impressiveness or dramatic pause." Knowing the possibilities inherent in the medium, he developed them to the very limits of their extent. Jeanette MacDonald might sing "Dream Lover" à la Ziegfeld Follies (happily *sans* the big staircase with tall girls

[23] In *Hound & Horn*, Winter, 1931.

What more logical way to make the transition from silence to sound than with the musical film? Lubitsch chose the operetta form, orchestrating his visuals with witty sound effects, dialogue, and ingratiating music. He didn't miss a beat. Jeanette MacDonald and Maurice Chevalier in *The Love Parade.* (1929)

in Pawnee Indian or Folies Bergères costumes stepping archly down, with which Ziegfeld would have embellished it!), but Lupino Lane and Lillian Roth, as valet and maid in the royal palace, burlesqued their master's and mistress's plaintive yearnings with the insolent bravura that only a director absolutely sure of his virtuosity could pull off.

The result was a resounding success with the public as well as the critics. One critic, a profound observer of the early American movie screen when he was not translating Gorky, was Alexander Bakshy who said: "More ingratiating with audiences than even Maurice Chevalier was its more telling comedy, produced by deft juxtaposition and contrasts of scenes provided by Lubitsch himself."

Such as the bored American tourists in a bus suddenly waking to interest when their guide tells them that the Sylvanian royal palace cost $110,000,000 (another Lubitsch dig at "money-as-money"); the cannons booming on the prince's wedding night and his futile efforts to stop them; the gibberish "Afghanese" of the Afghan ambassador, skeptical of a marriage in which the woman dominates the man, with his "No chongo!" (It won't work) as his final verdict; the prince, when told of his royal predecessor's cross-eyes on the medal he is wearing, saying: "Stanislaws the 22nd cross-eyed? They never taught that in school!"; the palace watchdog who barks a reprise of the chorus of a sentimental song to Paris in "musical barks"; a cabinet meeting discussing the necessity of the queen's marrying (and presided over by the queen), heard through the doorway (again) through which an admiral stalks out as the queen's voice is heard saying, "I certainly don't need any help from the Navy!"; the large staff used by the court chamberlain to announce with three dramatic knocks the entrance of the queen for her marriage, which is exchanged for a small wand that makes two little taps for the prince's entrance; the queen in her white uniform of the Radetsky Hussars, velvet dolman and all, like a female Prince Danilo, singing the "Grenadiers' Song" before her guard while the prince, with no official duties, sleeps the morning away; the servants in the kitchen who gossip over their masters' peccadillos (anticipating by a decade the acid parallel between masters and servants in Renoir's *La Règle de Jeu*); the prince walking the entire length of the palace, followed by the anxious queen, just to get his pajamas to pack, when he has decided to leave her—the camera doggedly following him every foot of the way; the charming "comeuppance" of the queen at the close when she and the prince try to determine a suitable "punishment" for her shrewishness, the tables now being turned. . . . These are but a few of many moments that made *The Love Parade* a Lubitsch picture more than a Chevalier one, though it did

establish them both (and Miss MacDonald, too) as an ir-
resistable team in films of this *genre* that they were to do
together again and again.

Lubitsch was now looking around for his next story. He
was under contract to Paramount, the studio that imported
Eisenstein,[24] and was "riding the crest of the wave," as they
say—he could do anything he wanted. He might have turned
to Alarcón's nineteenth-century sketch of Spanish life, *The
Three-Cornered Hat*, a merry charade about a miller, his
pretty wife, and the corregidor (a high official of the town)
who panted after her, which Manuel de Falla embellished
with a blazing musical score in 1919, or to Ravel's sardonic
one-act opera, *L'Heure Espagnole* (1907), about lovers being
hidden in grandfathers' clocks. What are their plots but delightful "Lubitsch scenarios," in effect? (The former was
subsequently filmed twice, by H. d'Abbadie d'Arrast in Spain
and in Italy starring Vittorio De Sica.)

He found his next plot, however, in an obscure German
stage work, *The Blue Coast*, by Hans Müller, which, together with an episode from Booth Tarkington's *Monsieur
Beaucaire*, he and his writers, Ernst Vajda and Vincent
Lawrence, fashioned into *Monte Carlo* (1930), another
screen musical.

But to say this was "another screen musical" is to say the
opposite of what it really was, a captivating flight of the
spirit in the guise of the traditional operetta, with an an-
tiphonal passage: the famous "Blue Express" scene that was
the talk of the movie world of the time. This was the episode
that introduced the hit song, "Beyond the Blue Horizon."
Commented Kenneth White:

Monte Carlo carried the methods of *The Love Parade* even
further. Objects about the players, an engine rushing through the
countryside, the figure in a clock-tower, became the instruments of
musical and amusing comment. Sounds and music, in *Monte Carlo*,
perform the same function for the ear that the camera does for the
eye; an auditory breadth and inclusiveness is achieved that could
not possibly be obtained in any other representational art. The epi-

[24] To whom Eisenstein submitted several scripts, all rejected. He
then went to Mexico.

sode in which the engine's flying wheels introduce the dramatic mood of a song Jeanette MacDonald is on the point of singing and musically sustain the visual and auditory effect of swift motion, is nothing short of a masterpiece of sound direction. In a sense, the episode can be called one of "sound montage," a stylistic method which leaves no effect unsupplied to the spectator. A German film called *Zwei Herzen im Drei-Viertel Takt* attempted to gain some of the effects of *Monte Carlo*, but failed precisely where Lubitsch succeeded: in blending sounds with the visual pattern.

With Jack Buchanan's English music-hall tenor substituting this time for the cognac baritone of Chevalier, Jeanette MacDonald slithering in and out of her boudoir, joining him in a love duet over the telephone (Lubitsch was now doing things no one ever even thought of before, such complete freedom of method had he already achieved in the new medium), Zasu Pitts as a querulous maid, and Claude Allister as the jilted baron delivering his patter songs, *Monte*

Now sure of his formula, he elaborated on it in a second film-operetta, *Monte Carlo*, again with Jeanette MacDonld and with the English music-hall star, Jack Buchanan. This film contained the memorable "Beyond the Blue Horizon" sequence. (1930)

Carlo had not only a quartet of raffish principals but as many raffish secondary roles. Long before Rex Harrison did his "talking" songs like "Why Can't the English?" and "I've Grown Accustomed to Her Face" in *My Fair Lady*, Claude Allister had done it in *Monte Carlo*—using what the Germans call *Sprechgesang*, literally "speaking-singing."

Not only is there not a wasted foot of film, there is not a wasted frame. Every second counts. A car starts and arrives in an almost imperceptible dissolve, scarcely five seconds on the screen, in the smoothest transition possible. Again, as would be irresistible to him in a film set in the gambling capital of Europe, Lubitsch has his wry comments about "money-as-money," as when Jeanette MacDonald, musing in the train on the would-be husband she has just run away from, grants that he had everything a woman could desire: "He's rich, he's wealthy, and he's got nothing but money!" Or, when she rubs a hunchback's hump for luck, just before she enters the casino, the hunchback turns to her, doffs his hat and smiles, "Fifty francs, please." (Stroheim in one of the casino scenes of *Foolish Wives*, a film obsessed with money, also set in Monte Carlo, has Karamzin rub the bank-note he's going to play on a hunchback's hump, but Lubitsch goes him one better.)

The intonation, the *timbre*, with which the repartee is delivered, has now become a meaningful part of the lines themselves, the elasticity of the lines being drawn to a tautness which sent them snapping back in surprise, as sudden and as unexpected as a jack-in-the-box popping up. Or lines are juggled and come down (or sometimes are left up in the air like the unfinished joke that the jilted baron starts to tell in the train till he realizes the joke's on himself)—come down where you least expect them or in a different "color" than when they went up. This playing with words, the free use of *non sequiturs*, *bon mots* that turned in on themselves, a veritable bengal lights of impish frolickings with seemingly the whole spectrum of the human voice (but never a solecism—*not ever*)—all this became also a part of the "Lubitsch touch" if, indeed, it was now possible to isolate these "touches" from anything else in the film. So closely integrated were they with the action that the whole film became a "Lubitsch touch." There was just no letup in the "touches." Each catapulted the next one into place.

All this betokened, too, a monstrous agility of mind, unique even at a time when the sound film was new and everyone was experimenting with it in that first rapture with this miraculous toy, that time to which Walter Kerr referred to so nostalgically as ". . . (the) never-quite-to-be-recaptured excitements of films when Chaplin and Keaton and Ernst Lubitsch were yearly promises . . ." [25]

Despite the encomiums of praise lavished on *The Love Parade*, the critics outdid themselves to express their delight with *Monte Carlo*, and were now vying with each other to find phrases that would convey the fact that *The Smiling Lieutenant* (1932), set in a superficially gilded, braided Vienna, and which came next, topped even those two. Was Lubitsch going to repeat the incredible feat he had accomplished with his silent films in surpassing himself with each picture?

"For just about the best time you've ever had in a motion picture theatre, rush right to see *The Smiling Lieutenant*," wrote Mildred Martin in *The Philadelphia Inquirer*. "It's a film that will linger long and lovingly in the memory. So much perfection comes along so infrequently that upon finding it one feels like tossing hats in the air and sending all one's best friends, and even enemies, to have one really good time. . . . It is a story as light as a meringue, as dainty as a lace valentine, and naughty enough to supply one with ample spice. It has all been done, however, in such beautiful taste and with so light a touch that scenes that might have been dangerous less delicately handled could not possibly offend the most puritanical. . . . Lubitsch has surpassed himself."

Hans Müller, he of *Monte Carlo's* source, again provided the source for this one, *Nux, the Prince Consort* (that made three "prince consorts" in a row for Lubitsch), which also served as the source for Oscar Strauss's world-famous turn of the century operetta, *A Waltz Dream*. It had already been lovingly filmed at Ufa in Germany by Ludwig Berger as a

[25] "The Movies Are Better Than the Theatre," *The New York Times*, March 3, 1968.

A third screen operetta followed, *The Smiling Lieutenant*, derived from Oscar Strauss's *A Waltz Dream*—three sound-film hits in a row, a feat duplicated only by René Clair in France with his own initial trio of sound films, also musicals—*Sous les Toits de Paris*, *Le Million*, and *A Nous la Liberté*. (George Barbier, Miriam Hopkins, and Maurice Chevalier.) (1932)

silent picture with Mady Christians and Willy Fritsch, and achieved international success second only to those other two silent film operettas, Lubitsch's *The Student Prince* and Stroheim's *The Merry Widow*, the biggest success of all three. Lubitsch's penchant for showing woman as the sexual aggressor, begun in his American silent films, was now continuing in his sound films, in the first three of which the man ends up as the queen's consort, chosen by the queen. One recalls that Stroheim, too, had a penchant (among his others) for this same situation, as in *Queen Kelly* when Seena Owen, as the choleric queen, catches Gloria Swanson (Kitty Kelly) and Walter Byron (Prince Wolfram, her fiancé) *in flagrante*. The queen, outraged at the prince's amorous dalliance on the eve of their wedding, lashes at him in fury with a riding crop. Bewildered at this revelation, Kitty Kelly whimpers to the queen, incredulously, "Is he marrying *you?*" To which the queen replies witheringly, "No, I'm marrying *him!*"

"Directed with frequent flashes of positive genius," wrote William Boehnel in *The New York Telegram*, "embodying some of the most brilliant of the famous 'Lubitsch touches.' . . . Here Lubitsch has done what René Clair did in *Le Million*. Like Clair, Lubitsch has allowed his music as well as his camera to work for him. There are long stretches when only a musical motif is used, and yet one is able to understand the action perfectly. Indeed, it is an excellent example of the use of the silent-picture technique and talking and sound-picture methods. The dialogue is sparingly, almost grudgingly, used."

"All the shrewd delights that were promised in *The Love Parade*," wrote Richard Watts in *The New York Herald Tribune*, "are realized in *The Smiling Lieutenant* and with an economy and sureness that give it a luster which no other American-made comedy–satire has achieved. One must look to René Clair's *Le Million* to find its peer."

"I do not hesitate an instant to call it Lubitsch's best talking film," said John S. Cohen, Jr., in *The New York Sun*, "largely for the reason that most of it is silent, most of it is pantomime with incidental dialogue, the whole last half being practically and refreshingly mute save for its synchronized score and its sound effects. . . . The production is beautiful with its exquisitely lighted marble interiors, its palatial marble stairways and its regal atmosphere, and several of the original waltzes are still lovely enough to melt you completely."

The point of all this is to indicate Lubitsch's originality, as first commented upon, and to bring to light again, after all these years, some of the honeyed phrases with which this originality was received—phrases that were uniquely reserved for him, as in Watts's opening line of his review which spoke of ". . . *The Smiling Lieutenant*, which rolled on exquisitely ball-bearinged wheels across the screen of the Criterion Theatre last night. . . ."

True, it was yet another variation on the mythical kingdom peopled by operetta characters, an eternal never-never land where the "trouble in paradise" was scarcely more than the momentary agitation of the moonlit garden pool ruffled for a fleeting instant by the darting goldfish in *Forbidden Paradise* (what a happier world, that could engender such delicate things!). But what more natural than that such an unreal place like Hollywood, dedicated to "make-believe," should so bewitchingly spin out farragos of Sylvanias, Ruritanias, Flausenthurms, and Graustarks. And when the setting was a "real" place, like the Vienna of *The Smiling Lieutenant*, it was a prop Vienna of prop bittersweet *amour* and gaiety, amidst whose swooning aura the love of Monsieur Chevalier and Mademoiselle Claudette Colbert—ah, those Viennese!—rose to its rose-leafiest ecstasy.

Elsewhere, we have described the checker-board scene between Chevalier and Miriam Hopkins. There is also the hilarious satire on court ritual in the preparation of the bridal couple's royal bedchamber on their nuptial night, and the scene where the princess threatens her father, the king, if he doesn't let her marry the handsome commoner, the lieutenant, with, "If you don't let me marry him, I'll—I'll marry an American!" There is one marvelous cinematic passage I must not fail to mention. When Franzi, the lieutenant's old flame, is summoned by the princess to the palace to give her lessons in how to win her husband's affection (he still pines for Franzi), she dutifully obeys. We see her running up the palace steps and, in an enchanting overlapping dissolve begun while she is still flying up the steps, we already see her at the piano as the camera glides across the keyboard in a continuing movement through the dissolve as Franzi's hands negotiate an arpeggio from lowest bass to highest treble, the whole thing done as a single movement from the bottom of the steps to the high treble of the keyboard. It is done so swiftly and smoothly as literally to take your breath away. After which, Franzi gets up, smiles at the princess, gives her a hefty slap for taking her lieutenant from her, then says, "Now let's get down to business."

Then a strange thing happened.

Lubitsch made a complete *volte-face* from the gay, frothy trifles that were so much more than that, and next filmed a dark, somber drama from Maurice Rostand's bitter pacifist play, *The Man I Killed*. Films didn't exist in a vacuum after all, but in a world where that periodic insanity, war, also existed. Two years before, Lewis Milestone had made *All Quiet on the Western Front*, and before that King Vidor had made *The Big Parade*; in Germany, G. W. Pabst with *Westfront 1918*, and in France, Leon Poirer with *Verdun: visions d'histoire* and Abel Gance with *J'Accuse*, not to mention the Russians—Eisenstein, Ermler, Pudovkin, and Dovzhenko—all had seemingly delivered the final condemnation of war as an instrument of national policy.

What was the director of *Kiss Me Again* and *The Love Parade* doing in this area of the human condition? True, he had ridiculed war in a satirical comedy years ago, in *Die Bergkatze*, but that was a comedy, almost a burlesque. Now he was in dead earnest, risking a brilliant career with a story so "off beat" that no other film director would touch it. Besides, the public was sated with war films by 1932. It sought escapist entertainment. The economic depression set off by the stock-market crash in Wall Street in 1929 had far-flung reverberations. How could it continue to be "business as usual"? In those parlous days Lubitsch revealed the serious man within the "frivolous artist"—the man "with a tragic sense of life" (in Unamuno's phrase), that had always been there.

With Rousseau he could say, "I, alone, know my heart." With *The Man I Killed* (1932) he had done an act of faith which is always an act of exorcism. Quite simply, it was something he had to do—to purge himself, if you will, of what John Grierson was to call his "desolate sophistication."

The Man I Killed employed a theme rare for the screen—contrition. A young Frenchman, who had killed a German youth in a shellhole during the war, is so conscience stricken,

Now that Lubitsch could do whatever he wanted, he chose a work that no one else would have touched—the bitter anti-war play, *The Man I Killed*, by Maurice Rostand. He didn't have to do it, he could have "played it safe," like many other directors, but there are times when the honest artist does what he feels he must do, like Vidor making *Our Daily Bread*, De Sica making *Umberto D*, Sternberg making *Anatahan*, or to quote the classic example, Stroheim making *Greed*. Ultimately, the validity of Lubitsch's somber statement in this film was proved only too true—Phillips Holmes, seen here with Nancy Carroll and Lionel Barrymore, was killed in World War II. (1932)

after the war, that he confesses to a priest as if he were a criminal. The priest glibly absolves him, assuring him that he merely did his duty. "Duty?" the young man asks. "Why is it my duty to kill?" He goes to Germany to seek out the parents of the youth he killed so that he may fall on his knees before them and beg their forgiveness. The problem here was how to tell a story in which not the actions of the characters but the dark violence of their thoughts was the important thing.

So immersed did Lubitsch become in the *morbidezza* of

the piece that Ernst Vajda, co-scenarist with Samson Raphaelson on the film, described a late afternoon in a cemetery, dead leaves swirling in the wind, with Lubitsch actually imitating the leaves blowing about the gravestones in the wind.

"It is further evidence of Mr. Lubitsch's genius," said *The New York Times.* "It is new and daring, something the movies always fear," wrote Florabel Muir in *The Motion Picture Herald.* "It's about war and war is a Hollywood phobia just now. But after seeing perhaps a hundred pictures in the last year, it seemed to be the most magnificent of all —the ripened fruit of the genius of the screen's first director." "A terrifically affecting motion picture," wrote William Boehnel in *The New York Telegram,* "which shows once again that of all the directors in Hollywood, Mr. Lubitsch is the finest. . . . A film that in its humanity, quiet comprehension and the sympathy which he brings to his characterizations, has never before been equaled for effectiveness on the screen." "A brilliant success," commented Richard Watts. "Assisted by a noble and poignant idea, Lubitsch has plunged valiantly into what is essentially poetic tragedy, mixed with genuinely bitter and ironic anti-war statement, and emerged with some of the finest direction of the screen. It is the best work Lubitsch has done in the sound-film."

Finally, there is the eloquent tribute paid the film by Robert E. Sherwood in *The New York Post:*

For more than ten years Ernst Lubitsch has managed to hold his position of pre-eminence among the movie directors of the world. On various occasions others have arisen to occupy his throne—but only during those periods when he himself was between pictures. Virtually every one of his productions from *Passion* to *The Smiling Lieutenant,* has served to re-establish his supremacy.

This supremacy has not been accorded him by vote of the great army of film fans, but by the professional denizens of Hollywood who are qualified to appreciate the delicacies of the director's art. Thus, while Lubitsch has been revered and applauded by his colleagues, and paid vast sums by his employers, he has been known as one who consistently soars over the heads of his audience (a feat which, alas, doesn't necessitate the breaking of any altitude records).

It is a great tribute to Hollywood that in this instance, at least, it has refused to measure genius in terms of the box-office yardstick. The veneration that it has lavished upon Lubitsch has been out of all proportion to the size of his grosses.

Now comes his latest and, perhaps, his greatest—*The Man I Killed*—and again the wise ones of the movie business are loudly proclaiming the news that, "It's a masterpiece—but it will lose money."

Whether this is or isn't so I am in no position to guess. The box office is a mystery which I long ago gave up the attempt to fathom. For all I know, or care, *The Man I Killed* may earn fabulous profits, or it may be drowned in a sea of red ink; but of its artistic importance there can be no question of doubt.

It is the best talking picture that has yet been seen and heard, for it is the closest approach that has been made to the true cinematographic ideal—precisely the same ideal that existed and was so infrequently realized in the old silent days. The moving picture's principal claim to recognition as an individual art is, as it always has been, its ability to express the eloquence of silence. In placing too much reliance upon words, printed in sub-titles or spoken in dialogue, it has neglected its own unique powers.

Lubitsch has accepted the power of speech conferred upon the cinema by courtesy of the Western Electric Corporation, and has used it merely as a means of emphasizing the fact that the greatest moments in a screen drama are those in which there is nothing to be said.

The armistice-day parade seen through the stump of a soldier's amputated leg; church bells tolling between booming guns; officers, kneeling in Notre Dame cathedral during a peace sermon, their spurs and sabres glistening as the camera glides from pew to pew; a cannon sounds a victory boom which wakes a wounded soldier in a hospital bed, and he screams in fright; gunfire over the crosses in a soldiers' cemetery. ". . . It was my duty to kill?" says the remorseful young man to the priest. "Is this the only answer I can get in the house of God?" The priest gives him absolution for his blasphemy. "I came here to find peace," the young man says, "but you haven't given it to me." Then: "Am I mad and this is what the world calls sane?" . . . The two mothers of sons killed in the war, standing over their sons' graves, swallowing their tears and exchanging recipes for cinnamon cake. . . . The "alert" sounded by the ringing of bells in the shops of the little German village as the young Frenchman goes down the street. . . . The father of the boy whom the young Frenchman killed, but who doesn't know this and who has received him in his home as his son's friend, tries to buy a round of beer in the local café only to be met by hostile stares from his old cronies. "Who sent them out to kill and be killed? We, the fathers! I stood here when my son marched away to his death, and I cheered!" Outside he contemplates the silent street over which we hear the thud of marching feet. . . . The young Frenchman takes up the dead German boy's violin and plays a lullaby (Schumann's "Traumerei") as the parents and the German boy's intended bride beam, for he has decided to stay, without revealing his secret to the parents, it is better so. . . .

And so the film ends. "The film and its story can easily raise havoc with those in the audience who lost heavily in the war," concluded *Variety* in its review.

All agreed that Lionel Barrymore was superb as the German father. Phillips Holmes, they said, was perhaps too pallid for the conscience-stricken young Frenchman who hated what the war made him do. Poor Phillips Holmes. He answered his critics unwittingly, by being killed in World War II.[26]

With *The Man I Killed* "off his chest," Paramount hoped Lubitsch would now return to his old *métier*, the making of gay, insouciant comedies again—preferably with music and, of course, "with a little sex." With hardly any respite, and certainly with no time to look for a story, in eight weeks there was a new Lubitsch film making its bow—*One Hour With You* (1932)—a musical remake of his old silent hit, *The Marriage Circle*. The duet of scrambled couples this time comprised Maurice Chevalier and Jeanette MacDonald (naturally), Roland Young and Genevieve Tobin, with Charles Ruggles this time as the fifth wheel on the cart. Once

[26] Compare *The Man I Killed* with Preston Sturges's jingoistic *Hail the Conquering Hero*, made in 1944 when America was at war again. Sturges was no Lubitsch disciple here. No more uncontrolled turd-kicking and frenzied flag-waving under war hysteria was ever seen in an American film.

The Man I Killed failed at the box office. Paramount asks Lubitsch for "a real Lubitsch film" again. And "what is a real Lubitsch film?" A comedy, of course. Lubitsch decides upon a musical remake of his early silent hit, *The Marriage Circle*, which reunites the successful team of Jeanette MacDonald and Maurice Chevalier, and adds the saucy Genevieve Tobin, seen here, as a filip. (*One Hour With You*, the famous "switch of the wrists" touch from *The Marriage Circle*, 1932.)

again the old formula of the *commedia dell'arte* worked, in which Harlequin and Columbine, Pierrot and Pierrette, pair off after considerable tiffs and miffs, with poor Punchinello left to fend for himself. It may have been an old formula but: "Ernst Lubitsch has scored again in *One Hour With You*," wrote *The Philadelphia Inquirer*'s Miss Martin. "He has given the screen, upon which he has already proved his supremacy in the direction of sophisticated comedy, a brand new form of musical entertainment. . . . He has mixed verse, spoken and sung, a smart and satiric musical background, asides to the audience, and sophisticated dialogue, as well as lilting and delightful songs, the music provided by Oscar Strauss. The result is something so delightful that it places the circlet of gilded laurel leaves jauntily upon the knowing and wise head of Hollywood's most original and knowing director."

That same month, in the March, 1932, issue of *Vanity Fair*, appeared a notable article "Field Generals of the Film" by Harry Alan Potamkin, a summing up of American and European directors as of that date. (The Soviet contingent was for Potamkin beyond criticism.) In it he spoke of "the false good taste of Griffith," the "jack-in-the-box" humor of Mack Sennett, and the "bad taste of De Mille, who borrowed from the phalanx of the Gospel and the flank of Mack Sennett with meretricious results." He spoke of the early films of Josef von Sternberg, of "the honest American idiom of their open attack," decrying "the cult of von Sternberg's later preoccupation with the navel of Venus rather than that of Buddha, for all his being, by his own token, a man of meditation. Sternberg has the smoke but not the flame of battle." King Vidor, he opined, "aspires to important expressions he cannot achieve—he has more zeal than intelligence." He speaks, complimentarily, of his "innocence." Lewis Milestone was commended because he was not "obsessed with himself." Dismissing John Ford, he spoke of "Murnau, who completed his great career with *Sunrise*." *Tabu* he regarded as "an unfortunate throwback." The most promising new director were for him Roland Brown (for *Stark Love* and *Quick Millions*), Irving Cummings (for *Dressed to Kill*) and Rouben Mamoulian (for *Applause* and *City Streets*). "All causes," he said, "have their Ichabods. In the movies they are lost souls. A Lubitsch, glib in his chit-chat, keeps remaking the self-same film. . . . A sensitive artist like Mauritz Stiller is slain with humiliation. Victor Seastrom, the greatest director before the Russians, is another eucalyptus tree in Siberia . . . James Cruze, a man of talent for humorous fantasy . . ." Erich von Stroheim was "over-rated by his cult and abused by the arbitrary ministry of the studio, but a man, in spite of many blind-spots, of backbone and purpose . . ." Maurice

Tourneur was one of the best. . . "In the meantime we have a host of drawing-room officers who use the new medium as so many epaulets, so many gold frogs." It is easy to agree with some of it, to disagree with other parts of it, but one must admire its patrician style. (He had not seen *The Man I Killed* when he wrote it.)

By this time one of America's most distinguished novelists, Theodore Dreiser, had taken a real interest in Hollywood, despite his difficulties with Paramount over the filming of his *An American Tragedy* the year before. His *Jennie Gerhardt* fared somewhat better. Interviewed at the time, he professed his admiration for Chaplin and the Russians, and some of Griffith's work, but his chief enthusiasms were for Mack Sennett and Lubitsch, the *alpha* and *omega* of screen comedy. And by this time, too, Lubitsch also had among his literary admirers such anti-Hollywood figures as H. L. Menchken, Theodore Dreiser, George Jean Nathan, Edmund Wilson, Ben Hecht, Alfred Kerr, and Thomas Mann.

"At one point in my career," wrote King Vidor in his autobiography, *A Tree Is a Tree*, "while directing Miriam Hopkins, I became infatuated with the soft Southern talk of this Georgia queen. One evening we had a dinner engagement which was known only to the two of us. Miss Hopkins told me she had been sent a new script by Ernst Lubitsch with the request that she give an answer on the following day. She asked if I would help her decide whether she should play the part. She read straight through and we were both elated with Miriam's part and with the sharp humor of the story. As Miriam read the final lines on the last page of the manuscript, her eyes fell on a scribbled notation at the bottom of the page. It read:

> King—
>> Any little changes you would like I will be happy to make them.
>
>> Ernst

A real-life 'Lubitsch touch' had exploded our secret world."

The picture was *Trouble in Paradise* (1932).

Trouble in Paradise . . . !

The time is the Depression. Marianne (Kay Francis) has lost her handbag and offered a large reward for its return. People with handbags galore come to claim the reward, among them the "Bolshevik"—unkempt, bitter—only he has no handbag.

BOLSHEVIK: So you lost a handbag Madame?
MARIANNE: (nervously) Yes.
BOLSHEVIK: And it had diamonds in the back.
MARIANNE: (impatiently) Yes.
BOLSHEVIK: And diamonds in the front.
MARIANNE: Yes.
BOLSHEVIK: Diamonds all over.
MARIANNE: Yes, have you found it?
BOLSHEVIK: No! (Then pounding his hand with his fist to empha-
    size his tirade, word for word—) But let me tell you—any

Now back in his old form and at the top of that form, he finds again in Europe (the source of almost all of his films) a Hungarian trifle that he and his scriptwriter, Samson Raphaelson, will turn into the most brilliant of all his sound films, *Trouble in Paradise*. Here he is with his feminine star, Miriam Hopkins, of the magnolia blossom accent. (1932)

woman who spends a fortune in times like these for a handbag
—Phooey! Phooey! Phooey!

BUTLER: (intervening) I must ask you—

BOLSHEVIK: (not through yet) And as Trotzky said—

(In Russian)

Any woman who spends a fortune for a silk purse
is a sow's ear.

(In English)

And that goes for you, too!

The contretemps with the "Bolshevik" is charmingly resolved by the sudden entrance of Gaston Monescu (Herbert
Marshall) who does have the bag, and why not?—since he
stole it. And he, too, has come to claim the reward, which
is bigger than what he could sell it for.

"Money-as-money"—this picture is very harsh and cynical
about money, and "sex-as-sex" (there is not the slightest concern with marriage in the whole film)—about this the picture is very gentle (though there is nothing mealymouthed
about everyone's biological impulses).

Grover Jones, a Hollywood writer noted for his screenplays for suspense melodramas, had been called in by Lubitsch to collaborate since the plot had to do with jewel
thieves. Although he contributed nothing to the final screenplay, he regaled Lubitsch and Samson Raphaelson, the film's
scenarist and dialogue writer, with so many merry yarns that
Lubitsch suggested he be given a courtesy credit, as "adapter."
The original play (from the Hungarian, naturally, of one
Laszlo Aladar—where *did* Lubitsch keep finding them?) bore
almost no resemblance to the finished script—save for the
barest idea.

This masterwork of sardonic humor was Lubitsch's own
favorite among all his films. It tells how a pair of charming
swindlers, man (Herbert Marshall) and girl (Miriam Hopkins), meet in Venice, fall in love, and get jobs on the house-
hold staff of a rich widow (Kay Francis) so as to rob her.
Jealous of her partner's infatuation with the widow, the girl
decides to rob her alone and ditch him. But the man, realiz-
ing that he and the girl truly love each other and that it's
"better for business that way," goes off with the girl—with

their separate hauls from the widow now combined in their happy reunion.

"It has the exhilaration of watching a championship tennis match," said Georges Sadoul. "It has the perfection, in its unrelenting ellipsis, of a surgeon's bistoury lancing an abcess," remarked Jean Mitry. "It is satire in the strongest sense of the word, employing an often cruel sarcasm aimed at moral institutions and principles. The badinage between the characters is only a device by which, without seeming to touch on them, Lubitsch demolishes more than other 'engaged' directors. . . . Yet there is nothing lighter than this film, light in its best, not superficial, sense. With it he became the most mordant, most subtle ironist of the cinema, with this almost evanescent work, perhaps his masterpiece."

Miriam Hopkins and Herbert Marshall in *Trouble in Paradise.* (1932) *See page opposite for dialogue from this scene.*

"Praise for Ernst Lubitsch's new picture cannot be too lavishly spread over the entire production from beginning to end. For me it is the sublimation of his art—better, perhaps, than any other of his many films." Thus eulogized Norbert Lusk in *Picture Play*. "A shimmering piece of work," extolled *The New York Times*. "The Lubitsch magic is again in evidence," wrote Richard Watts in *The New York Herald Tribune*, "and, thereupon, *Trouble in Paradise* becomes a thoroughgoing delight . . . a civilized, deft, silken and debonair comedy. . . . In his slyest and most knowing manner, Lubitsch—who is, taking one thing with another, the master of them all—lights upon a slender and less than novel tale of a gentleman bandit and his beautiful prey and by his great gift for the subtly amusing treatment of sex problems, trans-

LILY: When I came here it was for a little adventure—a little game you play tonight and forget tomorrow. . . . But I've got a confession to make to you . . . Baron, you are a crook. You robbed the gentleman in 253, 5, 7, and 9.

GASTON: Countess, believe me, before you left this room I would have told you everything. And let me say this with love in my heart—Countess, you are a thief. The wallet of the gentleman in 253, 5, 7, and 9 is in your possession. I knew it very well when you took it out of my pocket. In fact you tickled me. But your embrace was so sweet. . . . By the way (*handing it to her*) your pin.

LILY: Thank you, Baron.

GASTON: Not at all, Countess. There's one very good stone in it.

LILY: What time is it? (*She hands him his watch.*) It was five minutes slow but I regulated it for you.

GASTON: I hope you don't mind if I keep your garter. (*He holds it up.*)

LILY: Darling! Tell me all about yourself! Who are you?

GASTON: You remember the man who walked into the Bank of Constantinople and walked out *with* the Bank of Constantinople?

LILY: Monescu!

GASTON: Gaston Monescu.

LILY: Gaston!

(*In sheer delight, she throws herself into his arms.*)

Kay Francis and Herbert Marshall in *Trouble in Paradise*. *See page opposite for dialogue from this scene.*

forms it into a brilliant excursion into cinema light comedy.
. . . There have, with the passing of years, been innumerable
imitators of the Lubitsch manner, and what we inevitably
refer to as the 'Lubitsch touch,' but the German still remains
the unapproachable master of the frivolous spirit in the
cinema."

1933—Lubitsch becomes a naturalized American citizen,
and he had this to say that same year:

What so many people forget when they criticize the work of a
film director is that he has to cater for varying tastes, all over the
world. When a play is produced on the New York stage, for instance, the producer can stress certain points, introduce definite
"business" which he knows will appeal to the New York audience.
If he were to produce the same play in London, he might change
his method drastically, because he knows that London would appreciate certain situations that a New York audience would miss; and
vice versa. Imagine, then, the enormous difficulties that face a

MARIANNE COLET: I've got a confession to make. . . . You like me.
   In fact, you're crazy about me. Otherwise you wouldn't worry
   about my reputation. Isn't that so? . . . But I don't like you.
   I don't like you at all! I wouldn't hesitate one instant to ruin
   your reputation—like that!

   (*She snaps her fingers.*)

GASTON: You would?
MARIANNE: Yes, I would!
GASTON (*snapping his fingers*): Like that?
MARIANNE (*snapping her fingers again*): Like that!
GASTON: I know all your tricks.
MARIANNE: And you're going to fall for them.
GASTON: So you think you can get me?
MARIANNE: Any minute I want.
GASTON: You're conceited.
MARIANNE: But attractive.
GASTON: Now let me tell you . . .
MARIANNE: Shut up—kiss me!

   (*They kiss.*)

Wasting all this marvelous time with arguments. . . .

film-maker. He has to produce a screen play that will appeal, not only to New York and London, but also to the Middle West towns of America, the Irish and Scottish peasants, the Australian sheep farmer and the South African business man. This will give you some slight idea of the difficulties with which a film director has to contend and why so much time and thought are necessary if a worldwide reputation is to be secured.

He had now made six sound films in a row, each declared to be better than its predecessor which, itself, was unanimously acclaimed a perfect thing of its kind. How do you top that? Even Lubitsch couldn't top *Trouble in Paradise*.

He did a five-minute sequence with Charles Laughton in Paramount's *If I Had a Million* (1932), composed of seven sequences by seven directors, a set of variations on "the dreams that money can buy" (right up Lubitsch's "money-as-money" alley), and the ferocious joy with which the sequence ended—a calorific razz from the meek clerk to his

Miriam Hopkins and Herbert Marshall in *Trouble in Paradise*. See *page opposite for dialogue from this scene.*

boss—was echoed in ten million hearts around the world as the realization, at last, of the promise that the meek shall inherit the earth.

Here, in truth, was a "Lubitsch touch" *in excelsis.*

What next—and different? What about a straight comedy *without* music? A top-flight play, then? Why not? Noel Coward's *Design for Living,* which the Lunts and Coward, himself, had made memorable on the stage. Ben Hecht was engaged to collaborate on the screenplay. He would "do a Lubitsch" too—no Coward dialogue. "We'll rewrite it for the screen." In an interview with Alistair Cooke in the *London Observer* Lubitsch was quoted as saying that for the screen you cannot photograph people sitting around talking, especially about the past, as they did in this play. "Motion pictures should not talk about events in the past. That's why I've completely changed the beginning of the play. Even on the stage this was dull. One was told where they met, what they had done for many years, how they had loved. I have to *show* these things, in their right order. Things on the

GASTON: Are you insane? You have to get out of here at once! She may come back any minute.

LILY: What time is your rendezvous?

GASTON: Now, Lily—

LILY: Yes, M'sieu Colet.

GASTON: You *have* to get out of here!

LILY: That's what I'm here for—to get out, as far from here as a hundred thousand francs will take me. . . . (*Dialing the wall safe.*) 65 . . . 94 . . . 35 left . . . 63 . . . 8 . . . I wouldn't fall for another man if he were the biggest crook on earth. . . . 76 . . . 84 . . . 55. . . . What has she got that I haven't got?

GASTON: Lily, you *must* listen to me—

LILY: Shut up!

GASTON: But Lily—

LILY: Go ahead, say something! Come on—be brilliant! Talk yourself out of it—bluff yourself in!

GASTON: (*Starts to say something.*)

LILY: Shut up, you liar! (*She swings the safe-door open and takes out a wad of banknotes.*) That's what I want! This is real! Money! Cash!

If *Trouble in Paradise* was conceived on a high plane of mordant humor and whose mercurial fire blazed and crackled with a prodigality of sarcastic energy, the Lubitsch sequence for *If I Had a Million*, with just three words of dialogue, was conceived and carried out on the lowest humorous plane and with the simplest of means. Here Laughton, having just been made the beneficiary of a million dollars, gives his boss—which is to say, every boss in the world—a farewell razz. (1932)

screen should happen in the present. Pictures should have nothing to do with the past tense. The dialogue should deal with what is, not with what was." The action in a film was more dense than in a play. Something had to be *happening*, all the time. This was the spirit of the film, as opposed to the method in the theatre, where words were the thing.

Design for Living was even for Lubitsch a difficult feat, for he had to steer the tale of a lady, who loves two gentlemen simultaneously, past the censors while preserving as much of the work's original humor as possible. Somehow, it didn't come off this time. Nor were the players—Gary Cooper, Frederic March, and Miriam Hopkins, ingratiating enough in themselves—a match for the Lunts and Coward.

I recall one Lubitsch touch where Miriam Hopkins throws herself on a couch in mock despair, whereupon a cloud of dust rises from the couch to ridicule her emotion.

Lubitsch returned to the film musical, the operetta, for his next picture, *The Merry Widow* (1934), the rights to which MGM had owned since buying it for Stroheim. Now, with the advantage of sound, they could put the heady Lehár score on the soundtrack and Chevalier (who else as Prince Danilo?) and Jeanette MacDonald could sing the world-famous songs. And the cameraman would be the same one (Oliver Marsh) who had so beautifully photographed Stroheim's silent version.

Gary Cooper, Miriam Hopkins, and Fredric March in Ben Hecht's adaptation of Noel Coward's *Design for Living*. Good intentions somehow gone awry. But there were still "Lubitsch touches" like the anti-romantic one where Miriam Hopkins, torn between her two lovers, throws herself down on a couch to show her despair, and raises a cloud of dust that reduces her dramatic gesture to the purest slapstick. (1933)

Inevitably, Lubitsch had to do *The Merry Widow*. MGM owned the rights, and it had been filmed only once before, some twenty years earlier, as a *silent* film. Now with sound and the Lehár score and Chevalier and MacDonald to sing the honeyed songs—who could resist it? Curiously, audiences did. "Gone was the romance and sentiment of the original," wrote Theodore Huff in his Index on Lubitsch. "Lubitsch, with a cold and detached treatment, used the old operetta merely as a springboard for his customary shafts of satire and jesting about sex." Perhaps it should have been left to be wept over by the dandies of yesteryear. Certainly it was no match for the immensely popular Stroheim version, with John Gilbert and Mae Murray, which, despite the *bizarrerie* and withering wit that would have given its original librettists conniptions, was much closer to the "Lippen schweigen, flustern Geigen" witchery of the 1905 original. (1934)

This time the first "Lubitsch touch" came right under the credit titles as a magnifying glass sought in vain to find the tiny mythical kingdom where the action took place. But if ever a plot was rewritten, this was it. (Anyway, no one could possibly film the original libretto—you could only get away with that on the stage where *only* the music mattered.) Still it was, after a fashion, that sprig of rosemary, *The Merry Widow*, newly bedecked and bedizened with boas, flounces, Balkan officer-*chic* and all. I recall the portly King Achmed leaving the bedroom of Queen Dolores, walking across the palace parquet only to find, as he tries to buckle his sword-belt back on, that it is far too small. Whose belt does he have on then? Guess . . . Or the transformation of the sad rich widow, all in black mourning, even to her black pekinese, into the dazzling white "merry widow," even to her now white pekinese. But the picture lacked what Gaston Monescu in *Trouble in Paradise* said a love letter to a beautiful lady should have—"bouquet . . . mystery." Sumptuously produced, it cost too much for its box-office grosses to cover that cost. *The Merry Widow* was the last picture that Lubitsch and Chevalier made together. Oscar Levant, in his book *The Unimportance of Being Oscar*, mentions his surprise at Chevalier's negative reaction to two people during a discussion of "the old days." "When we talked of Lubitsch, I got the impression that his early director had been too overpowering for him." (The other negative reaction was to Shaw.)

Let us pass over *Desire, Angel,* and *Bluebeard's Eighth Wife* and highlight from that period a signal honor bestowed on Lubitsch—the red ribbon of the Legion of Honor, awarded him by the French government in recognition of his directorial achievements. The event was celebrated at a big party given him by his handsome wife, Vivian, on the occasion of his birthday, during which the surprise award was made. A second surprise was a sumptuous recording machine given him as a birthday present by Mrs. Lubitsch. A galaxy of stars representing the Hollywood and French movie colonies attended the festivities.

Where Stroheim was ironic, Lubitsch was sentimental, and vice-versa. It was a matter of emphasis. In Stroheim's version Prince Danilo has a riotous fling with the *houris* at Maxim's on the eve of his duel with the nasty Crown Prince over Sonia. In the Lubitsch version there is no duel (nor was there in the operetta) and Danilo sings his pledge to the pretty witches with their morning-glory eyes of a considerably more sedate Maxim's . . . "*Lolo, Dodo, Jou-Jou. . . . Margot, CloClo, Frou-Frou . . .*" Lubitsch's fastidious compromise with the rosemary of the original and his own healthy ebullience lost what *The Merry Widow* basically had had since that epochal night in 1905 when it had its world premiere at the Theater an der Wien in Vienna. For all the corrosive scorn the Stroheim version had for its skittish original plot, it exuded an aura of attar of roses. (1934)

"One thing a film-maker must always think of," he said in an interview in 1936, "is that the public has caught up with him. It is used by now to cleverness, to beauty, to drama, to ideas, to music, to dancing. A film that for its brilliance made a sensation a few years ago creates hardly a ripple today, is enjoyed in its time and then is forgotten. Excellence has become almost a commonplace. *The Last Laugh* is remembered because it was a brilliant and gripping film in a dull cinema year. But *Ruggles of Red Gap* was cleverer, just as satiric and entertaining . . . People want to laugh, want to feel, want to cry, want to be astounded, want to be pleased, want always to have life made vivid for them. And if a film can't do that, it lacks art, and it decidedly lacks showmanship."

As far back as 1932, Lubitsch had wanted to make a film with Greta Garbo. Mercedes de Acosta, in her autobiography *Here Lies the Heart* tells of going with Garbo to meet Lubitsch after Garbo had completed *As You Desire Me*, based on Pirandello's play. "*Mein Gott! Mein Gott!*" he exclaimed when he saw her in the doorway, then ran over to embrace her. They sat down on a sofa and he held her hand.

"Greta," he said, "Vy don't you tell those idiots in your studio to let us do a picture together? *Gott*, how I vould love to direct a picture with you!"

Smiling that sad smile that had sent countless adoring millions into crazy ecstacy the world over, Garbo answered, "You tell them, Ernst. I'm far too tired to talk to studio executives," and she sadly shook her head.

"Vat fools they are," he said, then turning to Miss de Acosta: "How vonderful Greta and I would be together. Vat a vonderful picture ve could make together!"

It was not to happen for seven years, not until the summer of 1939. It took two months to shoot. Again Lubitsch's source was a Hungarian, Melchior Lengyel, who became famous for a line worthy of La Rochefoucauld: "Kissing a woman's hand is never the right thing to do; it is either too much or too little."

Obviously, a team like that would set off sparks. What

Lubitsch and Josef von Sternberg, the two top directors at Paramount, visit the sound stage where De Mille is directing a scene for *Cleopatra*. An amusing and revealing study in reactions. (1934)

emerged from the corrosive humor of the screenplay by Charles Brackett, Billy Wilder, and Walter Reisch (with the usual assist from the director-collaborator) was a veritable arsenal of whooshing roman candles. Lubitsch was inspired as he had not been since *Trouble in Paradise*, and the picture showed it. It was called *Ninotchka*.

Garbo played a dour female Soviet commissar sent to supervise a trio of bumbling agents entrusted by her government to sell certain crown jewels for badly needed foreign exchange. The setting is Paris and, under the seductive ministrations of that city, Comrade Nina Yakushova melts and becomes Ninotchka, "dear little Nina," the darling of a Parisian charmer who has fallen in love with her.

What need to say more? The film is so well known that

ABOVE: Hollywood, O Hollywood! Lubitsch's home in Bel-Air, California. (1935) BELOW: The doting father and his daughter, Nicola, celebrate her fourth birthday at a party. Years later she wrote to me, "He was the most wonderful father anyone ever had."

Gary Cooper, Marlene Dietrich, and John Halliday in *Desire* (1936). *See opposite.*

Lubitsch is now production chief of Paramount and undertakes to supervise Frank Borzage's production with Dietrich under her renewed contract with the studio, following *The Devil Is a Woman*, her last (and most brazen) film with Sternberg, whose title Lubitsch had changed, for box-office reasons, from *Caprice Espagnole*. The choice of story is again Lubitsch's, as was true for all his films. This new film was *Desire*. It derived from a charming German film, *Die Schönen Tage von Aranjuez (The Beautiful Days at Aranjuez)*, by Hans Szekely, starring Brigitte Helm in the Dietrich role. The setting was still Spain but the humor became American, instead of Continental. Though Dietrich was still photographed beautifully, it was obvious that Lubitsch did not see in her what Sternberg had, and made so much of, in the seven paroxysmic films they did together that have since become the stuff of legend. She played her part as an exquisite jewel thief well enough, but that special *brio* was missing.

There was an ambivalence about Dietrich in her Hollywood films with Sternberg in which she exuded both masculine as well as feminine qualities. This made her "the total woman" and strengthened her characterization of the *femme fatale*, charging it to the highest power. A true fatal woman is no purely feminine thing— that would be almost a contradiction in terms. There must be something vigorous to balance the willowy blandishments. To take this important, nay vital, aspect of her playing away from Dietrich and ask her to be purely feminine is to lose the major part of the strength and humor she manifested with Sternberg, who understood this. Compare her in *Desire* and *Angel* (1937) with any of her Hollywood Sternberg films (not *The Blue Angel*—she was feminine there but it was a totally different and non-Hollywood kind of femininity—a sex machine like Wedekind's Lulu in *Pandora's Box*, with a "one-track mind," but what a track!). It is the difference between a Toulouse-Lautrec, whose women also had that duality, and, let us say, a Marie Laurencin or Berthe Morisot. Only in René Clair's *The Flame of New Orleans* did Dietrich play with something of the same quality found in her Sternberg films, but was this not reinforced by the duality of her role where she played both the "bad" and the "good" look-alike "cousins"? Clair must have sensed this polarity in her art. He was, after all, very clever—and very knowing.

Miss Dietrich honors the occasion of the 25th anniversary of Lubitsch's career as a director by giving a party, complete with anniversary cake and champagne, at the Paramount studio for the cast and technical crew of *Angel*. Here she offers slices of the enormous cake to Herbert Marshall and the director. (1937)

Lubitsch with the Viennese dancer, Tilly Losch, at a Hollywood party given by Basil Rathbone. (1937)

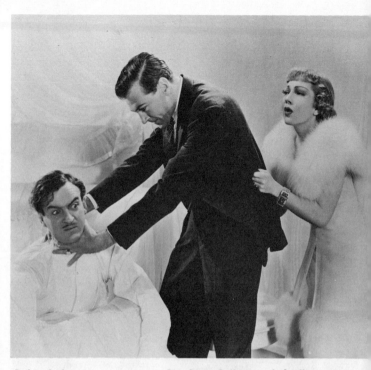

Lubitsch keeps a promise to Claudette Colbert and finally gets around to making the wacky *Bluebeard's Eighth Wife*, with David Niven, Gary Cooper, and Miss Colbert. (1938)

And then came *Ninotchka*, that good-humored satire on the *moeurs* of the U.S.S.R. Lubitsch and his writers did not set up a "straw man" the more easily to demolish him. The "Russians" in it (all played by non-Russians, of course) give as good as they take. And Garbo, to whom Lubitsch *was* sympathetic, played magnificently under his direction. Here is Garbo as the ascetic Nina Yakushova, envoy extraordinary sent to Paris to check on the representatives of the Soviet Board of Trade, all too susceptible to capitalistic luxuries, Sig Rumann (Iranoff), Felix Bressart (Buljanoff), and Alexander Granach (Kopalski). (1939)

ABOVE: Garbo, Melvyn Douglas, and Lubitsch go over a scene for *Ninotchka*. BELOW: The "Lubitsch touch" in action. The director sculpts a fleeting moment in *Ninotchka* during a rehearsal, like a musician conducting an orchestra during a passage marked *con amore*. His films were choreographed as much as they were directed.

each has his ineffable memory of it. One need only compare it with *Angel* the film Lubitsch made with Dietrich, to see with whom he was the more "sympathetic." When one compares it with a similar satirical comedy on the Russians, *Comrade X*, in which Hedy Lamarr (never more beautiful) played a Soviet lady trolley conductor in a script by Ben Hecht and Charles Lederer, directed by King Vidor, one realizes what an innately *un*humorous thing *Comrade X* was—the mercurial raffishness of the former versus the flatfooted orthodoxy of the latter, the prodigality of sardonic energy of one as against the pallid banality of the other. (Like Dietrich in any Sternberg film versus Dietrich in any non-Sternberg film.) All the savor was missing. Compare the hard-lipped rue, the futile laughter, with which Felix Bressart plays in *Ninotchka* and the querulousness with which he plays in *Comrade X*. Compare *"die göttliche"* (the divine), as Garbo was called, in *Ninotchka*, with *"die schönste Frau der Welt"* (the most beautiful woman in the world), as Lamarr was called by Max Reinhardt, in *Comrade X* . . . compare, compare . . . Hedy Lamarr needed one Lubitsch picture to "put her on the map" but, alas, this was not to be vouchsafed her. An attempt with Sternberg might have done it also—in a vehicle chosen by Sternberg for her, not the creaky *New York Cinderella* by Charles MacArthur assigned to them, which Sternberg gave up as hopeless.

In lieu of recounting excerpts from the reviews again, I have included in this book excerpts from the screenplay of *Ninotchka*, so that its inimitable tang may be savored once more.

We have seen, as in the instances cited from Jim Tully, Harry Alan Potamkin, and John Grierson, that some of our otherwise most perceptive critics had their blind spots even a generation ago, when Lubitsch was being assayed for the first time. A generation later discloses an equally astute critic of our own day, Kenneth Tynan, with his own blind spot. During a panegyric on Garbo, he singles out *Ninotchka*, alluding in passing to the "cellophane *kitsch* of the Lubitsch touch—how it dates!," then goes on to delineate ecstatically the beauty with which she plays the scene where, slightly

Paris and Melvyn Douglas as Leon, a very personable Parisian, thaw out the wintry attitude of Comrade Yakushova toward the frivolities and decadences of Western capitalism. (*Ninotchka.*)

tipsy with champagne during a *tête-a-tête* with Leon, she turns to an imaginary assemblage and says, "Comrades! People of the world! The revolution is on the march! I know . . . wars will wash over us . . . bombs will fall . . . all civilization will crumble . . . but not *yet* . . . please . . . wait, wait . . . what's the hurry? Let us be happy . . . give us our moment. . . ." Tynan cites this apparently completely unmindful of the fact that everything that has gone before in the film has been an inexorable buildup to that lovely scene, that Lubitsch collaborated in its writing, and that if Garbo played it luminously it was because Lubitsch directed it so (years later she was to say that he was the only great director she ever had in Hollywood). Mr. Tynan achieved here what must certainly be a world's record in the swiftness of forget-fulness.[27]

1940 . . . *The Shop Around the Corner.*

"It has a universal theme and tells a simple story," said Lubitsch. "I have known just such a little shop. The feeling between the boss and those who work for him is pretty much the same the world over, it seems to me. Everyone is afraid of losing his job and everyone knows how little human worries can affect his job. If the boss has a touch of dyspepsia, better be careful not to step on his toes; when things have gone well with him, the whole staff reflects his good humor."

The source was again Hungarian, a play by Nikolaus Laszlo, but which underwent a complete transformation in the screenplay by Samson Raphaelson. The setting was a little leather goods and novelty shop in Budapest in which the salesgirl (Margaret Sullavan) and head clerk (James Stewart) quarrel so much that they decide it must be love. Felix Bressart was again in it (by now a Lubitsch favorite) as Pirovitch, who also works in the shop. Marton (Jimmy Stewart) is confiding in Pirovitch about a girl he has been corresponding with in answer to her "Lonely Hearts" ad:

MARTON: Remember the girl I was corresponding with?

PIROVITCH: Ah, yes . . . about those cultural subjects.

MARTON: Well, after a while, we came to the subject of love, natu-rally, but on a very cultural level.

PIROVITCH: What else can you do in a letter?

MARTON: Pirovitch, she's the most marvelous girl in the world . . .

PIROVITCH: Is she pretty?

MARTON: She has such ideals, such a point of view on things . . . She's so far above the girls you meet today, there's simply no comparison.

PIROVITCH: So she's not so very pretty.

[27] Some time later in an interview Tynan said, "If I had to define what it is in American acting that I think I miss in English acting, I'd say it's Jewishness. Don't ask me what it means. A sense of humor that is the best in the world, the quickest in self-denigration, the most candid. The ability to go from being as sharp as you like to being sentimental. The English theatre has kept Jews out. It's anti-Semitic."

And back in Moscow, Nina, Iranoff, Buljanoff, and Kopalski reminisce about the "good old days in Paris." As in a Russian film the spring thaw symbolizes the breakup of the long (czarist) winter, here spring brings with it another kind of revolution—the triumph of love over ideology, but without moral compromise to the heroine or her loyalty to the Soviet ideal. "No one shall say," she smiles, steadfast to the end, "Ninotchka was a bad Russian." (*Ninotchka.*)

Winter in pre-war Budapest, a little café where young lovers have their rendezvous over coffee and cake. A book (*Anna Karenina*, of course), and a red carnation on the café table, an earnest conversation, more earnest that moment than anything else in the world. . . . In this *milieu* did Lubitsch find the setting for his next film, *The Shop Around the Corner*, with James Stewart and Margaret Sullavan. A *milieu* of which Max Ophuls was to become so fond, it served to show Lubitsch in a gentle and mellow twilight mood, reminiscent of Molnar's *Fashions for Men*. (1940)

Handsome is as handsome does. A rare formal portrait study of the maestro. (1940)

The Shop Around the Corner, another Lubitsch favorite, was an evangel, lowly and wistful, of little people, their woes and happinesses, as it concerned the shop which employed them, and their sorrows and joys outside of business. Frank Morgan was especially memorable as the stern but genial shopowner. For only the second time, Lubitsch was not dealing with his "high world" of princes and lackeys, but with "everyday people" with whom his audiences, for the most part, could identify. But the picture did not do well at the box office. Perhaps its humor was too gentle. Perhaps a Lubitsch picture without sassy sex wasn't what this public wanted—they doted on his princes and lackeys. Whatever the public thought, the film was utterly beguiling.[28]

[28] That year, Stroheim included Lubitsch among his favorite American directors, others being Milestone, Capra, Ford, and Victor Fleming.

That Uncertain Feeling (1941) was a return to sassy sex. It was supposed to be a remake of *Kiss Me Again*, but you'd never know it if you weren't told. Burgess Meredith, who co-starred in it, had a happy memory of it. "That was a fine experience, a haunting experience. Today I think it's haunting because I remember him so much from that time. I don't know when I had a better time in my whole career than during that period. He and I were very close, and we had a fine time together. He was an extraordinary director . . . he'd act everything out for you, and he'd act it out so funny, so definitely, that I would stand there as an audience. He would act it out in such a way, and so hilariously, that he would give you the *idea* of what he wanted without expecting you to do it necessarily just his way, because, first of all, he had a horrendous accent. Or he would stop in the middle when he was acting my lines and make some crack about my brother, with whom I was having trouble at the time, some other purely personal thing which in some psychic way he knew I was undergoing. He was very psychic. I'd fall down laughing because right away he'd improvise, in the middle of a scene he was doing for me, some very personal thing about my life, with his big cigar in his mouth, and he knew I'd come over and say, 'How did you know about that?' and he'd say, 'I have ways of knowing.' " [29]

For two years World War II had been raging in Europe. Hitler had overrun most of the continent. In an insane burst of megalomania he had opened a new front in the East by blitzkrieging Poland. Melchior Lengyel, who had provided Lubitsch with the core of the Soviet satire, *Ninotchka*, came up with a Nazi satire, this time, *To Be or Not to Be* (1942), about a company of Polish actors trying to carry on during the German occupation. "Running up against the same sort of criticism leveled at Chaplin's *The Great Dictator*," wrote Theodore Huff in his *Index to the Films of Ernst Lubitsch*, "the Lubitsch burlesque, laid in Nazi-invaded Warsaw, was called callous, a picture of confusing moods, lacking in taste, its subject not suitable for fun making. While others felt

[29] From *Film Fan Monthly*, February, 1968.

The Shop Around the Corner not having done so well, it was decided Lubitsch's next picture should be a sex comedy again, for that's what the public expected from him. What to do? Something tried and true—a remake again, this time of the legendary *Kiss Me Again*, for which Lubitsch asks for and gets Merle Oberon, shown here with the director and her then husband, Alexander Korda, the producer. (1940)

No remake was ever as good as the original, and *That Uncertain Feeling* was no exception. Americanized, over-written by its well-meaning scenarists, and relying chiefly on the Eurasian beauty of Miss Oberon and the antics of Burgess Meredith, it was frivolous *sans* the nobility which frivolity needs as a precondition of its existence, like a shadow needs an object to produce it. Lubitsch could not have had his heart in it. The first rapture that produced *Kiss Me Again* was gone. First rapture, like first love, cannot be duplicated. (1941)

that such merciless satire and subtle humor were good anti-Nazi propaganda, the picture was, perhaps, ill-timed, doubly so as it opened not long after the death of Carole Lombard, killed in an airplane accident at the height of a brilliant career. Her original style of clowning was here at its best."

In 1942 we did not have the term "black comedy." Lubitsch, always daring to do something new, gave his audiences just that—a morbid comedy, which they rejected, just as audiences were also to reject Chaplin's mordant *Monsieur Verdoux*.

Without its unintended overtones the picture is mostly melodrama and farce, of the recently popular kind that makes laughing matters of corpses and killings, with moments of high comedy, of satire, and—occasionally—of stunning realism. The melodrama concerns the exploits of a band of Polish actors working with other patriots to sabotage their Nazi conquerors, and particularly their escape from extirpation by the Gestapo. The farce lies in the burlesquing of the Nazi and in the character which Jack Benny brings over from radio, and the inevitable fantastic twists such elements give to the plot. And above the level of all this is Carole Lombard, with her talent for comedy maturing into lovely perfection.

It all adds up to a remarkably entertaining show, skillfully devised for its comic aims and full of laughs. On the surface the Gestapo seem to be easily and almost incredibly fooled by a few false beards and disguises—made plausible enough for comic purposes by showing a group of actors in the beginning rehearsing a Nazi play and later on simply carrying their stage characterizations into the main plot. But there is something sharper than mere farcical invention in this—what fools the Gestapo is not the beards but their own jitters, their constant fear of their higher-ups, of betrayal in their own ranks. This is sound, though subtle, comment, as well as a lot of fun.

The jolt comes in the bombings and the invasion, and the flashes of underground revolt against the brutal conquerors. Chaplin's theory that the most serious matters are the best material for comedy gets a pretty tough test here. Sensitive people won't like it.

Naturally the whole thing is done slickly and cleverly. Jack Benny is at once the Jack Benny of the air-waves—slightly but sufficiently ham—and a Lubitsch character—a surprising amalgamation that is

To Be or Not to Be had a good idea, from an original story by Lubitsch and the Melchior Lengyel of *Ninotchka*—actors remain actors though the world comes tumbling down around them (a keen observation). Set against the Nazi bombing of Warsaw, it was unjustly attacked in some quarters as a callous subject for humor although its sharp satire, edged with somber glints of Polish gallantry in the face of the German holocaust made the film a salutary anti-Nazi work. The tragic death in a plane crash of Carole Lombard, seen here with Jack Benny as the theatrical couple, shortly before the film's release, dampened one's ardor for the film, however. (1942)

Nicola and Daddy. Wrote Sir Richard Steele in *The Spectator*
(1712): "Certain it is, that there is no Kind of Affection so pure
and angelick as that of a father to a Daughter. He beholds her
both with and without Regard to her Sex. In Love to our Wives
there is Desire, to our Sons there is Ambition; but in that to our
Daughters, there is something which there are no Words to express. Her Life is designed wholly domestick, and she is so ready a
Friend and Companion, that everything that passes about a Man
is accompanied with the Idea of her Presence."

a director's triumph. Sig Ruman is a dynamo of coarse fun, and Tom Dugan's Hitler, with its indescribable skirted overcoat, has moments that rival Chaplin's. Stanley Ridges is the one sinister figure that holds up the dramatic tension.

Carole Lombard is so luminously alive that only afterwards do you remember what the screen has lost. Not the least of her minor triumphs is that she makes you forget Jack Benny is not talking to Mary Livingstone at moments; for the rest she shows better than ever before those rare qualities of a fine comedienne, an intelligent mind and a blithe spirit expressing themselves easily and gracefully through an assured technique of acting. And you can't think of her except in the present tense.[30]

Laurence Olivier, who was in Hollywood for a while during the war years, tells of a night when Lubitsch, who was the "block warden" one week (residents of Beverly Hills and Bel Air volunteered to do "night watch" duty, seeing that blackouts were preserved, and so forth), saw a house ablaze with lights, the blinds up, curtains parted, a perfect "target." In a flood of German and thickly accented English mixed with German oaths, he shouted to the people inside to pull down their blinds, "Donnerwetter!", and douse their lights. Olivier, hearing this, looked out his window at the darkened street below, then called out to a neighbor who had also opened his window to see who was shouting, "Have we been invaded already? Sounds like the Germans are here!"

Nicola, his daughter, tells of his frequent visits to Walter Reisch's house, adjoining his in Bel Air, for the excellent *himbeeresaft* (a cold raspberry juice drink) Reisch prepared. There he would discuss the respective merits of Vladimir Horowitz and Jascha Heifetz during such happy hours of relaxation. One of his most brilliant disciples, Preston Sturges, paid him a charming tribute in his *Sullivan's Travels* when he has Veronica Lake, as a girl trying to break into the movies, say to Joel McCrea, a Hollywood director who has asked her what he can do for her, "Introduce me to Lubitsch." In straight deadpan, he answers, "Who's Lubitsch?" Later, the director, wishing to please her, says: "I'll introduce you to Lubitsch."

[30] James Shelley Hamilton in *The National Board of Review* magazine, March, 1942.

Then came *Heaven Can Wait* (1943), from still another Hungarian play, *Birthdays*, by Laszlo Bus-Fekete, again just a glimmer of an idea that Samson Raphaelson, his scenarist, and he expanded into what Huff in his *Index* called "a series of animated tintypes, poking sly fun at the manners, decorations and naughtiness of the gay nineties, the locale moving, in a vein of fantasy, from Hades to old New York and Kansas as the career of a mild Casanova is traced." It was Lubitsch's first film in color, and his use of it earned him the praise of no less than D. W. Griffith. It was also a favorite of Lubitsch's. He said it was a "three hair-cut" picture, that being the length of time it took to make it. The story covered three generations and each sequence had to be carefully weighed for the changes in speech, in furniture, in background—changes not so great as to interfere with the continuity but sufficient to establish the passing of time.

In March, 1946, a special "Oscar" was awarded him for his "contributions to the art of the motion pictures."

In June of that year, *Cluny Brown* made its debut—"a bright and amusing light satire on the smugness of British society," as Huff described it. For once the source was not Hungarian or even middle-European, but an arch English novel by Margery Sharp. A fine cast, handpicked from Hollywood's "British colony," was headed by a delectable Jennifer Jones, as a lady plumber, with just the right fey edge to her playing, and an especially droll performance by Richard Haydn.

The last scene was charming, in the true Lubitsch style, in which Charles Boyer and Jennifer Jones, now married, are suddenly surrounded by a group of people on the street, after she has fainted, and Boyer smilingly indicates to a policeman who is there, too, that it's all right, nothing serious, it is just that his wife is pregnant. It is all done in pantomime, as seen through a shop window and we do not hear a word of the excited conversation, but at this news everyone breaks into smiles, and in this little flurry the music rises, the end title comes on the screen, and the audience is smiling, too.

After all the skirmishing, after all the "beating around the

Another derivation from the Hungarian (ah, those Hungarians!) was *Heaven Can Wait* which, as Huff described it in his Lubitsch Index, was "a series of animated tintypes poking sly fun at the manners, decorations, and naughtiness of the Gay Nineties, the locale moving in the vein of fantasy from Hades to old New York and Kansas as the career of a mild Casanova is traced." Once again, Lubitsch and his now favorite writer, Samson Raphaelson, who worked so marvelously together, spun out of a Continental trifle a gossamer tale whose point was that it had no point—except to be disarmingly charming on the theme of a gay Lothario and his light o' loves, tinged with Shavian, Schnitzlerian, and Molnaresque glints. (Charles Coburn, Gene Tierney, and Don Ameche in *Heaven Can Wait*, 1943.)

bush," Venus was finally made pregnant, which is what it was all about all the time.

1947 · · ·

When he started making *That Lady in Ermine*, a fantasy in the form of a comic ghost story in which ancestors come to life at midnight, assuming very corporeal form (deriving from an obscure European operetta), Lubitsch stated in an interview: "Unfortunately, we have neglected the camera greatly in the last few years. We have failed to tell the story in visual terms. Naturally, the spoken word is a great asset and carries great power, but we have become so engrossed in dialogue that we have neglected to take full advantage of the expressive power of the silent approach. In my next picture, I hope we will have a chance to give more attention again to visual effects. I will take full advantage of dialogue and speech, but I also would like to leave enough room for the valuable things we learned and have partly forgotten from the silent days."

He never really forgot those wonderful silent days.

But there was not to be a next picture, there was not even to be this picture. A recurrent heart attack took him off the film somewhere before the midway point. Some two weeks of shooting remained, which Otto Preminger took over. There was a long convalescence and Lubitsch recovered. On Thanksgiving Day at Jeanette MacDonald's house he joked and bantered and was his old ebullient self again. But he did get serious at one point when the subject of the House Unamerican Activities Committee came up. This mad-dog committee infuriated him, and he took a strong unequivocal stand against it.

On November 30th, at his home in Bel Air, he was stricken again. He had been under medical care for a heart condition for several years, yet even when he began to show physical signs of exhaustion he refused to "slow down" or "take it easy." Nor would he give up his cigars. Efforts of his physician and a fire department pulmotor to resuscitate him were futile. His secretary, Steffi Trondle, notified his now-divorced wife, Vivian, in New York. He had been expecting his nine-

If Kräly was Lubitsch's pet scenarist during his silent period, Samson Raphaelson, shown here, was certainly his favorite scenarist during his sound period; they made nine films together. Self-portrait made by Raphaelson in 1960.

If a lamp falls and the bulb does not break, the sudden shock will make the lamp burn brighter than before . . . but the remaining minutes of this lamp are very brief. Lubitsch has already had several heart attacks and had seemingly recovered. He came back with *Cluny Brown*, a merry charade, his spirits higher than they had been since *Ninotchka*. Satirizing British "high society," his cast (especially Jennifer Jones and Richard Haydn) played with all the old Lubitsch raffishness. And the closing scene, played in frantic pantomime, was touched with the old charm. It was all very sweet, and it was a nice note for "the Lubitsch story" to end upon—a high trill with bells and violins. (Charles Boyer, Billy Bevan, Reginald Gardiner, and Jennifer Jones in *Cluny Brown*, 1946.)

He tried once more, with *That Lady in Ermine*, but it was no use, and he had to abandon the film. He had burned himself out. A new heart attack proved fatal . . . a month short of his 56th birthday.

Lubitsch as caricatured by Ali Hubert in 1928. Reproduced by permission of Verlag E. A. Seemann, Leipzig.

year-old daughter, Nicola, who lived with her mother, for the Christmas holidays.

They say that when Michelangelo was brought the news of Raphael's death, he exclaimed in astonishment, "Raphael dead? How is it possible?"

There were many who felt the same way about the great director. All that protean vitality gone? The genial, gay, jolly Lubitsch dead? How, indeed, was it possible? There are deaths one simply refuses to believe—it takes getting "used to." Didn't Cocteau say, "Artists only pretend to die . . ."?

.   .   .

As much as anyone, as much as Griffith and Chaplin, Lubitsch was a seminal figure in the cinema's formative years. He was also the only European director who succeeded in making a successful compromise with Hollywood without compromising himself. Though he became achetypical of the successful Hollywood director by Hollywood's own standards, he became also "the directors' director," for none admired his skill more than other directors, remaining, as in Polonius's dictum, always true to himself. That self was one with integrity, a quality as rare as were the other American directors who had it—Flaherty, Stroheim, Sternberg, Chaplin, Griffith, Welles, and their kind. There were never very many whose integrity was held on that high a plane. And, withal, he was genuinely modest and would disclaim praise showered upon him, because he could never quite understand being praised for something that not only came so easily to him but which he enjoyed so much, for no one ever enjoyed his work more.

Lubitsch "wore his heart on his sleeve," as they say. It was there for all the world to see. He hid nothing. If Sternberg, for example, was an introvert, Lubitsch was an extrovert; if Sternberg's films were too "gamey" for some, they found "lighter" fare in Lubitsch's, though the true cinema *gastronome* savored them all.

In 1958, Billy Wilder instituted the Ernst Lubitsch Prize, an annual award of the Club of West Berlin Film Journalists for the best acting in a film comedy, for acting mattered most in a Lubitsch film. Had he not himself begun as an actor in comedies? If the director made a good comedy, he would win instant recognition; the prize was meant to help the actors (or actresses) to whom equal recognition might not come so swiftly. For Lubitsch, the erstwhile actor, who practically acted out every role he ever directed, it is a fitting memorial. It is awarded every January 28th on the anniversary of his birthday.

In 1967 an extensive retrospective of his films was given at the Berlin Film Festival, and was repeated that year at the Cinémathèque Française in Paris. This year, another retrospective is scheduled for showing at the Museum of Modern Art in New York.

The man alone in the arena may sometimes falter, he may commit an error, but as Cocteau has again noted, out of this syncope, out of this chance encounter between his attention and inattention, a breach will open unaware and, in some inexplicable manner, something marvelous will have transpired which rapturously transports those spectators with the capacity for wonder. You get nothing for nothing.

Excerpts from the Screenplay
of NINOTCHKA *

So that some idea of a typical Lubitsch satire may be obtained, herewith are extracts from the screenplay by Charles Brackett, Billy Wilder, and Walter Reisch for *Ninotchka*, adapted from a story by Melchior Lengyel. Lubitsch, of course, collaborated in the writing of the film, which reflects the characteristic dry wit of his phrasing.

A screenplay differs from a printed play in that it does not exist in its ultimate form until it is filmed, its visual expression being as much a part of it as the text. It has been written with the visuals in mind. A play is complete in its printed form whether it is performed or not. A screenplay *needs* fleshing out—hence even the most accomplished scenario requires the personal vision of the director who, therefore, occupies a more strategic function in bringing a film to life than does the stage director in similarly bringing a play to life. The screen director also, under ideal conditions, exerts a greater autonomy over the various elements that combine to make up the finished work—the choice of actors, the *décor*, lighting and photography, music (when it is called for), etc. Nor should we forget the unpredictable inspiration of the moment, the sudden improvisation of a bit of "business" on the set which has resulted in so many felicitous "touches" characteristic of the best screen directors, frequently "at the expense" of the original script, which, again under the most ideal conditions, should be expendable as often as the whim and fancy of the director wishes. This aspect of improvisation is far more characteristic of the screen director than his theatre counterpart. Besides which, the former, with his close-ups, medium and long shots, moving

* Reprinted with the authorization of Loew's, Inc. and Metro-Goldwyn-Mayer, owners of the copyright, and Dodd, Mead & Co.

camera, and the like, *controls* his audience by these emphases more than the stage director does. (Obviously, it is only the most salutary uses of these devices which apply.) Finally, the screen director, again ideally, should collaborate on the screenplay for, by its very nature, it becomes, in the last analysis, a part of the direction.

Camera directions, and the like, have been omitted and the condensations of transition passages appear as published by Dodd, Mead & Co. in the volume *The Best Motion Pictures of 1939-40*, edited by Jerry Wald and Richard Macaulay.

With this *apologia pro excerptis* out of the way, here then are characteristic parts of the score of the "operetta," *Ninotchka*, which Lubitsch brought to such glowing "musical" life. (Author's note.)

. . .

We fade in on an establishing shot of Paris in the month of April. Over this shot is superimposed the following title: "This story takes place in Paris, in those wonderful days when a siren was a brunette, and not an alarm—and when a Frenchman turned off the lights, it wasn't for an air raid."

We dissolve to the lobby of the luxurious Hotel Clarence. Through the revolving doors comes Comrade Buljanoff, a member of the Russian Board of Trade. Despite the spring climate of Paris, he still wears his typical Russian clothes, consisting of a coat with a fur collar, a fur cap, and heavy boots.

Buljanoff glances around the lobby, obviously overwhelmed by its magnificence. The manager, puzzled by Buljanoff's strange appearance, approaches him and politely asks if he can be of any service. Buljanoff says, "No, no," and exits to the street. This performance is repeated by two other similarly attired Russians—Comrades Iranoff and Kopalski. Each assures the puzzled manager he wants nothing, then disappears through the door.

In front of the Hotel Clarence, we find the three Russians in heated discussion, as a taxi awaits them at the curb.

KOPALSKI—Comrades, why should we lie to each other? It's wonderful.

IRANOFF—Let's be honest. Have we anything like it in Russia?

ALL THREE (*agreeing with him*)—No, no, no.

IRANOFF—Can you imagine what the beds would be in a hotel like that?

KOPALSKI—They tell me when you ring once the valet comes in; when you ring twice you get the waiter; and do you know what happens when you ring three times? A maid comes in—a French maid.

IRANOFF (*with a gleam in his eye*)—Comrades, if we ring nine times . . . let's go in.

BULJANOFF (*stopping him*)—Just a minute—just a minute— I have nothing against the idea but I still say let's go back to the Hotel Terminus. Moscow made our reservations there, we are on an official mission, and we have no right to change the orders of our superior.

IRANOFF—Where is your courage, Comrade Buljanoff?

KOPALSKI—Are you the Buljanoff who fought on the barricades? And now you are afraid to take a room with a bath?

BULJANOFF (*stepping back into the taxi*)—I don't want to go to Siberia.

Iranoff and Kopalski follow him reluctantly.

IRANOFF—I don't want to go to the Hotel Terminus.

KOPALSKI—If Lenin were alive he would say, "Buljanoff, Comrade, for once in your life you're in Paris. Don't be a fool. Go in there, and ring three times."

IRANOFF—He wouldn't say that. What he would say is "Buljanoff, you can't afford to live in a cheap hotel. Doesn't the prestige of the Bolsheviks mean *anything* to you? Do you want to live in a hotel where you press for the hot water and cold water comes and when you press for the cold water nothing comes at all? Phooey, Buljanoff!"

BULJANOFF (*weakening*)—I still say our place is with the common people but who am I to contradict Lenin? Let's go in.

Several days later, we find the Russians, attired very much like Parisian men of the world, returning from the races to the Royal Suite. There they find a telegram from the commissar, advising them of the arrival of an envoy extraordinary, and canceling their authority.

Excitedly the Russians dash to the railroad station, not forgetting first to have themselves moved to the smallest room in the house and engaging the Royal Suite for the envoy.

At the railroad station, where the train has already arrived, the three Russians hurry down the platform, searching the crowd for some clue as to the identity of the Envoy Extraordinary. After making several mistakes, they finally note a woman, who obviously is also looking for someone. The Russians go to her and identify themselves. Ninotchka introduces herself as "Nina Ivanovna Yakushova, envoy extraordinary, acting under direct orders of Comrade Razinin." As they all shake hands, Ninotchka's grip is as strong and forthright as a man's.

IRANOFF—What a charming idea for Moscow to surprise us with a lady comrade.

KOPALSKI—If we had known, we would have greeted you with flowers.

NINOTCHKA (*sternly*)—Don't make an issue of my womanhood. We are here for work . . . all of us. Let's not waste time. Shall we go?

The Russians are taken aback. As Ninotchka bends down to lift her two suitcases, Iranoff calls:

IRANOFF—Porter!

A porter steps up to them.

PORTER—Here, please. . . .

NINOTCHKA—What do you want?

PORTER—May I have your bags, madame?

NINOTCHKA—Why?

KOPALSKI—He is a porter. He wants to carry them.

NINOTCHKA (*to* PORTER)—Why? . . . Why should you carry other people's bags?

PORTER—Well . . . that's my business, madame.

NINOTCHKA—That's no business . . . that's a social injustice.

PORTER—That depends on the tip.

KOPALSKI (*trying to take* NINOTCHKA'*s bags*)—Allow me, Comrade.

NINOTCHKA—No, thank you.

Ninotchka takes both suitcases and walks away with the three Russians, whose nervousness has increased with every word from the Envoy Extraordinary.

BULJANOFF—How are things in Moscow?

NINOTCHKA—Very good. The last mass trials were a great success. There are going to be fewer but better Russians.

The three comrades exchange troubled glances, as we dissolve to the lobby of the Hotel Clarence, where we find Ninotchka, followed by the three Russians coming through the lobby. She observes every detail of the unfamiliar surroundings. Suddenly she stops before a showcase in the lobby which features a hat of the John-Frederic's type. Ninotchka demands to know what the strange object is and Kopalski apologetically explains that it's a woman's hat. Shaking her head and clucking her tongue Ninotchka says "How can such a civilization survive which permits women to put things like that on their heads? It won't be long now, comrades!"

By the time they get to the Royal Suite, the Russians are thoroughly apprehensive over Ninotchka's reaction to such elegance.

BULJANOFF—This is the apartment we have reserved for you, Comrade Yakushova. I hope you like it.

NINOTCHKA (*glancing around the tremendous room*)—Which part of the room is mine?

IRANOFF—You see . . . it is a little different here. They don't rent rooms in pieces. We had to take the whole suite.

Ninotchka begins to unpack her things and puts her typewriter on the desk.

NINOTCHKA—How much does this cost?

IRANOFF—Two thousand francs.

NINOTCHKA—A week?

IRANOFF—A day.

NINOTCHKA—Do you know how much a cow costs, Comrade Iranoff?

IRANOFF—A cow?

NINOTCHKA—Two thousand francs. If I stay here a week I will cost the Russian people seven cows. (*With an outburst of emotion.*) Who am I to cost the Russian people seven cows?

BULJANOFF—We had to take it on account of the safe.

IRANOFF—For ourselves . . . we are much happier now since we moved to a little room next to the servants' quarters.

Ninotchka takes Lenin's picture from her bags.

NINOTCHKA—I am ashamed to put the picture of Lenin in a room like this. (*She puts the photograph on the desk.*) Comrades, your telegram was received with great disfavor in Moscow.

KOPALSKI—We did our best, Comrade.

NINOTCHKA—I hope so for your sake. (*She sits at her desk and starts to type her report.*) Let us examine the case. What does the lawyer say?

BULJANOFF—Which lawyer?

NINOTCHKA—You didn't get legal advice?

BULJANOFF—We didn't want to get mixed up with lawyers. They are very expensive here. If you just say hello to a lawyer . . . well, there goes another cow.

KOPALSKI—We dealt directly with the representative of the Grand Duchess. I am sure if we call him he will give you a very clear picture.

NINOTCHKA—I will not repeat your mistake. I will have no dealings with the Grand Duchess nor her representative.

Ninotchka continues to type. The three Russians watch her nervously. Each click of the typewriter pounds on their consciences.

NINOTCHKA (*looking up*)—Comrade Buljanoff . . .

BULJANOFF—Yes, Comrade?

NINOTCHKA—Do you spell Buljanoff with one or two f's?

BULJANOFF (*with fright in his voice*)—With two f's, if you please.

That evening, Ninotchka, equipped with a street map, starts out to see Paris. Outside of the hotel, she consults her map, then starts across the street. In the center of the street is a little safety island. As Ninotchka reaches this island, Leon also steps onto it, coming from the other direction. They pass on without noticing each other, but the whistle of a traffic policeman releases a flood of automobiles in their direction and both Ninotchka and Leon have to step back onto the safety island. Completely impersonal, Ninotchka asks Leon, merely as a point of intellectual curiosity, how long they have to wait between the traffic policeman's whistles. She is mildly contemptuous of Leon when it appears that he has never considered this matter carefully enough to know the answer. Leon, however, attracted to Ninotchka, volunteers to help her in any other way he can. Taking him at his word, Ninotchka has Leon hold the map for her while she consults it.

NINOTCHKA (*engrossed in her geography*)—Correct me if I am wrong . . . we are facing north, aren't we?

LEON (*bewildered*)—Facing north . . . I'd hate to commit myself without my compass . . . pardon me . . . are you an explorer?

NINOTCHKA—No . . . I am looking for the Eiffel Tower.

LEON—Is that thing lost again? . . . Listen . . . if you are interested in a view . . .

NINOTCHKA—I am interested in the Eiffel Tower from a technical standpoint.

LEON—Technical . . . I couldn't help you from that angle. You see, a real Parisian only goes to the top of the tower in moments of despair to jump off.

NINOTCHKA—How long does it take a man to land?

LEON—Now, isn't that too bad! The last time I jumped I forgot to clock it! (*Looks at map.*) Let me see . . . Eiffel Tower . . . Your finger, please.

He takes her finger and points to the map with it.

NINOTCHKA (*skeptically*)—Why do you need my finger?

LEON—Bad manners to point with your own . . . here . . . the Eiffel Tower.

NINOTCHKA—And where are we?

LEON (*shifting her finger back to the hotel*)—Here . . . here we are . . . here you are and here I am. . . . Feel it?

NINOTCHKA—I am interested only in the shortest distance between these two points. Must you flirt?

LEON—I don't have to but I find it natural.

NINOTCHKA—Suppress it.

LEON—I'll try.

Ninotchka starts to fold her map.

NINOTCHKA—For my own information would you call your approach toward me typical of the local morale?

LEON—Madame, it is that kind of approach which has made Paris what it is.

NINOTCHKA—You are very sure of yourself, aren't you?

LEON—Nothing has occurred recently to shake my confidence.

NINOTCHKA—I have heard of the arrogant male in capitalistic society. It is having a superior earning power that makes you like that.

LEON—A *Russian!* I *love* Russians! Comrade . . . I have been fascinated by your Five Year Plan for the past fifteen years!

NINOTCHKA—Your type will soon be extinct.

At the very top of the tower we find the elevator door opening and Leon emerges, obviously reconciled to waiting at the top of the staircase for Ninotchka. To his great amazement, he sees her standing at the balustrade, looking out over Paris. Recovering from his surprise that Ninotchka has climbed the stairs while he ascended in the elevator, Leon approaches her. Ninotchka is very matter-of-fact.

NINOTCHKA—You gave me some very valuable information. Thank you.

LEON (*looking at the dazzling view*)—And thank you for getting me up here. I've never seen this before. Beautiful, isn't it?

NINOTCHKA—Yes, it is.

LEON—I'm glad I saw it before becoming extinct.

NINOTCHKA—Do not misunderstand me. I do not hold your frivolity against you. (*She looks him up and down.*) As basic material you might not be bad, but you are the unfortunate product of a doomed culture. I feel sorry for you.

LEON—You must admit that this doomed old civilization sparkles . . . it glitters!

NINOTCHKA—I do not deny its beauty, but it is a waste of electricity.

LEON—What a city! There are the Grands Boulevards . . . blasted out of the heart of the old streets. The Arc de Triomphe . . . made to greet Napoleon's army. The Opera! And Montmartre . . . Montparnasse . . . La Bohème . . . and now I'll show you the greatest attraction! (*He steps to a telescope and taking some money from his pocket drops a coin in the slot.*) It will cost me a franc but it is worth it. (*He adjusts the telescope.*) The most wonderful spot in all Paris—unique! Here, look . . . (*She looks in telescope.*) What do you see?

NINOTCHKA—I see a house that looks like any other house. What's remarkable about it?

LEON—It's not the structure but the spirit which dwells within. There are three rooms and a kitchenette dedicated to hospitality.

NINOTCHKA—So that is your house?

LEON—Well, let's say I live in it. Such a pleasant place . . . all kinds of comfort, easy to reach, close to street car, bus, and subway . . .

NINOTCHKA (*straight from the shoulder*)—Does that mean that you want me to go there?

LEON (*feeling that he has offended her*)—Please don't misunderstand me. . . .

NINOTCHKA—Then you don't want me to go there.

LEON (*in a pickle*)—Now I didn't say that either . . . naturally nothing would please me more.

NINOTCHKA (*simply*)—Then why don't we go? (*Looking at him.*) You might be an interesting subject of study.

LEON—I will do my best.

> As they walk toward the elevator, we dissolve them to the entrance hall of Leon's apartment, where Gaston, Leon's elderly, dignified butler, admits them. Ninotchka looks over every detail of the apartment with a lively technical interest. Her principal attention, however, almost immediately centers upon Gaston.

NINOTCHKA—Is this what you call the "butler"?

LEON—Yes.

NINOTCHKA (*takes* GASTON's *hand*)—Good evening, Comrade. (*To* LEON.) This man is horribly old. You should not make him work.

LEON—He takes good care of that.

NINOTCHKA—He looks sad. Do you whip him?

LEON—No, though the mere thought makes my mouth water.

NINOTCHKA (*to the completely flabbergasted* GASTON)—The day will come when you will be free. Go to bed, little father. We want to be alone.

> Leon is all for turning on the music as an aid to romance but Ninotchka seems more interested in the dimensions of the room. Resigning himself to the constant statistical activity of Ninotchka's mind, Leon says, "If there are any special aspects of the room you wish to study, I have nothing to conceal. Just look around. That's my desk. Those are my books, and here am I. Where shall we begin?" Ninotchka replies, "I will start with you."

LEON—That's great. I'm thirty-five years old. Just over six feet tall. I weigh a hundred and eighty-two pounds stripped.

NINOTCHKA—And what is your profession?

LEON—Keeping my body fit, keeping my mind alert, keeping my landlord appeased. That's a full time job.

NINOTCHKA—And what do you do for mankind?

LEON—For mankind not a thing—for womankind the record is not quite so bleak.

NINOTCHKA—You are something we do not have in Russia.

LEON—Thank you. Thank you.

NINOTCHKA—That is why I believe in the future of my country.

LEON—I begin to believe in it myself since I've met you. I still don't know what to make of it. It confuses me, it frightens me a little, but it fascinates me, Nin-otchka.

NINOTCHKA—You pronounce it incorrectly. Ni-notchka.

LEON—Ni-notchka.

NINOTCHKA—That is correct.

LEON—Ninotchka, do you like me just a little bit?

NINOTCHKA—Your general appearance is not distasteful.

LEON—Thank you.

NINOTCHKA—Look at me. The whites of your eyes are clear. Your cornea is excellent.

LEON—Your cornea is terrific. Tell me—you're so expert on things—can it be that I'm falling in love with you?

NINOTCHKA—You are bringing in wrong values. Love is a romantic designation for a most ordinary biological, or shall we say chemical process. A lot of nonsense is talked and written about it.

LEON—Oh, I see. What do you use instead?

NINOTCHKA—I acknowledge the existence of a natural impulse common to all.

LEON—What can I possibly do to encourage such an impulse in you?

NINOTCHKA—You don't have to do a thing. Chemically we are already quite sympathetic.

LEON (*bewildered, and yet completely intrigued*)—You're the most improbable creature I've ever met in my life, Ninotchka, Ninotchka . . .

NINOTCHKA—You repeat yourself.

LEON—I'd like to say it a thousand times.

NINOTCHKA—Don't do it, please.

LEON—I'm at a loss, Ninotchka. You must forgive me if I appear a little old-fashioned. After all, I'm just a poor bourgeois.

NINOTCHKA—It's never too late to change. After all, I'm just

a poor bourgeois myself. My father and mother wanted
me to stay and work on the farm but I preferred the
bayonet.

LEON (*bewildered*)—The bayonet? Did you really?

NINOTCHKA—I was wounded before Warsaw.

LEON—Wounded? How?

NINOTCHKA—I was a Sergeant in the Third Cavalry Brigade.
Would you like to see my wound?

LEON (*dumbfounded*)—I'd love to. (*She pulls the blouse
off her shoulder and shows him her scar.*) Tsk, tsk, tsk.

NINOTCHKA—A Polish lancer. I was sixteen.

LEON Poor Ninotchka. Poor, poor Ninotchka.

NINOTCHKA (*readjusting her blouse*)—Don't pity me. Pity
the Polish lancer. After all, I'm alive.

More and more puzzled and fascinated, Leon sits down
close to her.

LEON—What kind of a girl are you anyway?

NINOTCHKA—Just what you see. A tiny cog in the great wheel
of evolution.

LEON—You're the most adorable cog I ever saw in my life,
Ninotchka, Cogitska, let me confess something. Never
did I dream I could feel like this toward a sergeant.

A clock strikes.

LEON—Do you hear that?

NINOTCHKA—It's twelve o'clock.

LEON—It's midnight. One half of Paris is making love to the
other half. Look at the clock. One hand has met the
other hand. They kiss. Isn't that wonderful?

NINOTCHKA—That's the way a clock works. There's nothing
wonderful about it. You merely feel you must put yourself in a romantic mood to add to your exhilaration.

LEON—I can't possibly think of a better reason.

NINOTCHKA—It's false sentimentality.

LEON (*trying desperately to make her mood more romantic*)
—You analyze everything out of existence. You analyze *me* out of existence. I won't let you. Love is not
so simple. Ninotchka, Ninotchka, why do doves bill
and coo? Why do snails, coldest of creatures, circle in-

terminably around each other? Why do moths fly hundreds of miles to find their mates? Why do flowers open their petals? Oh, Ninotchka, Ninotchka, surely you feel some slight symptom of the divine passion . . . a general warmth in the palms of your hands . . . a strange heaviness in your limbs . . . a burning of the lips that is not thirst but a thousand times more tantalizing, more exalting, than thirst?

He pauses, waiting for the results of his speech.

NINOTCHKA—You are very talkative.

That is too much for Leon. He takes her into his arms and kisses her.

LEON—Was that talkative?
NINOTCHKA—No that was restful. Again.

Leon kisses her again.

NINOTCHKA—Thank you.
LEON—Oh, my barbaric Ninotchka. My impossible, unromantic, statistical . . .

At this point the telephone rings.

NINOTCHKA—I must go.
LEON—Ninotchka, or shall I say Special Envoy Yakushova. . . .
NINOTCHKA—Let's forget that we ever met.
LEON—I have a better suggestion. Let's forget that the telephone ever rang. I never heard that you are Yakushova . . . you are Ninotchka . . . my Ninotchka . . .
NINOTCHKA (firmly)—I was sent here by my country to fight you.
LEON—All right, fight me, fight me as much as you want, but fight me tomorrow morning! There's nothing sweeter than sharing a secret with a bitter enemy.
NINOTCHKA (uncompromisingly)—As a representative of Moscow . . .
LEON—Tonight let's not represent anybody but ourselves.
NINOTCHKA—It is out of the question. If you wish to approach me . . .

LEON—You know I want to . . .

NINOTCHKA—Then do it through my lawyer!

LEON (*desperately*)—Ninotchka, you can't walk out like this. . . . I'm crazy about you, and I thought I'd made an impression on you. You liked the white of my eye.

Ninotchka looks at him for a second, then pulls herself together.

NINOTCHKA—I must go.

She starts for the door.

LEON—But, Ninotchka, I held you in my arms. You kissed me!

NINOTCHKA—I kissed the Polish lancer too . . . before he died.

We are now back in Ninotchka's suite.

The lawyers leave and, left alone with the Russians, Ninotchka relaxes still more.

NINOTCHKA—Well, it means another two weeks in Paris.

IRANOFF (*with exaggerated efficiency*)—Too bad we have to waste all that time.

KOPALSKI—I acted on your suggestion and got in touch with the Power and Light authorities. Whenever you want to visit their plants they are open to you.

NINOTCHKA (*a little bit dreamily*)—Oh, yes, Power and Light. Thank you.

BULJANOFF—There's something else which I know will appeal to you. A visit to the Paris sewers. They tell me it is extremely instructive.

NINOTCHKA—Huh? . . . Why don't you get a haircut, Buljanoff? You all look so wintry, Comrades. And why do we always keep the windows closed? (*She opens the window.*) Isn't it amazing, at home there's still snow and ice and here . . . Look at the birds. I always felt a little hurt that our swallows deserted us in the winter for capitalistic countries. Now I know why. We have the high ideal but they have the climate. . . .

The living room of Leon's apartment. It is evening, and Leon is walking nervously up and down while Gaston putters over the drink table. Noticing Leon's nervousness, Gaston comments on it, complaining that Leon has acted very strangely since meeting Ninotchka. Among other things, Leon has taken to making his own bed, and doing a thoroughly bad job of it.

GASTON—May I add, sir, that it was with great amazement that I found a copy of Karl Marx's "Capital" on your night table. That is a socialistic volume which I refuse to so much as dust, sir. I view with alarm, sir, the influence over you of this Bolshevik lady.

LEON—I can't follow you, Gaston. Isn't it about time that you realized the unfairness of your position? You being my servant? Wouldn't you like to stand on an equal footing with me?

GASTON—No, sir.

LEON—Isn't there any revolt in you? Sometimes when I order you around don't you feel like kicking me in the pants?

GASTON (emphatically)—No, sir.

LEON—Oh, you're a reactionary! Don't you look forward to the day when you can come in here and stand square on your two feet and say, "Hey, you, d'Algout! from now on it's going to be share and share alike"?

GASTON (outraged)—Emphatically not, sir. The prospect terrifies me. Now, don't misunderstand me, sir, I don't resent your not paying me for the past two months, but the thought that I should split my bank account with you . . . that you should take half of my life's savings . . . that is really too much for me.

The doorbell rings. Gaston starts for the door. With a gesture Leon stops him.

LEON—Go to bed, little father, go to bed.

Gaston exits, and Leon admits Ninotchka, who timidly wears her new hat, as well as a completely new and very chic outfit. It takes Leon a few seconds to digest her new splendor. He looks at her again and kisses her hand.

NINOTCHKA—I don't look too foolish?

LEON—Foolish? If this dress were to walk down the Boulevard all by itself I would follow it from one end of Paris to the other, and when I caught up with it I would say, "Just a moment, you charming little dress, I want you to meet Ninotchka . . . you two were meant for each other."

Ninotchka feels more comfortable, and Leon leads her into the living room, where she pauses a second and looks around.

LEON—You remember this room?

NINOTCHKA—I've never been here before. I wonder whom you're thinking of. Oh, I know, a girl with a map, figuring out each step, worrying about north and south. Today . . . now this might shock you . . . I went up to a taxi and said, "Eight Rue du Bois" . . . and here I am.

LEON—You see? Life can be so simple.

NINOTCHKA—For twelve francs, seventy-five.

LEON—Twelve seventy-five from the Clarence? The son-of-a-gun made a detour! . . . (*Charmingly.*) But he got you here.

At this moment the clock starts to strike the hour of nine. Leon wants to take her in his arms. She resists a little.

NINOTCHKA (*reprimanding him*)—It's nine o'clock.

LEON—That's when one half of Paris says to the other half, "What are your plans for this evening, madame?"

NINOTCHKA (*getting more and more in the spirit of her change of appearance*)—Well, first I should like to take off my hat and jacket. (LEON *takes them.*) Then could we have some music?

LEON—A wonderful idea! Radio or records?

NINOTCHKA—Not radio. Let's have music that's just for ourselves.

Leon turns on the victrola.

LEON (*with great feeling and sincerity*)—I'll play it softly because I have things to tell you about which I can't shout.

He walks back to Ninotchka, who by now is seated in an armchair. He sits on the arm of the chair. He tries to make a declaration of love. He stammers several words.

LEON—Well, my darling . . . I . . . we . . .

It is no use. In a sudden outburst of emotion he takes her in his arms and kisses her.

LEON (*as they come out of the kiss*)—You see I couldn't shout that.

NINOTCHKA (*with great feeling*)—Leon, you know the jokes you told me a few days ago? I wake up in the middle of the night and laugh at them. Now, Leon, that's wrong. I know they're not funny, they're silly. They're stupid. And still . . . I laugh . . . and when I look at Buljanoff and Iranoff and Kopalski I know they are scoundrels and I should hate them—then I realize who made them like that, and instead of sending my report to Moscow I tear it up and go down and buy a ridiculous hat . . . and if this keeps on . . . am I too talkative?

LEON—No . . . go on.

NINOTCHKA—Leon, I want to tell you something which I thought I never would say, which I thought nobody ever should say, because I thought it didn't exist . . . and, Leon . . . I can't say it . . .

They kiss again, then with guilty happiness, she produces lipstick and a little mirror. Leon watches her tenderly as she makes up her lips.

LEON—What a gesture for a Sergeant.

As soon as she is finished, Ninotchka slips the mirror and lipstick back into her handbag and as she does so, glances at the top of the desk.

NINOTCHKA—When I was here before I noticed a photograph of a woman on the desk in a wide silver frame. I thought what a waste of silver. That's all that interested me then. Now I would like to know . . . what happened to the woman?

Leon too is completely serious by now. For answer he
quietly opens the drawer of the desk. Ninotchka looks
in and takes from the drawer the photograph. As she
looks at it she rises.

NINOTCHKA—The Duchess.

Leon nods gravely.

NINOTCHKA *(looking at the picture)*—She is very attractive.
She has great elegance. *(She looks back at* LEON.*)* She's
what you call a woman of the world, isn't she?
LEON *(after a little pause)*—Ninotchka, I love you.
NINOTCHKA—I suppose she is very entertaining. . . . It must
be lots of fun to be with her, so witty, so glamorous . . .
LEON—Ninotchka, you're jealous.

Ninotchka nods sadly.

NINOTCHKA *(with great feeling)*—Leon, don't ever ask me
for a picture of myself. . . . I couldn't bear the thought
of being shut up in a drawer. . . . I couldn't breathe, I
couldn't stand it.
LEON—My darling.

As we fade in on the interior of a smart night club, Swana
enters with a party consisting of General Savitsky and five
other smartly dressed people. Swana notes the crowded condition of the room and asks the head waiter if he can man-
age a table near the floor. The head waiter replies that Count
d'Algout made the reservations that afternoon—it is only a
small table but it will be no trouble to put in some extra
chairs. Grasping the situation, Swana says, "No, that's another party." Trying to save an embarrassing situation, one
of the ladies in the party suggests that since the place is so
crowded why don't they go somewhere else? Swana however
is delighted at the chance to have a look at "that female
Bolshevik."

SWANA—I'm going, Leon . . . *(She rises, as does* LEON, *delighted to get rid of her.)* . . . but before I leave I must

compliment you on your gown, Madame Yakushova. Is
that what they're wearing in Moscow this year?

NINOTCHKA—No, last year, Madame.

Swana sits again, as does Leon.

SWANA—Isn't it amazing! One gets a wrong impression of the
new Russia. *(Cynically.)* It must be charming. I'm glad
conditions are so improved. I assume this is what the
factory workers wear at their dances?

NINOTCHKA—Exactly. You see, it would have been embarrassing for people of my sort to wear low cut gowns in
the old Russia. The lashes of the Cossacks across our
backs were not very becoming, and you know how vain
women are.

SWANA—You're absolutely right about the Cossacks. We
made an unpardonable mistake when we let them use
their knouts. They had such reliable guns.

Leon has grown more and more uncomfortable as the
two ladies fence.

LEON—Will you do me a favor? Stop talking about the good
old days.

SWANA—A very wise suggestion, Leon. I'm afraid Madame
and I will never agree. *(She plays her trump card.)* The
only thing we have in common is our lawsuit and that
will be decided next week. I understand everything will
be over by Thursday. Am I right?

Ninotchka and Leon realize the malice and yet the truth
of her words.

NINOTCHKA—You're right, Madame, it will all be over by
Thursday.

We dissolve to the living room of the Royal Suite, as Ninotchka and Leon, both very tight, enter. Leon carries a
bottle of champagne wrapped in a napkin. They sit down
together on a couch. They talk nonsense about a house they
plan to build. In deference to Ninotchka's political connec-
tions, Leon agrees to paint the house red rather than white.

NINOTCHKA—No, don't let's have it any color . . . no color
. . . just a house house . . . let's form our own party.

LEON—Right! Lovers of the world, unite!

NINOTCHKA *(delighted)*—And we won't stretch up our
arms. . . .

LEON—No! No!

NINOTCHKA— . . . and we won't clench our fist. . . .

LEON—No! No!

NINOTCHKA *(tenderly)*—Our salute will be a kiss.

LEON—Yes . . . a kiss . . . salute!

She sinks into his arms and they kiss.

NINOTCHKA—I am so happy. No one can be so happy without being punished. I will be punished and I should be
punished. *(She gets up.)* I want to confess, darling.

LEON—I know . . . it's the Russian soul.

NINOTCHKA *(her gaiety mixed with sadness)*—Everyone wants
to confess and if they don't confess they make them
confess. I am a traitor. When I kissed you I betrayed the
Russian ideal. Leon, I should be stood up against the
wall.

LEON *(sympathetically)*—Would that make you any happier?

NINOTCHKA—Much happier.

LEON—All right.

Still carrying the champagne bottle, Leon leads her to
the end of the room and stands her against the wall.
Tying a napkin over her eyes, he pops the champagne
cork and Ninotchka sinks gently into a chair.

NINOTCHKA *(happily)*—I have paid the penalty. Now let's
have some music.

Leon, in an alcoholic fog, tries to find the radio. Ninotchka, getting drunker by the minute, keeps repeat-
ing, "A little knob . . . a little knob." She lurches toward the safe, opens the concealing door and both are
delighted as they see the dial of the safe. With radio
tuning and safe combination all mixed up in her mind,
Ninotchka directs Leon how to open the safe. The
door swings open and both are disappointed when no

music is forthcoming. As they look into the safe, Ninotchka, through her haze, becomes aware of the case containing the jewels.

NINOTCHKA (*bitterly*)—There it is . . . Thursday . . . you can't rip it out of the week. . . .

LEON (*helpfully*)—But I can throw it out of the window.

NINOTCHKA (*philosophically*)—It wouldn't be fair to the man in the street. (*She pushes back the lid.*) There they are . . . they are terrible things, those jewels . . .

LEON— . . . but big.

NINOTCHKA— . . . they are the tears of old Russia. . . . See that stone?

LEON—Who cried that one?

NINOTCHKA—Czar Peter gave it to his wife, Catherine the Great. For it he sold ten thousand serfs in the market.

LEON—Now, darling, don't get impatient, wait until we are married. You know that worthless butler of mine . . . that reactionary? Some day when I come home to you I may say, "Darling, I drove Gaston to the market and look what I got for him!"

From the case of jewels he takes a beautiful diadem and holds it in front of her.

NINOTCHKA—First ten thousand serfs . . . now just Gaston. It is very encouraging.

LEON—Let me put it on you. You will teach these jewels. For the first time they will learn how they can look.

NINOTCHKA—They belong to the people.

LEON (*in a ceremonial voice*)—I give them back to the people. . . . (*As formal and steady as possible under the conditions he puts the diadem on her head.*) I make you Ninotchka the Great . . . Duchess of the People! . . . Grand Duchess of the People!

Ninotchka falls in with the spirit of this imaginary coronation.

NINOTCHKA—Is this the wish of the masses?

LEON—It is their wish.

NINOTCHKA—Thank you, Leon . . . thank you, masses. (*In a low voice.*) Can I make a speech now?

LEON—Please.

Ninotchka turns to an imaginary assemblage.

NINOTCHKA—Comrades! People of the world! The revolution is on the march. . . . I know . . . wars will wash over us . . . bombs will fall . . . all civilization will crumble . . . but not yet . . . please . . . wait, wait . . . what's the hurry? (*Mixing reality with fantasy.*) Let us be happy . . . give us our moment. . . . (*Turning to* LEON.) We are happy, aren't we, Leon?

LEON (*fondly*)—Yes, sweetheart. (*He holds her in his arms.*)

NINOTCHKA (*her voice getting dimmer and dimmer*)—So happy and so tired.

She falls asleep in his arms. Leon gathers her up and carries her into the bedroom, the diadem still on her head. He puts her down on the bed. She is now sleeping soundly. He kisses her once more and then starts toward the door to the corridor and exits with a slam of the door.

On the night table beside Ninotchka is a photograph of the stern-faced Lenin. The crash of the slamming door awakens Ninotchka for a moment. Completely content and happy, she turns around and sees the disapproving face of the photograph.

NINOTCHKA (*charmingly*)—Smile, little father, smile.

The photograph of Lenin starts to smile in approval, as we fade out.

Next day, Ninotchka lies on the bed, still in her evening dress. The diadem is no longer on her head. The door buzzer is ringing persistently and Ninotchka finally half wakens, calling out, "Come in!" in a weak voice. The Duchess Swana enters. She permits herself surprise and amusement at the state of the room, then walks over to the bed where lies

Ninotchka, still not equal to the effort of getting up. Swana is obviously delighted to have caught Ninotchka in this position.

SWANA—How stale last night's gaiety looks! It has the taste of a dead cigarette.

NINOTCHKA—If you were encouraged to come here by our meeting last night I am afraid you misunderstood my attitude.

SWANA—Don't worry, you were quite rude enough. (*During the following speech, she draws the curtains and opens the windows.*) Do you mind if I let in a little fresh air and sunshine? I'm sure it will make you feel better and I want you to be at your very best. In full possession of your faculties, at least.

NINOTCHKA (*regaining her usual firmness*)—Please come to the point. What is it you want?

SWANA—I just dropped in to have a little heart to heart talk with you.

NINOTCHKA—We have nothing to discuss.

SWANA—Now there you are completely wrong. If we sit down for a little chat, I'm sure we won't run out of conversation and what's more it won't be dull.

NINOTCHKA—Madame, what is it you people always say, regardless of what you mean . . . "I am delighted to have you here"? I have not reached that stage of civilization.

SWANA—That's all right . . . I grow on people.

NINOTCHKA—I must ask you to leave.

SWANA—Leave? That's exactly what I came here to ask *you* to do. Leave! I don't mean this hotel and I don't mean Paris . . . I mean France. There's a plane for Moscow at five-forty.

NINOTCHKA (*puzzled*)—Madame, if you . . .

SWANA—Don't worry. I have already made reservations. It's perfect flying weather. They assure me there's a fine tail wind which will sweep you back to Moscow in no time.

NINOTCHKA (*still not understanding*)—If this is meant to be a joke it is not funny. Or do you still think you're issuing orders from your palace in Petrograd?

Ninotchka's words for the first time sting Swana out of her apparently superficial attitude.

SWANA (*bitterly*)—My palace in Petrograd . . . yes, you took that away from me. You took away my czar, my country, my people, everything I had . . . (*With emphasis.*) . . . but nothing more—I warn you.

NINOTCHKA (*simply*)—People cannot be taken away, Madame, neither a hundred and sixty million nor one. Not if you have their love. You hadn't. That's why you're not in Russia any longer, and that's why you came here this morning.

SWANA—Very interesting, my dear, but couldn't you write all that from Moscow? A dissertation on love on Soviet stationery—would be an amusing paradox.

NINOTCHKA—It is not enough to be witty, Madame. People grow tired of being entertained. You made that mistake before. Problems were never solved by bowing from a balcony.

SWANA—My dear, you don't know how impressive I could be. Did you ever see me in my regalia with my diadem and all my jewels?

The word diadem startles Ninotchka. She remembers the night before and looks toward the safe, which is closed by now. Ninotchka continues to stare in the direction of the safe as Swana chatters on.

SWANA—You can't deny we gave the people their money's worth—almost—eight tumbling Romanoffs—eight!

NINOTCHKA (*desperately*)—I must insist that you leave.

SWANA—Not before you agree to use those reservations to Moscow.

NINOTCHKA—In that case I can only say good-by.

Abruptly she goes into the bedroom, where she is horrified to find the diadem missing—nor are the other jewels in the safe.

NINOTCHKA—Where are they?

SWANA—You were very careless with our precious jewels, my

dear. They're too expensive a toy for two children to play with.

NINOTCHKA—Where are they?

SWANA—Don't worry. Fortunately last night a very trust-worthy friend kept his eyes open. Perhaps he overstepped his function as a waiter but he fulfilled his duty as a Russian. (*She draws back the fur scarf she is wearing, revealing a diamond star, one of the jewels we have seen.*) I just put this on for sentiment. The rest are absolutely safe. I assure you. But if you feel like notifying the police . . .

NINOTCHKA—You leave me no choice.

SWANA—Won't it be rather embarrassing for a Soviet Envoy to disclose the circumstances under which she lost them?

Swana freely admits that France will uphold the Soviet Republic in every court which she will drag it through —and, she adds warningly, she will certainly drag the case through every court available, which should consume a matter of two years. Ninotchka doubts that Swana has enough money to endure such court expense. Swana replies, "I may run out of money, but you have already run out of bread. Two years is a long time for your comrades to wait." Ninotchka scornfully says, "I see. You have calculated in terms of hunger."

SWANA—No, I just wanted to be absolutely impartial. Both of us are faced with two rather uncomfortable years. We can condense these two years to two minutes if you want to accept my proposition.

Ninotchka now realizes what she is after.

NINOTCHKA—Go on.

SWANA—I am willing to hand over the jewels and sign the necessary papers if you take that five-forty plane to Moscow.

NINOTCHKA (*quietly*)—That's not the way to win him back . . . not Leon.

SWANA—I think I know Leon quite as well as you . . . possibly a little better. Leave that worry to me. Five-forty leaves you time enough to close the deal with Monsieur Mercier but naturally you'll be too busy for any farewells. I'll see to it that everything is done in the most expeditious manner and I will also see you to the air-port. That's my proposition, Comrade Yakushova.

OFFICIAL (*into phone*)—Yes . . . Comrade Cazabine? No, I'm sorry . . . he hasn't been with us for six months. He was called back to Russia and was investigated. You can get further details from his widow.

LEON (*horrified; as the official hangs up*)—Pardon me, I am very interested in what you just said—you mean when an envoy goes back to Russia—if they don't like what he has done they put him out of the way?

OFFICIAL—Not always . . . look at me . . . I've been back twice. (*He knocks on wood.*)

LEON (*his alarm growing*)—Here's my passport. . . . Please give me a visa. I have to leave for Russia immediately.

OFFICIAL—Count Leon d'Algout . . . a count! . . . a noble-man!

LEON—Don't hold that against me . . . please!

OFFICIAL—Why should an aristocrat want to go to Russia?

LEON—Business.

OFFICIAL—What business?

LEON—Private.

OFFICIAL—There is no privacy in Russia. This whole thing seems very suspicious. What's the real reason? If you ever want to get into Russia, take my advice . . . confess!

LEON (*dismayed*)—Confess what?

OFFICIAL—Are you sympathetic to the former Czaristic gov-ernment—the white Russians?

LEON—On the contrary—I don't want to have anything to do with them.

OFFICIAL—You believe in our cause?

Leon, feeling that he has to go to the rescue of his girl, whips up an enormous enthusiasm for the cause.

LEON—Oh . . . I think it's great! Everyone works—every-one contributes—that's what I want to do—work! I make my own bed—you can call up my butler! I don't believe in the right of the individual. I like the Bolshevik ideal—everyone being the same. You just like me—me just like you—I use your comb—you use my toothbrush —oh, it's a great life . . . please . . . give me that visa!

OFFICIAL—No!

LEON—Listen, I want to be absolutely frank with you. I have no business in Moscow.

OFFICIAL—I think so too.

LEON—I want to see a friend of mine . . . a very dear friend. . . . It's a personal matter which has nothing to do with politics or social philosophies . . . it's a girl.

OFFICIAL—So it's love which drags you to Moscow.

LEON—Yes!

OFFICIAL—No visa.

LEON (*fighting for his point*)—I *must* get into that country of yours!

OFFICIAL—Oh, no. No visa.

LEON (*more aggressively*) That's impossible! Nobody has the right . . . you can't do that! . . . If you don't give me that visa . . .

OFFICIAL (*ironically*)—You're going to force us . . . huh?

LEON (*growing violent*)—Now look here . . . you advertise all over the world that you want people to go into your country and when someone tries to get in, you keep him out!

OFFICIAL—Why should I take a chance?

LEON—On what?

OFFICIAL—How do I know you don't want to blow up a factory?

LEON—What for . . . why?

OFFICIAL—Or a tunnel or a bridge . . .

LEON—Suspicions . . . nothing but suspicions! . . . that's the trouble with you! If you don't let me in I'll stand in front of this office of yours and warn people to keep away from Russia! . . . I'll picket your whole country. . . .

The official laughs in a superior way.

LEON—I'll boycott you, that's what I'm going to do! . . . No more vodka . . . no more caviar . . . no more Tchaikovsky . . . no more borscht . . . wait a minute, I know something better than that. . . .

The official leans forward sarcastically.

OFFICIAL—What?

With a knockout blow, Leon sends him to the floor, then leaning over the counter he shouts.

LEON—And you can tell the Kremlin that's just the beginning!

He strides out.

The official's head emerges from the counter. As he adjusts his bruised jaw, he speaks.

OFFICIAL—No visa.

We are back in Russia. Anna tells Ninotchka that ever since she has returned from Paris, she has been acting queerly and making other people feel queer. Ninotchka says stoutly, "I have nothing to hide." Anna says, "You should." She walks over to a cupboard and takes out a piece of lingerie which she shows to Ninotchka. She tells Ninotchka that when she passed through the laundry yard today, all the women in the building were huddled around this piece of lingerie, so Anna removed it from the line and brought it into the apartment. Anna warns, "Things like this create a bad feeling. First they didn't know whose it was. Then they saw the Paris label and did it cause a commotion! . . . It undermines our whole cause." Wearily, Ninotchka says, "I see. Thank you, Anna. I'll dry it up here when I wash it next. I should hate to see our country endangered by my underwear.

Unable to contain her curiosity, Anna asks Ninotchka what else she had in Paris in the way of clothing.

NINOTCHKA (*enjoying the thought*)—Well, a hat . . .
ANNA—What was it like?
NINOTCHKA—It was very silly . . . I would be ashamed to wear it here.
ANNA—As beautiful as that? What else? Come, tell me.
NINOTCHKA—An evening gown.

ANNA (*puzzled*)—Evening gown?

NINOTCHKA—A dress you wear in the evening.

ANNA—What do you wear in the morning?

NINOTCHKA—When you get up you put on a negligee and then you change to a morning frock.

ANNA—You mean to tell me you wear a different dress for different times of the day?

NINOTCHKA—Yes.

ANNA—Now, Ninotchka, you're exaggerating.

NINOTCHKA—No, my dear, it is true. That's how they live in the other world. Here we dress to have our bodies covered . . . to keep warm . . .

ANNA—And there?

NINOTCHKA—Well, sometimes they're not completely covered but . . . they don't freeze.

ANNA (*fingering the piece of lingerie*)—They must have wonderful materials to make a thing like this so soft . . . something you don't even see.

NINOTCHKA—You feel it though.

ANNA (*hesitantly*)—Ninotchka, I wouldn't bring this up if we weren't such good friends.

NINOTCHKA—What is it, Anna?

ANNA—You know I told you that Pavlov and I are going to get married when he comes back from maneuvers. Would it be asking too much . . .

NINOTCHKA—You want this?

ANNA—Just for the honeymoon.

NINOTCHKA—You can have it for good. It is my wedding present.

Anna is for a moment speechless over this generous gift. She embraces and kisses Ninotchka.

ANNA (*ecstatic*)—Am I going to play that cadenza tonight! (*She leaves with her cello.*)

At this moment the door opens and Buljanoff, Iranoff, and Kopalski enter. The four greet each other warmly, then a moment of silence follows and they look at each other as people do who share a secret.

KOPALSKI (*wryly*)—Well, we're back home.

BULJANOFF *(sourly)*—You know what they say—there's nothing like home.

IRANOFF—That's right . . . and we might as well face it.

NINOTCHKA—Sssh! Once and for all, we're in Moscow!

KOPALSKI *(walking over to the window)*—Yes, there's no doubt of that. . . . *(Sarcastically.)* Just look out of the window and there it is.

NINOTCHKA—And it's great! Think what it was a few years ago and what it is now.

Iranoff and Buljanoff have joined them at the window.

IRANOFF—She's right . . . *(Under his breath)* . . . anyhow let's talk ourselves into it.

BULJANOFF—Just see how happy the people look . . . from here . . .

KOPALSKI—Can you blame them? . . . at least the May Day parade is over!

BULJANOFF—That's another thing . . . it's spring.

NINOTCHKA—The same spring we had in Paris. Just as good.

KOPALSKI—Even the swallows are back.

BULJANOFF AND IRANOFF—Yes, that's right.

IRANOFF—Maybe that's the same swallow we saw in Paris.

BULJANOFF—It is, Ninotchka! It is! He must have been in Paris! You can see it in his whole attitude! He just picked up a crumb of our black bread, shook his head and dropped it.

KOPALSKI—If you asked him why he left France I bet he couldn't name one good reason.

BULJANOFF—I should be a swallow! Right now I would be sitting in front of the Café de Paris picking up flakes of French pastry that would melt in my bill.

NINOTCHKA—Now, Comrades . . . there is something better in life than crumbs of French pastry.

KOPALSKI *(the realist)*—Yes, a good piece of apfel strudel. . . .

NINOTCHKA—We will get that . . . we'll get everything . . . maybe a little bit later but we'll get it . . . we must be patient . . . finally we got the spring, didn't we? We got the swallows, and you will get your apfel strudel too.

BULJANOFF (*consolingly*)—And if it is too late for you your children will eat it.

IRANOFF (*breaking the mood*)—Let's forget the future . . . let's stop being sentimental . . . let's start that omelet.

The office of Razinin, Commissar on the Board of Trade. As we fade in, Ninotchka enters the office, carrying several folders. Razinin tells her that she will have to turn over her work to someone else—it seems that Kopalski, Buljanoff, and Iranoff are in some kind of trouble. Razinin complains that he sent them to Constantinople on an important fur deal solely on the strength of Ninotchka's Paris report on these gentlemen. Up to now, the three comrades have not only failed to sell a single piece of fur, but are dragging the good name of Russia through every café and nightclub in Constantinople. He reads from a report, "How can the Bolshevik cause gain respect among the Moslems if your three representatives, Buljanoff, Iranoff, and Kopalski, get so drunk that they throw a carpet out of their hotel window and complain to the management that it doesn't fly?" Ninotchka suppresses a smile and asks if Razinin is sure the report is correct. Razinin replies dryly, "It gives details which couldn't be invented. Naturally I want to verify it and that's why I need you." Apprehensively, Ninotchka says, "You want me to go to Constantinople?" Razinin says, "Yes—leaving immediately."

NINOTCHKA (*her one object to escape the mission*)—I appreciate the confidence you show in me, but I must ask you to entrust someone else with this mission. I should hate to interrupt my present work. I am positive that my survey is more important than finding out whether three of our comrades have been drinking some extra glasses of champagne.

RAZININ (*austerely*)—That is for me to decide, Comrade Yakushova.

NINOTCHKA—I am sorry, I don't want to overstep my position —but please . . . don't send me.

RAZININ—I don't understand.

NINOTCHKA (*making a last effort*)—How can I make myself clear . . . it is difficult to express but I'd rather not go to foreign countries any more. Please, Comrade . . . let me stay here . . . let me finish my work . . . I am in the rhythm of it now . . . I don't want to go away. I don't want to be sent into that foreign atmosphere again. It throws one out of gear . . . let me finish my work . . . I have concentrated everything in it . . . please . . . don't make me go.

RAZININ—Please don't waste my time, Comrade. Do your duty. Good-by.

NINOTCHKA—I will do my best.

We dissolve to the Constantinople airport, where we find Buljanoff, Iranoff, and Kopalski standing in the crowd. All three of them are dressed elegantly and gaily and seem to be in the happiest mood. One of them carries a large bouquet of flowers with which to greet Ninotchka.

We next find the Russians as they usher Ninotchka into a luxurious hotel suite. The Russians are anxious to have her praise the suite, but Ninotchka feels duty bound to protest. She is shocked that her friends seem to have no concern for consequences, and only gradually does it become clear to her that they have no intention of ever going back to Russia. They reveal to her that they have opened a little restaurant.

NINOTCHKA (*completely bewildered*)—Who gave you this idea? What is responsible for all this?

KOPALSKI (*with a gleam in his eye*)—There's something in Constantinople . . . something irresistible . . .

IRANOFF— . . . it is in the air . . . it may come around the corner as you walk down the street . . .

BULJANOFF— . . . it may step out of a bazaar . . . it may wait for you in a corridor . . . it may hide in the shadow of a minaret . . .

KOPALSKI (*pointing to the balcony*)—Right now it's on the balcony.

Ninotchka looks toward the balcony and is dumbfounded as she sees Leon standing there smiling at her. He walks quietly toward her.

LEON—They wouldn't let me in, so I had to get you out.

NINOTCHKA (*still taken aback*)—So—you're behind all this. I should have known.

> Leon takes her hand and kisses it. The three Russians exchange glances. The CAMERA PANS WITH THEM— leaving Ninotchka and Leon as the Russians walk discreetly out of the room and close the door behind them.

LEON—Trying to keep me away from you! It couldn't be done. Naturally I couldn't go on forever punching passport officials in the nose—but I found a way, didn't I? Darling, I had to see you. I wrote and wrote but all my letters came back.

NINOTCHKA—The one I got they wouldn't let me read. (*Carried away by emotion.*) It began, "Ninotchka, my darling," and ended, "Yours, Leon."

LEON—I won't tell you what came between . . . I'll prove it. It will take a long time, Ninotchka . . . at least a lifetime.

NINOTCHKA—But, Leon, I am only here for a few days.

LEON—If you don't stay with me, I'll have to continue my fight. I'll travel wherever Russian commissions are. I'll turn them all into Buljanoffs, Iranoffs, and Kopalskis. The world will be crowded with Russian restaurants. I'll depopulate Russia. Once you saved your country by going back. This time you can save it by staying here.

NINOTCHKA—Well, when it is a choice between my personal interest and the good of my country, how can I waver? No one shall say Ninotchka was a bad Russian.

An Interview with
Samson Raphaelson *

Lubitsch's favorite screen writer during his American sound
film period was Samson Raphaelson, with whom he made
eight pictures: *The Smiling Lieutenant, The Man I Killed,
The Merry Widow, Angel, One Hour with You, Trouble in
Paradise, The Shop Around the Corner, Heaven Can Wait,*
plus a ninth, *That Lady in Ermine,* which the author completed just before the director's last illness. Three—*Trouble in
Paradise, The Shop Around the Corner,* and *Heaven Can
Wait*—the director counted among his major productions,
especially the first two. *Trouble in Paradise* Lubitsch regarded
as his best work.

Samson Raphaelson's brilliant dual career as playwright
and screen writer was also reflected in such successes on the
Broadway stage as *The Jazz Singer, Young Love, Accent on
Youth, Skylark, Jason and Hilda Crane,* among others, and
in his screenplays for Alfred Hitchcock's *Suspicion, Green
Dolphin Street,* etc. He has just completed a new play which
Broadway will soon see.

. . . .

*To what degree was the finished picture reflected in the
script before the direction began, because the script is almost
like the finished film—the film appears to have been directed
on paper first. To what degree did Lubitsch participate in the
writing and to what degree is the famous "Lubitsch touch"
seen in the script first, as frequently happened, so that the
"Lubitsch touch" often appears to be a contribution of the
writer?*

* This interview took place in Samson Raphaelson's New York
apartment on December 3, 1967, expressly for this book.

Lubitsch was the most literary of directors—not that he wasn't terribly aware of film and enormously capable of handling film—but he thought like a writer and functioned like a director, so that if there were words or interplay of dialogue values on the most sensitive level, that would enhance what he had to say in his film concept, he sought those values and wasn't content until he got them.

He was aware that such values existed, then.

He was very much aware. And if you couldn't find them, he'd find someone else who could.

He knew what he was looking for.

That's right. If he could do it himself, of course, he could do without the writer. But he knew what a writer could do, once he got the hang of that writer. I think almost every writer who ever worked with him wrote his best. Lubitsch didn't necessarily make him write like Lubitsch, but he brought out what the fellow had; he pressed him more than the fellow might himself. That doesn't mean that my own best writing was done with Lubitsch—my best writing in the *vein* of Lubitsch was done with him—I had other values to express in the theatre. But to a remarkable extent, the film was in the script. Lubitsch prepared a foolproof script that you'd say almost any director could direct. That's not true, of course, but it's comparatively true. Seventy-five percent of his work was done when that script was done. And he already had the performances in mind and they weren't just performances that he superimposed on actors, they were performances that he knew those actors could give. And very rarely did any actor fail to give his best performance with Lubitsch, and that's why they loved working with him. At the moment of working with him they might not be happy because he wouldn't waste much time getting it done his way. He'd know how they should do it and he'd show them, frequently acting out the parts himself, and, once they saw that, they couldn't do it any other way because it was so right, so superior.

What about the so-called "Lubitsch touch"? Did you find yourself contributing "Lubitsch touches" that he retained?

A meeting between Lubitsch and a writer was usually one of mutual respect. I enormously admired him from what I had seen of his previous work. I had fallen in love with *The Love Parade*. I thought it was the most delightful picture I'd ever seen. The only picture in my life I ever saw twice. So I had a notion how Lubitsch would approach things, and I loved that approach. It belonged to me even though he had thought of it first. I wished *I* had thought of that *way* of telling things . . . like his use of doors. . . .

Doug Fairbanks, Jr., was interviewed on Lubitsch's method right after That Lady in Ermine *and he said that not only did he act out all the parts including the female parts, but he put great stress on the importance of doors. He said doors in a film can often be as important as actors.*

Yes, but I never caught Lubitsch ever thinking in terms of a formula; that is, he wouldn't say, "How can ve use a door in this scene?" Never once would he say that. He would face the problem and say, "Vat do ve do here? How do ve lick dis? How do ve say it vit style? How do ve say it *different*? How do ve say it *different* and *good*? Different and true?" But he was also one of the few great practitioners who was not a victim of his own inventions and of his own style. In *The Smiling Lieutenant*, for instance, he used a minimum of dialogue and only at the high moments—this was soon after talking pictures came in, still using the rich resources of silent invention, so that the dialogue would become the cream, the peak of a scene. For a while he thought that was the way to go. He began to shift with *One Hour with You*—read the script, it's a dialogue show. It has some touches but it's a dialogue show.

He began to use dialogue more and more after the first experiments integrating sound and silence in the period of transition.

Right. In *Trouble in Paradise*, which followed, there were those nice shots in the beginning, but after that it's pretty much a dialogue show. After that, you knew the characters *from the script*, you could also read the full story in the script for *Shop Around the Corner*, in *Heaven Can Wait*. Right up to *That Lady in Ermine*, in which Lubitsch was a very sick man plodding along on formula and I couldn't fight him. What I had to do there was deliver what a worn-out man expected and I did it as an act of compassion, knowing it was going to be warmed-over Lubitsch and a repetition of his formula. I couldn't fight a man who had had two heart attacks. I wouldn't count that picture. But I think the *Shop Around the Corner* and *Heaven Can Wait* are as fine on the Lubitsch chart as anything he's ever done. To get back to your question: in a way it's difficult to say what his end of it was. He would set the standard and then we both began laboring. Right at the start of the picture. "How do ve get into it?" Lubitsch would ask. "How do ve open? It gotta be brilliant!" Like the garbage-gondola at the start of *Trouble in Paradise* or the magnifying glass looking on a map for the tiny principality in which *The Merry Widow* is set, which opens that film, right under the credits. And that sort of thing. It was fun.

May I pinpoint this question? Before actual shooting started, he'd collaborate with a writer on the script so that a script suitable for him would emerge?

I'll tell you how it happened. We met every morning. I didn't sit off in a corner and write. There was a secretary in the room. We wrote it together, that's all. You couldn't trace it. If the problem was, "How do we get into this scene?", whoever finally found it wasn't necessarily the author of it because he might not have found it if the other hadn't said two other words before. But the dialogue, usually, when it came right down to it, came out of me because I work by talking, anyway, you see. I can't write by myself, I always have a secretary as a "sounding board." But it often could have come from him. Then the girl would type it out (she'd know when to take it down), and then we'd read it back and throw it away or like it or take part of it and re-shape it and discuss it. I wish to God the tape recorder had been in existence in our time, to take it all down—it would have been wonderful to have had an actual recording of these sessions—that would have been a great thing.

That sure would . . .

To see the evolution of a scene . . .

Well, we're trying to reconstruct that right now.

It's very hard to because my memory betrays me; I don't remember so many things. One secretary we had might be able to remember—Helen Harrelson. She worked with us on several pictures, very observant she was—she had to be to know what to take down and what not to. We never told her.

. . .

Sometimes we'd get stuck, dead end. A concept we'd had in our outline wasn't working. And then he devised a way out which I've used frequently since myself, and it helps. "I tell you what ve do, Sam," he once said, "ve write it dull, like in life—just like people talk in real life—real dull —and see if ve get any ideas from dat." That was a wonderful idea because out of that sometimes came an unexpectedly fine scene—or, the opposite, seeing how long-winded it was and how truly dull, we'd realize how it *shouldn't* be done— and suddenly we'd find the answer. I've used that time and again since, in my own work—it's helped enormously.

To say what were his touches, I'd say this: It's very easy for me as a writer to think I remember the things I did and take credit for them. Actually, I don't. I must have been of great value to him, otherwise he wouldn't have insisted on having me, time and again and again. All I can say is this: if I'd done the same job with almost any other di-rector (don't forget Hitchcock and *Suspicion*) it wouldn't have been that good.

It wouldn't have been the same thing, certainly.

No . . . so that whatever it was that he contributed, whether it was to inspire me or actual writing . . . whatever I contributed . . . and, good God, how could you help, over a period of nine pictures, how could I help not contributing *some* shots that were known as "Lubitsch shots"? And how, in God's name, could this very, very, *very* talented man not help but contribute some goddam good lines of dialogue? Or concepts of dialogue? It ultimately becomes a question of: in which field is which man more likely to contribute; which is his specialty?

Would you say that his scripts were so tightly knitted that he very rarely overshot on his films?

Very rarely. He would say, "Dis time ve are spending here, writing, is de cheapest time ve got. All ve are paying now is your salary and mine. But the minute ve are on de set, ve are paying de stars, de dis, de dat, ve are paying $50,000 a day . . ." or whatever the amount was.

So that the editing was really done in the writing of the script.

That's right.

When the script was finished, that was pretty much it, wasn't it?

The shot-making was done. This reminds me of the time when we were at Twentieth Century Fox, on *Heaven Can Wait*, or whatever it was, and we were going to the commissary for lunch and, going there, coming in the opposite direction, was Zanuck. They paused to greet each other and Zanuck said, "How's it going, Ernst?" And Lubitsch says, "Vell, I tell you—slow but good." And Zanuck says, "That's fine," he says, "the only thing I'd rather hear than that is —*very* slow and great!"

Which was nice of Zanuck—you'd think he'd have said "fast," but he didn't—that was his attitude toward Lubitsch —deep respect.

We had one sequence—I wish to God I could find it, I don't think I have it—in *Heaven Can Wait* we had one sequence when this cavalier fellow became an old man; he was kind of a sexy old guy, he got into a mess with the nursemaid of his grandchild, or something, and this was a scene of grisly humor, inspired completely by Lubitsch; it came out of *his* knowledge, out of his European savvy. Once I got the idea, I was delighted and helped him express it. But it was so harsh, it was so mean, that Zanuck said, "We can't possibly dare to use this." It was the only time anything by Lubitsch was ever—that we both thought was good—that was ever rejected by the head of a studio. Then we rewrote it.

Do you remember what the scene was? Because that's an interesting sidelight.

I know the scene that we replaced it with. A little bit of real detective work at Fox in their filing department would locate the original. It would be kept on record.

I think it's a very interesting sidelight on him to know that he could do a harsh scene—just because he was such a great comic director.

It was a vicious scene which he didn't fully realize was vicious because he so loved lecherous old men, so he made him the way he knew such old lechers were—and the way he liked them. Doubtless, if it had been let pass, he would have been accused of bad taste. Then, but not today.

As in the case of that line in To Be or Not to Be, *in which the Nazi officer equates what the actor playing Hamlet did to Shakespeare with what the Germans were then doing to Warsaw. He was shocked by accusations of "bad taste," a thing he never thought himself capable of. Anyway, I am reminded of what Picasso once said, that so-called "good taste," what the mass public generally regards as "good taste," is the enemy of art.*

The scene we replaced it with is the one between the son and his aged father discussing the possible engagement of a reader-companion for the old fellow. The son suggests a nice quiet young man from Yale or Harvard but the old boy still has girls on his mind, even a specific young woman whom he says would make a perfect reader-companion. Their conversation is interrupted by a telephone call that comes for the father. The son answers the phone. "Hello," he says, "What? . . . Just a moment." He goes over to his father. "It's for you, *poochie.*" Visibly embarrassed, the old fellow picks up the phone and very meekly says, "Hello . . ." We then dissolve to a close-up of a newspaper with a picture of a girl lying on a couch in a negligee, holding a book, her legs very luringly displayed. The camera pulls back and we read the caption under the picture: *"Reader's Contract Settled for One Hundred Thousand Dollars."*

Another facet: imagine this man, who was better able to write a line, if he had to, than any other director who ever existed—and this anecdote indicates his respect for the writer—was shooting something that we had written together. One morning the studio called: "Mr. Lubitsch apologizes for waking you so early but it's important. We're sending a car for you to take you on location. Will you—?" "Of course," I replied. On my arrival at the set, a movie town, I waited for him to finish a shot and then he came over. He had just wanted to change one line—which no other director in his right mind would dream of consulting a writer about, let alone taking all that trouble. But he had the intelligence to know that maybe the change that he wanted to make might have something to do with something he had forgotten, about some character, about some value, which this change might contradict. He wanted my memory of the whole script, and my sense of the character. No other director I ever heard of would dream of taking that trouble—*one line.*

If you had to sum up the significance of the so-called "Lubitsch touch," since that's the name of this book and I'll be writing considerably about that, how would you sum it up?

People would cite certain shots as the "Lubitsch touch," like the opening shot of the garbage-gondola in *Trouble in Paradise*. . . .

Whose idea was it to open the film that way?

I couldn't tell you. If it were a clean-cut Lubitsch inspiration, I would remember. If it were a clean-cut inspiration of my own, I would remember. In other words, there were times when Lubitsch would say, "Sam, here's how ve get into dis. Listen to dis!" And I'd say, "Wonderful!" This wasn't one of those times. We labored for three days and we had terrible ideas and we had almost-ideas and then the minute we got this one, whoever got it, we knew we had it . . . but I have no idea now beyond that.

To what degree did the final versions of these several Central European plays, mostly by Hungarians, as it seems, did the final scripts depart from their original sources?

That's a swell question. I want to tell you: there was so incredibly little resemblance between any movie I ever made with Lubitsch and the original material, that the original material at best could be reduced to a page-and-a-half synopsis. The characterization became brand new. Take *The Shop Around the Corner*—I've got the original play, you can read it—nothing, not one scene, not one line of dialogue, coincides with the film. I remember this because I had to go over the orginal again for legal reasons once; also the source play of *Heaven Can Wait*, fantastically a case of no resemblance, and *Trouble in Paradise*, a completely new creation, compared to the original. But each had an idea, and that's really all we needed to begin with. Lubitsch saw in each what might be done with them. Then things began to happen, we got going.

What was Lubitsch's opinion of Von Sternberg?

Well, he would say, "Vell, you know, he vorks different dan de vay I vork, Sam—you see, he goes for other kinds of qvalities dan I go for. He certainly is doing some tings dat nobody else is doing and you gotta give him credit for dat."

He was very fond of Willie Wyler, personally, and Wyler, of course, had enormous respect for Lubitsch. Everybody of his time felt the same way. He was The Master and there were no two ways about it. As guests in his home or in his presence, wherever, they were in awe of him, yet Lubitsch never acted "important." There wasn't a trace of pretentiousness in him.

One more thing, about what Ben Hecht reported. Lubitsch never got ill during a story conference, lay down, and was incapable of talking. I never saw anything like that happening in all the time I was with him.

I didn't quite believe it either when I read it. That's Hecht's way of being whimsical.

Whimsical, you say? Extravagant—and a false picture of how Lubitsch worked. Hecht never overawed Lubitsch by sitting there with a frozen expression on his face and made him nervous—that's preposterous. Lubitsch was such a profoundly intelligent and poised man. Now here's Lubitsch's account of working with Hecht. I had asked him, "How did you get along with Hecht?" And he said, "Oh, fine, fine, Sam, fine—he's very able, very able." "No problems?" I said. "Vell, in the beginning," he said, "you know, ve vasn't used to each udder. I'd say to him, 'Look, de vay I usually vork, Ben, is ve get together, ve meet in the morning at a reasonable hour, ve have a secretary and ve vork together.'" And Hecht replied, "Not me, I'm not going to sit around and have you tell me how to write my stuff. I go home and I write the stuff and I bring it to you. Then, if you don't like it, we fight it out." "So I say, 'O.K. Ben.'" said Lubitsch, "'Go ahead. Dis is de general feeling how I vant, how I feel, de opening scene.'" And he explains it. "'You agree?' " " 'Sure,' " said Hecht, " 'I'll work on it.' " "So he comes two days later vit de scene," says Lubitsch. "And *you* know, how can a man, in two days . . . do anything . . . anyway I vas interested so I read it and I say, 'Now come on, Ben, for God's sake, you don't call dis writing.' And he says, 'What's the matter with it?' He gets sore. So ve talk a little bit, and ve talk a little bit more, and den ve talk a little bit more, and pretty soon Hecht and I are vorking every day from ten o'clock in the morning." Because Lubitsch's intelligence, his demands, and his capacity to develop what he wanted suddenly reached Hecht's mind and from then on they worked together. Some years later, Lubitsch and I met Hecht on the Fox lot, where we were all working. We were again on our way to lunch. We paused and chatted with him a moment and Hecht wasn't superior or uppity at all with Lubitsch, he was mild and shy and humble. Lubitsch even kidded him a little. Lubitsch was the one who was doing the needling—but not brutally. Then when we left, he turned to me and said, "If dis man vould put half as much energy into writing a good script as he does into bamboozling everybody, he vould be a really great writer."

I remember Hecht writing back to a friend in the East, "I'm making a fortune out here writing swill for the movies." Of course, Hecht admits his debt to Lubitsch in that little effusion of his on him. He says, "I learned everything I know about the screen from Lubitsch—I've forgotten what it was I learned, but I'm sure I learned it."

He *had* to admit that, because he was a very superior fellow. But that whole picture of Lubitsch getting ill and being incapacitated—oh, nonsense!

The way it's written, I don't think he intends you to believe it literally.

Probably not, probably not.

It's tongue-in-cheek.

You felt it was Hecht having fun . . . maybe?

Yes . . . I think so. Hecht was a great kidder, too.

But when Hecht and Charlie MacArthur got together, they did something for each other. *The Front Page* was a marvelously fresh original play in its day.

Oh yes, they were quite a team.

They did a lot for each other.

. . .

Well, now, an interview on Lubitsch, like a Lubitsch picture, should end with a comedy tag line.

Sir Cedric Hardwicke, at a dinner party given by Alfred Hitchcock, was defending the merits of English provincial cooking, which Lubitsch thought terrible. "Well, I don't know," said Sir Cedric, who was playing a humorless English general in a Hitchcock picture at that time: "It all depends on one's taste—for instance, in women, there are women who are perfumed and made-up and their clothes expensively designed for them—and there are other women, wholesome and artless and healthy and simple . . ." Whereupon Lubitsch broke in: "Who vants dat?"

An Interview with
Walter Reisch *

Walter Reisch, who collaborated on the scenario of *Ninotchka*, and wrote the scripts of those two "*echt*-Lubitsch"
charmers, *Maskerade* and *Episode*, which latter he also directed, was for many years an intimate friend of Lubitsch
in Hollywood where he had a long and distinguished career,
as writer-director of *Men Are Not Gods* and as coauthor of
the scenarios of *Titanic* (for which he shared an Academy
Award), *That Hamilton Woman*, and *The Great Waltz*,
among others. His original screenplay for *Comrade X* was
an Academy Award nominee, while his *Zwei Herzen im
Dreivertel Takt* (*Two Hearts in Waltz Time*), for which he
did the original screenplay, and the title-song lyrics, swept
the world. The hit song of *Das Lied Ist Aus*, "Frag' nicht
warum" ("Don't Ask Me Why"), introduced by Marcel
Wittrisch, and more recently one of the hits of Marlene
Dietrich's concert tour, has lyrics also by him. He is still
active in Hollywood.

. . .

What projects did Lubitsch have which he did not realize?

A good question, because at the height of his career Ernst
Lubitsch had such a position that he could practically realize
any project that he dreamed of.

There was one dream I know of that he never could put
on the screen: *Der Rosenkavalier*.

In a strange way, it was I who, in my hometown, Vienna,

* This interview took place in the Winter of 1967 in the study
of Mr. Reisch's home on Amapola Lane in Los Angeles expressly
for this book. Directly across the garden could be seen the house
where Lubitsch lived and died (268 Bel-Air Road). The interview
contains information hitherto unrevealed.

had to break the news to him that this "Rosenkavalier" project might be impossible for him to materialize. His wish to make the comic opera by Richard Strauss the crown of all his musical achievements in pictures he kept a closely guarded secret.

He didn't want any publicity, in fact not a word was to leak out to the press about his plan before he actually could contact Richard Strauss, himself, and acquire the motion picture rights.

Lubitsch had already approached the filmization of musicals with Viennese or pseudo-Viennese backgrounds in *The Smiling Lieutenant*, *The Love Parade*, and *The Merry Widow*. They all showed definite accents of the classic Austrian operetta. At the beginning of his career he had also made a silent picture of *Die Fledermaus*, which he not only directed but in which he played one of the important parts himself. The title of this Johann Strauss operetta was, in Lubitsch's version, *Das Fidele Gefängnis* (*The Merry Jail*). So the jump from Johann Strauss to Richard Strauss was almost a foregone conclusion, but yet who could have predicted it?

In the spring of 1936 he returned from America to Europe after an absence of many years. At the Studio L'Étoile in Paris he saw a picture with Paula Wessely, which I had written, *Maskerade*. This picture had a genuine Viennese background, and Lubitsch seemed very much taken with it. Through the Paris office of Paramount he contacted me in Vienna, announcing his arrival there on April 2. He was on his way to Russia, probably one of the first American visitors to get permission from Moscow. This was thirty-one years ago, and therefore rather extraordinary on the .part of the Russian authorities, who recognized Lubitsch's world fame by issuing him a visitor's permit.

The reason he wanted to talk to me was that he regarded me as a sort of expert on Viennese color and local customs.

I met him on April 4, 1936, at the old Hotel Bristol on the Kärntner Ring, opposite the State Opera House. It was, of course, a memorable moment for myself, especially since he immediately showered me with compliments on *Maskerade*. Actually, I suspected that it wasn't so much the

picture that he loved, but the reunion with his native language, which for the first time he confessed he had heard in
a sound film.

I arranged that same afternoon a showing of another picture I had written, *The Unfinished Symphony*, with Hans
Yaray and Martha Eggerth, and the next day I ran for him,
early in the morning and in a cold projection room, a second
Paula Wessely picture I had written and directed, *Episode*.
On the screen he recognized many actors' faces from his
former Max Reinhardt days, old friends and comrades-in-
arms with whom he had played on the stage. He was immensely moved at this *Wiedersehen* with Otto Tressler,
Erica von Wagner, Walter Janssen, and, since all these three
pictures were unmistakably of Viennese background, texture,
and musicality, he finally confided to me the true reason for
his stopover in Vienna. I don't think he had even told
Paramount in Hollywood about his project, but it was the
Rosenkavalier that he had in mind. Richard Strauss's waltzes
were for him the quintessence of all Viennese melodies, and
he contemplated having Jeanette MacDonald act and sing
the immortal part of the Marschallin, with Emil Jannings
penciled in as Baron Ochs von Lerchenau. Needless to call
to mind here that Jeanette had her biggest triumphs in
Lubitsch's pictures, and it was, of course, under Lubitsch's
direction in *Anna Boleyn*, *Madame Du Barry*, and *Das Weib
des Pharao* that Emil Jannings first became a world star.

But Lubitsch's great problem was the part of Octavian,
the young Cavalier of the Silver Rose himself. In the original
opera score this part was conceived for a mezzo-soprano.[1]
Lubitsch had heard Jarmila Novotna in the part and fell in
love with the role, but on the screen he could never visualize
a slim young mezzo-soprano playing the masculine Octavian.
To find an actor who could sing her great arias was plainly

[1] The part was a *hosenrolle* ("pants part") for a female singer
but Lubitsch wanted a young man for the young man's role. The
singing could be dubbed in later. Lubitsch intended to persuade
Richard Strauss to reduce the singing passages of the *Rosenkavalier*
as much as possible for the screen version and let Jeanette Mac-
Donald, as Marschallin, carry most of the arias. A proper voice,
matching his Octavian's personality, would, of course, have had to
be found.

unthinkable. Much heavier even than these misgivings was the blow I had to deal him in the projection room of the Sievering-Sascha Studios that rainy morning, because what never would have occurred to Lubitsch was the fact that the rights to the *Rosenkavalier* were unavailable. The picture had been made as a silent movie by, of all people, none other than Robert Wiene, director of the famous *Cabinet of Dr. Caligari*, in 1926, right here in Vienna. Huguette Duflos had played the Marschallin—no singing, of course; these were still the silent film days. Michael Bohnen, the baritone of the Met, had played Baron Ochs without singing a single note, either. Octavian was played by the handsomest *jeune premier* of the Paris theatre, Jacques Catelain.

Lubitsch was crushed. He at once wanted to see this silent opera, but no print could be found. Then he started to map out a campaign to acquire the remake rights for sound and color—and a new complication arose. Just in those April days of 1936 rumors reached Vienna about the peculiar, ambivalent position of Richard Strauss in Hitler's Germany. Dr. Goebbels had offered Strauss the complete supervision of the musical scene in all Nazi Germany; apparently Strauss had not rejected Goebbels's offer outright. Richard Strauss's loyalty to his Jewish librettists, Hugo von Hofmannsthal and Stefan Zweig, was above suspicion. Still, Lubitsch instantly gave up any wish to approach Richard Strauss personally, and he was the only one who could dispose of the rights or remake rights of any of his works.

The same evening, Lubitsch left Vienna for Moscow,[2] and only a year later in Hollywood, at the Chateau Marmont, where I was staying at that time, did the talk of *Rosenkavalier* come up again. In fact, Lubitsch admitted not having abandoned the project at all, but would reconsider it only if the prerequisites should be met: to find the young Octavian first, and then start negotiations for the rights.

It was as good a pretext as any. Rudolph Valentino was long since dead, and there simply could not be found an actor who could take over the Octavian role. In his heart, Lubitsch had moved away from the project. World War II

[2] I have been unable to find out any details of his Moscow trip. (H.G.W.)

was imminent, Hitler's legions started to march, soon the news came that Emil Jannings had died, and never in all the years to come, with the Battle of Britain, the Siegfried Line, Stalingrad, and Pearl Harbor, was the *Rosenkavalier* idea ever again mentioned by Ernst.

But one day the war was over and, on an afternoon in my house, Jarmila Novotna, with her beautiful daughter, had dinner with us. At that very dinner Marlene Dietrich, who spent almost every Sunday that she was in Hollywood in my house, mentioned the name of a Parisian actor, and the way she described him made Lubitsch most attentive. He exchanged a quick look with me, and I knew exactly that his fast mind was thinking again of Octavian, the Cavalier of the Silver Rose, when he heard Marlene describe Gérard Philipe, whom she had seen in Nice in a picture called *Le Diable au Corps*. This certainly was a coincidence that, with Jarmila Novotna present, Marlene, whose instinct for casting was infallible, should bring up the name of this new French personality.

But the climax of this story was more than a coincidence. No motion picture could have a more rounded denouement than the happening of another Sunday afternoon. A year after that dinner in my house, one of the dearest friends of Lubitsch, Margaret Wyler, wife of the famous director of *Wuthering Heights*, arranged a private showing in their house at 1121 Summit Drive in Beverly Hills. They would run the print of *Le Diable au Corps*, which had just arrived in Hollywood, the same *Le Diable au Corps* with Gérard Philipe of whom Marlene had spoken so highly.

The date was November 30, 1947. Margaret Wyler had invited everybody who was in my house that afternoon to come up to 1121 Summit Drive at 8:30. Marlene was in my house that afternoon, Mady Christians, Otto Preminger, Billy Wilder, Charles Brackett, Joan Harrison, Yvonne de Carlo, Mary Loos, Salka Viertel, Walter Wanger, Mervyn Leroy, Gottfried Reinhardt, Gene Markey, Edmund Goulding, Vanessa Brown, Helmut Dantine, Eva Gabor, Miklos Rozsa, Sidney Skolsky, John McClain, Michael Romanoff, and the Paul Kohners. Lubitsch did not come. He had died at 2:40 in his house, which was next door to mine, but at

8:30 we all were up there in the Wyler projection room on Summit Drive, and there played Gérard Philipe, the young Octavian of the *Rosenkavalier* indeed, the only one who could have played it in that Lubitsch dream that never came true.

What were Lubitsch's opinions of other directors? What was his favorite film of his own? What was his favorite film by others?

The favorite film of his own was usually the one he had just finished. Anyway, that's what he used to say. Whether he meant it or not, I can't tell. But certainly I can tell which picture by another had found his unqualified applause. Oddly enough, it was also the very last picture in his life that he ever saw. (I exclude here the rushes of the film he was working on.)

In September of 1947, exactly two months before his death, there was a special showing of an Italian picture in black-and-white, as yet without subtitles, and I'm almost sure that Lubitsch had never heard the name of the director of this picture: Vittorio de Sica. The picture was *Shoe Shine.* There were not more than four or five people with us: Billy Wilder, who at that time was Lubitsch's house guest and who had arranged the screening; Mary Loos was present; Dr. Maximilian Edel, who at that time was practically the permanent companion of Ernst, officially as a friend, but much more likely as a physician who worried deeply about Lubitsch's deteriorating heart condition. Maybe because the *milieu* of those little shoeshine boys was so many light years removed from the elegant drawing rooms in Lubitsch pictures, and the brilliantly lit throne halls, or Viennese wine gardens, the impact of that cruel, merciless Italian postwar desolation upon Lubitsch was tremendous. This was the first, as it was to be the last, time that he ever witnessed on the screen the message of total human misery, the unspeakable horror of street tragedies.

When it was all over, he sat as if mummified. He couldn't talk, he wouldn't participate in the controversy that broke out among us. He didn't want to believe what he had to believe, because he knew it was true, what he had just seen on the screen.[3]

Very late that night, when we drove him home, he decided not to send a cable to De Sica, but to write to him. He wanted to find a perfect translator, so that the letter should be in Italian. Whether he ever got around to writing that letter I don't know. Maybe De Sica can tell. One thing is clear. He never saw another De Sica picture, and never another picture of his own.

Were there any notable differences in Lubitsch's professional relationships with Dietrich and Garbo?

The best way to answer this loaded question is the fact that on November 30, 1947, when Lubitsch died at 2:40 P.M., the first person who found him dead in his library was his butler, Otto, who called Dr. Loos, Mary Loos's father, who closed his eyes—and another nineteen minutes later, it wasn't three o'clock yet, Marlene stood by the couch onto which Otto had lifted him. I had picked Marlene up at the nearby Shoreham Apartments, where she had been staying briefly. I took her over to 268 Bel-Air Road, and here were these two, both born in Berlin, in houses less than five minutes' walking distance from each other: life met death. Marlene was still in her house robe, with her gray mink flung over it. Of course they had had their little skirmishes during their Paramount days, when he directed her in *Angel* and other pictures. She claimed he had bullied her; he claimed she had contrasted him with Josef von Sternberg.

The truth is that he was as proud as a peacock that a Berlin girl had made good here in Hollywood and in the world. It was all kidding, teasing, and honest threshing out of problems between the two. Whether he liked directing Garbo better than Marlene is purely a matter of speculation, because there were so many years between the Lubitsch pictures with Marlene and *Ninotchka*, in which he directed Greta. Both of them, Marlene and Lubitsch, were then out of Paramount; there was hardly any production company on

[3] Orson Welles, too, was similarly moved. He regarded it as an utterly naturalistic, flawless work. [Author's Note.]

the map of Hollywood that would have contemplated his directing Marlene again. Anybody who had seen Marlene standing by his dead body that Sunday afternoon at 268 Bel-Air Road would know what she had felt for that man, who had already been a giant when she was a struggling tyro carrying a violin case on the Kurfürstendamm in Berlin.[4]

About Lubitsch's two marriages . . . ?

He divorced his first wife in the early thirties in Hollywood. Afterwards she married a flyer and disappeared completely from the film world, as far as I know. Lubitsch had no children by his first wife. I had asked Otto occasionally about the first Mrs. Lubitsch, however he never revealed any details about her.

The name of the second Mrs. Lubitsch is Sania (no spelling mistake, it is *S-a-n-i-a*). I believe they married in 1935, more likely at the beginning of 1936. He always called her Vivian. She is British.

They divorced towards the end of World War II. For many years she lived in Copenhagen, then she married again and made her home in Haiti. She is very well known in diplomatic circles, in Denmark, and in the Caribbean Islands.

From this marriage Lubitsch had a child, whose name is Nicola.

(The first Mrs. Lubitsch never married Hans Kräly as rumored. He had been Lubitsch's screenplaywright for decades. Lubitsch never forgave Kräly the intrusion into his private life. Kräly never wrote for Lubitsch again.)

What other incidents can you recall?

There were two incidents in which I had seen Lubitsch without a smile. Ernst had met every event in his life with his hearty laugh and counteracted even the gravest occurrences with his sharp wit and unfailing optimism. Twice I

---

[4] Marlene, probably inexplicably even to herself, carried a new record album of hers, under her arm, when she stood at Lubitsch's deathbed. Perhaps she had planned to play it for him that afternoon. . . . ?

saw him chalk-white and tightlipped. Not even during his many heart attacks did he fail to come up with a joke. Here are the jokeless moments:

a) On September 4, 1939, the *S.S. Athenia* of the Donaldson Atlantic Line was underway from Glasgow bound for Montreal when 200 miles west of the Hebrides an explosion suddenly ripped her hull, killing more than 100 passengers and crew. She started sinking fast, blasted, according to one version, by a torpedo from a German U-boat, according to another by a German mine.

Lubitsch's baby, Nicola, had been with her mother in London to visit her grandmother. Sania stayed on in London for another week; Nicola embarked with her nurse on the *Athenia* to return to her father.

It was Labor Day in the United States. All the programs on the radio were interrupted. Walter Winchell had the *Athenia* story; right after him Raymond Graham Swing reported the passenger list of the *Athenia*, among them Nicola Lubitsch. Ernst had not heard the radio report. It was Sam Katz (of the Balaban & Katz theatre chain in Chicago), who at that time was an executive at MGM, who rushed over to Lubitsch's house to break the dread news to Ernst.

Halfway up Bel-Air Road Sam Katz picked me up. We both entered the house. What followed was a study in efficiency on the part of the MGM executive. Sam Katz had taken over the telephone. Five MGM employees were called back from their holiday and tried, simultaneously with Katz himself, to establish some contact with the high seas, to find out about the rescue actions. The name MGM worked magic, even in a catastrophe not staged by any Culver City director, but by the German navy. For three hours Lubitsch stood leaning against the piano in his living room, holding onto the silver frame with his baby's picture. (There was only one other picture on his piano, that of Jeanette MacDonald in *The Love Parade*.) When, at the end of that day, Sam Katz finally handed Lubitsch the receiver to hear for himself what the MGM office in New York transmitted, Lubitsch was incapable of holding the receiver. So Otto, his butler, pressed it to his ear.

Nicola and her nurse had been picked up by lifeboats. The

nurse herself had performed the heroic act of saving Nicola's life. One of the first ships to reach the rescue scene was the *Southern Cross*, picking up some survivors. Later, the Norwegian freighter *Knute Nelson* finished the rescue action.

The last Sam Katz saw of Lubitsch that day was Ernst staggering away from the piano and locking himself up in his study, without his cigars, without finding any words, without a smile.

b) The other incident in which his proverbial humor froze up and nothing could thaw it out was at the beginning of 1942. He had previewed his picture, with Jack Benny and Carole Lombard in the leads, called *To Be or Not to Be*. It was produced by Sir Alexander Korda for United Artists; Lubitsch had written it, himself, in collaboration with a Hungarian playwright. It was the story of a theatrical company. Jack Benny and Carole Lombard were a husband and wife team, and Robert Stack was the third in the triangle. Sig Ruman, whose heavy German accent played a supporting role in several Lubitsch pictures, had an important scene in which, as a Nazi general, he said the following sentence: "What he [Jack Benny] did to Shakespeare, we are now doing to Poland." That night we had a sneak preview at the Westwood Village Theatre near Beverly Hills. The theatre had been cracking up with laughter, except when Sig Ruman's line was heard from the screen. After the sneak preview, we all had a drink at a nightclub on Sunset Boulevard, which since has closed its doors. Present were Mrs. Lubitsch, Brackett and Wilder, Sir Alexander, Henry Blanke, and others of Lubitsch's inner circle. Unless my memory fails me, S. N. Behrman was also present. It was Sania Lubitsch who was the first one, after a long series of noncommittal, evasive trivia and comments, to suggest eliminating the line in question. Ernst was absolutely aghast, but when the chorus of his intimates almost in unison picked up Sania's cue, and not only suggested but insisted that this line should be cut from the finished print, Lubitsch simply couldn't parry the reproach of his faithful that perhaps for the first time in his whole artistic career he had stooped to a tasteless crack. If we had said that the laugh just didn't come off, he would have been angry but would have slashed out the line from the film with his own hands; but to be accused of lack of taste made his face waxen and the long cigar tremble in his mouth. Other people came into the nightclub that evening, and, passing the table, looked the other way. Finally Sam Hoffenstein, a great wit and poet in his own right, came in and bent down to the Master, expressing his grief that the fate of Poland, the destruction of a country, the annihilation of millions, should have been grabbed up for the sake of a laugh. Lubitsch had no answer to that, no further argument, no smile. Later on, when practically every review in the American press, with the exception of *Time* magazine, took exception to this very line in *To Be or Not to Be*, Lubitsch wrote an open letter to *The New York Times*, in which he defended himself. He took full responsibility for the dubious line, explained in convincing paragraphs that nothing could have been more remote from his mind than to make a joke out of the tragedy of a whole country, a whole nation.

In Defense of
TO BE OR NOT TO BE

Apropos the matter of *To Be or Not to Be*, referred to by Walter Reisch in his interview, here is a letter from Lubitsch to a journalist that reveals his very sensitive feelings on the subject.

. . .

August 25, 1943

Miss Mildred Martin
Philadelphia Inquirer
Philadelphia, Pennsylvania

Dear Miss Martin:

I feel extremely sorry that my picture *Heaven Can Wait* has caused you two such uncomfortable hours.

I am not writing this letter with the intention to make you reconsider your criticism—nothing is farther from my mind. I am merely writing this letter to point out to you that several times in your criticism you resort to what one calls in sports circles a "foul."

In order to support your argument against me you feel it necessary to refer to the "Berlin born director." Not that I am trying to conceal my place of birth, but I feel at this point in your review the reference to my birth place is a little dragged in by the heels.

The purpose becomes very clear when in the next sentence in regard to *To Be or Not to Be* you call attention to my "callous, tasteless effort to find fun in the bombing of Warsaw."

Being an experienced newspaper woman you are surely aware of the effect such an allegation must have on the reading public, particularly at a time like this. Such propaganda is not very gracious, but when it is based on false facts it becomes outrageous.

Naturally, your statement that I "find fun in the bombing of Warsaw" is completely untrue. When in *To Be or Not to Be* I have referred to the destruction of Warsaw I have shown it in all seriousness; the commentation under the shots of the devastated Warsaw speaks for itself and cannot leave any doubt in the spectator's mind what my point of view and attitude is towards those acts of horror. What I have satirized in this picture are the Nazis and their ridiculous ideology. I have also satirized the attitude of actors who always reman actors regardless how dangerous the situation might be, which I believe is a true observation.

Never have I said in a picture anything derogative about Poland or the Poles. On the contrary I have portrayed them as a gallant people who do not cry on other people's shoulders in their misery but even in the darkest day never lost courage and ingenuity or their sense of humor.

It can be argued if the tragedy of Poland realistically portrayed as in *To Be or Not to Be* can be merged with satire. I believe it can be and so do the audience which I observed during a screening of *To Be or Not to Be*; but this is a matter of debate and everyone is entitled to his point of view, but it is certainly a far cry from "the Berlin born director who finds fun in the bombing of Warsaw."

I repeat again, I have no quarrel with your opinion of *Heaven Can Wait* or my ability as a director in general, but I feel I have a right to protest against such insinuations which are so completely contrary to my real beliefs.

Sincerely yours,
Ernst Lubitsch

EL–s

Last Memories
by Walter Reisch *

Lubitsch's first heart attack occurred in 1945, during a walk with his daughter in the gardens of the old Arrowhead Springs Hotel in California.

His second heart attack took place—maybe ten months later—in Otto Preminger's former house at 333 Bel-Air Road. It was a stag party for a high official of the prosecution team at the Nuremberg trials. I remember Lubitsch sitting between Clifton Webb and Leon Shamroy during the afterdinner conversation, which, of course, focused on the jurist, who had just returned from Nuremberg and was full of fascinating though cruel information regarding Hermann Goering and the rest of the war criminals in the dock. At one point during the jurist's narrative, Lubitsch beckoned me stealthily to his chair. I didn't have to wait to hear what he wanted to whisper to me; I saw by his distorted face that he was in the throes of another heart seizure.

Fortunately everybody else's attention was completely riveted on the jurist from Nuremberg, so nobody actually noticed how Ernst's lips and cheeks had changed color. I told him *sotto voce* that I would bring my car to the kitchen entrance, and he should try to meet me there in a few minutes. I knew he would hate to break up the party, just as much as he was always most anxious to conceal his growing heart weakness from others. When I came out on the Bel-Air Road triangle, I found my Oldsmobile squeezed in by Billy Wilder's car and two more station wagons. (By the way, Joan Harrison, now Mrs. Eric Ambler, was the only woman present at the stag.) I knew I could never drive my Oldsmobile out of the huddle. But I was lucky enough to

* This is from a second interview with Mr. Reisch that took place a few days later.

find a Buick parked in the clear, with the keys in the ignition. Without hesitating a second, I borrowed the Buick and arrived in time at the kitchen door to meet Lubitsch. Both his hands pressed to his chest, he stood doubled over on the threshold. Even Preminger's chef and servants were listening to the Nuremberg story without having noticed Lubitsch's exit. How I got him into the back seat of the Buick I don't know to this day. From Preminger's house to 268 Bel-Air Road it would ordinarily be a two-minute drive. Slumped in his seat, Ernst begged me to drive as slowly as possible, which was easy the first few yards; that's where Bel-Air goes downhill. But up his driveway it got very steep, and the slightest elevation seemed to aggravate Ernst's condition immensely. All in all, it took me eleven minutes to negotiate the brief stretch from Preminger's to Lubitsch's home. Otto, the butler, had the night off. It was the Finnish housekeeper who succeeded in reaching by phone Dr. Nathanson, the great heart specialist on the West Coast. Lubitsch was lying on a wooden bench, an antique Salzburg piece of furniture, a gift from his friend Henry Blanke. All Lubitsch muttered was, in German: "Es ist aus mit mir, es ist aus mit mir." ("I'm done for.")

I was too busy to contradict him. I don't think I said anything. I was untying his shoelaces, unbuttoning his collar, but the wool sweater that he always wore at night I couldn't pull over his head. Neither would I dare to bring him water or anything, since I had absolutely no experience in how to cope with somebody suffering a heart attack. Dr. Nathanson came soon and sent me out of the room. Meanwhile Otto, the butler, had been called back from his night off by the Finnish housekeeper. (To be sure, Lubitsch was already divorced from Vivian at that time.) Nicola was spending the night at a girlfriend's house.

When, half an hour later, Dr. Nathanson came out into the yard, he seemed most optimistic. He expressed hope for a quick recovery of the sick director. Provided, of course, that the *patient* Lubitsch would stop being the *director* Lubitsch, refraining from any excitement, agitation, physical work, and any smoking. A few weeks later Lubitsch started a new picture, *That Lady in Ermine*, for Twentieth-Century

Fox, with Betty Grable and Douglas Fairbanks, Jr. He never finished it. (He had not heeded Dr. Nathanson's advice.) I returned the borrowed Buick to the driveway of 333 Bel-Air Road, but I never found out whose car I had used from among the guests at Preminger's party.

Lubitsch's pallbearers in December, 1947, were: Otto (the butler), Mervyn Leroy, Billy Wilder, Richard Sale (Mary Loos's husband), and I; the list of honorary pallbearers was endless, and they all were present, including Louis B. Mayer, Gene Raymond (Jeanette MacDonald's husband), and scores of actors who had appeared in Lubitsch's pictures.

Charles Brackett delivered the eulogy at the Forest Lawn Cemetery.

Jeanette MacDonald sang Lubitsch's favorite songs.

Steffie Trondel, Lubitsch's secretary for many years, is buried a few feet away from his own burial plot at Forest Lawn in Glendale. She had saved all her life for this post-humous privilege, to sleep in death next to her boss. It was only a short time after 1947 that her wish was fulfilled.

Ernst Lubitsch's enormous cigar collection—the cigar, of course, was his trademark on all his photographs—was auctioned off in 1948. Ernst Lubitsch's famous Marc Chagall, with the flying angel over a *shtetle*—a Jewish village—had disappeared. Nobody knows where.

Lubitsch never learned how to drive an automobile. His butler-chauffeur was Otto.

I, myself, never addressed Lubitsch by his first name, Ernst. I always called him Herr Lubitsch.

Evaluations

¶ THE FILM WIZARD OF EUROPE *

by Herbert Howe

This was one of the earliest interviews with Lubitsch, done in Germany by the foreign correspondent of *Photoplay* magazine while the director was engaged in filming his last film there, *Die Flamme*, released in America as *Montmartre*.

. . .

The man who gave fame to Pola Negri, to Louis XV of France, and to Henry VIII of England . . .

The German film wizard, master of tragedy, and the man who makes history live . . .

"The Griffith of Europe," as he is sometimes called, because of the genius with which he made *Passion*, *Deception*, and *The Loves of Pharaoh* . . .

Ernst Lubitsch, star maker and king maker, sat opposite me in the lunchroom of his Berlin studio, his face beaming like a harvest moon over a platter of *Kalbsschnitzel*.

The broad smile broadened . . .

"My hobbies . . . my hobbies?" He lingered over the unfamiliar English word. "*Ja*, my hobbies is d'piano, d'cello, and d'shimmy."

"Good dancer," he blinked, his little black eyes crinkling out of sight. "Every night I dance in New York.

"Pretty girls in America. Ya, Ziegfeld Follies. Um!"—many ecstatic blinks—"Ya, I vill like to work in America."

He was beaming from every pore. His secretary, a German

* Excerpted from *Photoplay*, December, 1922.

boy whose English still has the flavor of German idiom, suddenly asked me if I had any chewing gum for Mr. Lubitsch.

"He is a great friend of the chewing gum," said the secretary.

Lubitsch demanded to know what was being said and then endorsed with, "Ya—California Fruit." Emphatic nods and blinks.

"It is very difficult getting him this California Fruit," sighed the secretary. "It is not much in Berlin. Sometimes I must go all over town looking. And it is all my fault. It is not allowed to smoke on the 'set,' and Mr. Lubitsch did not know what to do without his cigar. So I say, 'You must chew.' He say, 'Ya, but what I chew?' I say, 'Chewing gum.' And now I spend all my time looking down this California Fruit."

Such is the master of tragedy. "The man who never stops smiling" is what they call him around the studio. A plump, alert, restless little fellow of thirty with a broad humorous mouth, a hooked Semitic nose, crinkling bead eyes, and a lock of ink hair sprawling Napoleonically over a high forehead.

As he wheels restlessly to and fro on the "set," one arm behind him, his head cocked on the side, his eyes on the floor, he looks like a Dutch comedian doing a burlesque of Napoleon.

Over a neat business suit he wears a loose linen duster, the sort his carpenters wear. He seems to have no particular place or significance on the stage. He has no puttees, no megaphone, no director's chair with his name emblazoned across the back. In fact, he might be called a director without a country.

No sooner do you get him focused in the crowd of players and workingmen than—poof!—he has vanished like a genie. Ah, there he is!—popping up like a jumping jack beside Pola Negri. He whispers a suggestion. You wonder how she could have caught it, he is gone again so quickly.

The extras have crowded around to see the great Negri do her scene. From somewhere Lubitsch has let out a terrific bellow—"*Drehen!*" meaning "Camera!" The players are in action. Extras and workmen crowd closer to watch. Pretty soon you notice a little man darting around like a terrier on the outskirts of the crowd trying to get a peek. He can't see a thing on account of the extras, so he jumps upon a chair and looks over their heads. It's the director, the great Lubitsch. In a second he's off the chair and diving between the legs of the camera. He lets out another horrifying whoop. Something is wrong. He contorts his brows at fearful angles, making a diabolical face which is funnier than the smiling one of the minute before. Then he grins—as though amused by his fearful countenance, which has had no effect upon anyone but himself. He bounds among the players to act a "bit" for a little girl playing a *cocotte*. He is a very funny coquette, but he knows the business, every glance, every wink, every instinctive gesture of the flirt. . . . Then off again on a feverish pace as if he had lost all interest in the affair.

I pinioned him behind the piano upon one of these excursions—he always has music with his scenes. Seeing me, he plopped down on the stool and commenced playing very sour snatches from *The Music Box*.

"You know the *Moosic Box* sonks?" he asked, grinning. "Und *Sally?*"—more soggy notes, with Lubitsch beaming over them as if to coax them into melody by the sunshine of his smile.

We talked of American films. I asked him which of our stars he considered best.

"The best of all—the greatest actor in the world—*le plus grand*," he emphasized in three languages, "is—Ch'pln. Great tragedy actor—Ch'pln."

"Chaplin a great tragedy actor?"

"Ya—Ch'pln greatest actor of everything."

If Chaplin is the great tragedian, Lubitsch, the tragedy maker, is the great comedian.

But he is entirely serious in his appraisal of our films and players.

"Harold Lloyd—" he blinked his pleasure. "I saw him in New York—good—*good*—*very* good!"

Of the women—

"Ah, Pickford," he nodded.

"And Miss Lillian Gish, Mr. Lubitsch," interposed the secretary.

"Ah—Lillian Gish—*Orphans of the Storm*—Lillian Gish —ah, ah, ah," he teetered on his heels and went into a veritable paroxysm of blinks.

It was noon and everyone was awaiting the arrival of Pola Negri. She usually makes her entrance at about twelve o'clock. Someone came in and told Lubitsch that she was actually in her dressing room employed in making up. He celebrated the fact by taking another drink of raspberry juice and bursting into song.

Things grew a little more tense in expectancy. Lights were adjusted. Players began to take their places in the "set," which was an exact reproduction of a famous Parisian café of 1860. A huge bar maid in *décolleté* took her place behind the glasses and bottles, her shoulders looming over the bar like a range of the snowcapped Alps. The camera men began to jimmy with their instruments, as camera men always do. And then—somehow—you felt La Negri had arrived.

I couldn't see her, but the presence was conveyed, psychically and by murmurs. The secretary scurried past me whispering, "She's here—back there by the door to the café." I kept my position, however. It was peaceful and secure, and I'd been told that Pola was not feeling very well.

After the usual interminable wait, while lights and cameras and extras were changed all around again, Lubitsch came clambering into view. He took a place behind the cameras. Gave a quick squint and then—"Nay-*gree!*"

Swish, whish of silken skirts. A voice, somehow suggesting Camille, called tremulously, " 'Allo! 'Allo!" And Negri came strolling flirtatiously into view, casting mesmeric eyes to right and left, tapping an old gentleman on the ear with her pert green parasol, finally pausing at the steps to greet a gallant who rushed forward to kiss her hand. Then she rolled her great black eyes and winked—the wickedest wink a woman ever wunk.

The scene was enacted as though it were entirely impromptu. Unless you hear the camera click or observe very closely you never realize Negri is acting; her naturalness is perfection. She requires no direction.

"All she needs to know is the story," observed the secretary. "She does not need to study or think about it. It is instinct with her."

The same appears true of Lubitsch. He directs by instinct.

The part Pola was playing was that of a Parisian demimondaine who falls in love after a life of amorous adventure. Her lover, whom she inspires to success, is about to put her aside because she is a handicap to his position. When she realizes the insincerity of his love she throws herself from a balcony onto the pavement below and is killed.

But here comes the good old Americanizing touch.

There will be two endings, one happy and one sad.

I don't know exactly how the tragedy will be turned into a happy-ever-after comedy. Perhaps there will be a shot showing Pola falling onto the studio mattress instead of the supposed paving blocks.

The American public—the American public with the mind of a twelve-year-old child, you know—it must have life as it ain't. Yet that public swept *Passion* into one of the greatest successes of film times. And *Passion* ended with the lovely Negri head beneath the blade of the guillotine—and no pardon on horseback to save her.

However, there are *two* endings. It's entirely up to you. Drama is supposed to be Life. Unfortunately we have no choice as to our endings in Life.

As a director Lubitsch is a dervish. He can whirl through more work in a day than most directors can get past in a week. The most spectacular scene of *The Loves of Pharaoh* was shot in three days. He doesn't rehearse his players before starting a picture, as Griffith does. And he does not rehearse very much during actual filming.

Before he turns a camera upon the production, however, every detail of the story has been charted and all the research work has been completed by the art director. In collaboration with Lubitsch the scenarist has turned the story into continuity. I saw the bulky script lying in state on a table some distance from the "set." Lubitsch never went near it. It was like a lovely white corpse awaiting final disposition. Yet every detail of that scenario was being observed as scrupulously as the last wishes of the dead. Lubitsch does not improvise as many directors do. Chaplin, for instance, starts with a seed which gradually germinates. Lubitsch has written the story in carbon on his mind; every phase is indelible.

He has an uncanny memory. I will never forget the awe-stricken look upon the face of Frederick James Smith, *Photoplay's* managing editor, when Lubitsch recognized him in the crowd at the premiere of *Orphans of the Storm*. The astounded Frederick swore it was the first time a director had ever recognized him. The little film wizard had met hundreds of interviewers and film people during his few weeks in America yet he could remember a face and a name in an instant. His secretary told me that he could call any extra man by name who had worked for him years ago.

If Lubitsch is a fast stepper on the "set" he certainly is a shimmy dancer in the cutting room. You would imagine that he was mad at the film. He tears at it until you almost think you hear him growl. Now and then he holds it up to the light and gives it a blink—swish, crackle, zipp—and another five hundred feet goes areeling. *The Flame of Love*, the Negri picture he just finished, required about three days to cut and assemble. Any other director I've ever observed would take two weeks for an ordinary program feature. *The Loves of Pharaoh*, originally in ten or twelve reels, required less than a week.

This faculty for rapid cutting must be attributed to a supernatural memory, one which carries the story so perfectly that lightning decisions are possible. Some directors spend as much time on assembling a picture as upon photographing it, for it is generally conceded that this part of the production is of vital importance.

Lubitsch cannot work slowly. He must work while enthusiasm is ablaze. Ask him which he considers his best pictures and he will always reply that it is the one he is working on. That is his real conviction; if it weren't he couldn't keep at it.

I chose a happy time to visit Ernst Lubitsch, and perhaps a little of his exuberance was due to his approaching marriage to Irni Kraus, a Berlin girl who has played small parts in several German pictures but who has yet to make her debut in a Lubitsch film.

Very few people around the studio knew of the dramatic moment approaching in the life of the little director. No one had been informed officially. I did not learn of it until the day before. Then I accounted for the puzzling scene between Negri and Lubitsch on the first day I called. I had told Lubitsch that we had heard he was married to Pola. All brimming over with glee, and afraid lest he would burst before he told her, Ernst scampered off to where his gorgeous *Nay-gree* was sitting. He blurted out what I had said, and chuckled as Pola tossed back her head, her hand on her breast, in a typical gesture of laughter. He also looked very pleased when she quickly leaned forward and patted him affectionately on the cheek.

"A wonderful, wonderful woman," is the expression Lubitsch uses again and again about Negri. There is no one in the world like her—no one. He thinks *Deception* his best directional effort—next to *The Flame of Love*—but I objected that Negri was not in it to raise it to the stellar heights.

"Of course Henny Porten is good," I added, "but—"

"Pola is better!" shot Lubitsch, triumphantly. "No one like Pola—no one."

They have had their temperamental skirmishes. I wish I might have witnessed one. As a battler Lubitsch must be as funny as Chaplin, Pola as divine as Duse. These tilts always have the same ending, I'm told, Pola awarding a pat or a kiss upon the again-happy countenance of Ernst . . . Catherine the Great and her prime minister.

While Lubitsch was shy about confiding the joyful news of his marriage he was outspoken in his delight over the possibility of coming to America to work. "America by Christmas" is his banner cry. He may arrive for Thanksgiving, as Paramount is planning to grant his wish and allot him a few acres of floor in the Long Island studio. He wants to do modern stories of American life as a relief from the long series of historical dramas and as proof of his versatility. His ability doubtlessly can make the transfer, but I wonder if he will be as preeminent in the modern field as in the period. Still, what man wants to be without a rival?

It's a little bit mean of him, though, just when we were progressing so well in our history to drop us back into kindergarten. I never realized what a good teacher Professor Ernst was until I visited Versailles. If it hadn't been for *Passion* I would have had no appreciation for the bedroom of Louis XV. I might have thought that the little secret door by the bed was to the closet where the king kept his Sunday crown. But having seen *Passion* I knew that it was the door through which Madame du Barry came each evening at bedtime to shake hands with the king and wish him goodnight.

Perhaps the fact that Mr. Lubitsch has become a staid married man also has something to do with his desire to abandon the life of kings. Kings are bad company for married men.

I inquired of the secretary if Mr. Lubitsch had ever contemplated doing the rather exciting life of ex-Kaiser Wilhelm.

"Better you should not ask him that," advised the secretary. "The Kaiser is Mr. Lubitsch's pet dislike."

Before coming to America he will do one picture based on the life of Johann Strauss, the waltz king.

No honeymoon interrupted production activities at the Lubitsch plant. Indeed, Albert E. Kaufmann, Paramount's general manager of foreign productions, was wondering whether at last Lubitsch would stop work for an entire day. The secretary was of the doleful opinion that there would be only the usual half hour for lunch, Lubitsch muttering the nuptial vows between helpings of *Kalbsschnitzel*.

Perhaps you remember seeing Lubitsch as the hunchback in his production of *One Arabian Night*. But he made his fame as an actor by playing comedy roles, on both stage and screen. He's a natural comedian and has that constitutional shyness and modesty for which Harold Lloyd, as well as Chaplin, is distinguished among the tribe *histrionique*.

His friendliness is real and eager—"Be sure you come and see me when I come to America," he urged, as though he expected to have a rather lonely time of it.

Ernst Lubitsch, a Napoleonic little gnome, a Dutch comedian who can make the whole world weep, a little man with a big smiling heart. If he isn't a genius he's what a genius ought to be.

And if you don't think he's a hundred percent American, just bring on the jazz, the chewing gum, and the shimmy.

¶ *THREE WOMEN* *

by Robert E. Sherwood †

The first really memorable movie of the season is *Three Women*—a product of the same amazingly nimble brain that produced *The Marriage Circle*, and before that, *Passion*, *Deception*, and *The Loves of Pharaoh*.

Ernst Lubitsch is, in many ways, the greatest director of them all. He has a delicately tuned sense of comedy, great control of the forces of drama, and an instinct for literary construction. He knows exactly what he is shooting at, and he shoots straight.

Three Women lacks the fragile grace of *The Marriage Circle* and makes a few more concessions to Hollywood tradition; but even the most obvious movie tricks, like the discovery by the embattled heroine of a revolver in the villain's desk drawer, are accomplished so skillfully that they actually look new.

Perhaps the greatest tribute to Lubitsch's directorial genius is to be found in the work of the various players— Pauline Frederick, Lew Cody, and Mae McAvoy, in particular—who rise above themselves and contribute admirable performances. Miss Frederick and Miss McAvoy are both

* From *Life*, October, 1924.

† For a short period before he became one of America's most distinguished playwrights, Robert E. Sherwood held the post of film critic on the old humorous weekly, *Life*.

superb in unusually exacting roles, and Mr. Cody proves that he can be a fine actor when given half a chance.

Lew Cody has the part of a bounder, a homewrecker and inveterate cad—the sort of character that he has impersonated in countless pictures before. Compare his work in *Three Women* with his work in *Souls for Sale* and you will gain an idea of the gap that exists between the directors of these two pictures.

Referring to notes published in this department last week, I may say that *Three Women* is one of the pictures that I am anxious to see again.

¶ A NOTE ON *THREE WOMEN* *

by Hanns Sachs †

A young worlding has become, for the sake of her money, the lover of an elderly woman. Having achieved his expectations he no longer considers it worth while to go on convincing her of his love. She has no suspicions, refuses to have any, and perpetually offers herself to the reluctant lover. The situation is delicate, one not easy to represent even upon the stage; upon the film, where things appear without the mitigating veil of words, in all their brutal reality, its representation would appear to be an insoluble problem. How has the producer found it possible to film this situation without sacrificing anything of its poignancy?

The two are sitting side by side upon a sofa. The woman leans against the man, caresses him, toys with his clothing. She flings her arms round his neck. Playfully she plucks at his tie and at last draws it out so that it hangs over his

* Excerpted from "Psychology in the Films" in *Close-Up*, November, 1928.

† Dr. Sachs was a practicing psychiatrist and a pupil of Freud.

waistcoat. The man restores it to its place and is once more irreproachably correct.

In this case the representation is simple and short. There is no question of creating a tension, only of making the inexpressible expressible by means of displacement onto a small incidental action. The woman says: "Undress yourself," and the man, "I don't want to," but the treatment is so contrived that both can act as if the behavior of the other were simply the playfulness of idle fingers. The man does not choose to understand what the woman wants, the woman will not see that the man does not choose to understand, but the onlooker gives to the little episode its true value and knows in a moment more than could be revealed to him by means of a long caption. For him the proceedings are clear enough, and this "displacement" is exactly one of those means of expression, to which Freud first called attention, used by the unconscious everywhere, for instance, in dreams and in jest, to elude conscious recognition. The film seems to be a new way of driving mankind to conscious recognition.

In his *Traumdeutung*, page 263, Freud gives an explanation of the symbolic meaning of the tie, which, certainly, neither the onlookers of the film, nor the director, who created it, knew. But, all the same, it fits exactly into the thinly veiled meaning of the "slip action."

¶ *FORBIDDEN PARADISE* *

by Paul Rotha

Following in the path of Chaplin's *A Woman of Paris*, with a hint of the James Cruze domestic comedies, he made *The*

* Excerpted from *The Film Till Now*, 1930. (Jonathan Cape & Harrison Smith, London.)

Marriage Circle, a witty, superficial, amusing, intimate commentary on modern life in Vienna and Paris, as Hollywood conceived it. Lubitsch contrived to continue where Chaplin had left off, leaving out the cynicism and inner meaning and concentrating on the lightness of the framework. With this frippery, Lubitsch set off all the young men in Hollywood in the same vein, making himself from time to time several other comedies of a similar nature, such as *Three Women, Kiss Me Again, Lady Windermere's Fan* (from the Wilde play), and *So This Is Paris,* all delightful, effervescent movies. In between these sweetmeats came Lubitsch's one really brilliant film, a satire on Hollywood so subtle and so crafty that to this day many Americans cannot perceive wherein lay its sting. In the first place, *Forbidden Paradise* was conceived by Famous-Players-Lasky as a rollicking Ruritanian melodrama, with good opportunities for spectacle and a reliable box-office appeal. Ernst Lubitsch, however, for once forgetting that he was being clever on an American salary, treated this farce, in a moment of inspiration, in such a manner that it satirized with a nicety of wit the entire American movie system. The scenario was adapted by that admirable scenarist Hans Kräly from a play called *The Czarina,* which dealt with the amorous intrigues of Catherine of Russia, but Lubitsch brought the thing up to date, putting it in a Ruritanian setting. The amorous moods of the queen, the fiery revolutionary disturbances suppressed by handy checks, the delightful ins-and-outs of the court intrigues were handled by Lubitsch with a perfection of satire. The continuity was pleasingly smooth, and he employed deft touches in the use of the particular to reinforce the general that have seldom since appeared in his work. . . . He chose for his players Pola Negri, whose talents he knew well, and whose playing of the impassioned queen, exquisitely regal when in the presence of the court, and sexually alluring when alone with her favorite lieutenant, has never been surpassed in its kind; Adolphe Menjou, of Chaplin's schooling, magnificently subtle—his wide-hearted acceptance of the decorations that emblazoned the breast of the young lieutenant and the French ambassador will not be forgotten; Rod la Rocque, the essence of dashing lieutenants, innocent, good-looking, and slender; and Pauline Starke, angelic as the virginal lady-in-waiting.

He had built the vastest of palaces in which to house his regally passionate queen, with shining floors, massive columns, and great sweeps of drapery that seemed to hang from heaven. He had the roundest of full moons; the most luscious of roses; the blackest of velvet for the Negri's imperial dresses, with trains that swished across the mirrored floors; and an exquisite chorus of uniformed officers and bearded revolutionaries. Beyond being a commentary on the frailty of women (in particular of queens), on sly chancellors and gallant officers, *Forbidden Paradise* was a most satisfying exposure of the false glamor in which Hollywood lived.

AN INTERVIEW *

by Jim Tully

Lubitsch came to America with the greatest opportunity ever given a director but was inveigled into directing Mary Pickford in *Rosita*.[1] Miss Pickford has never needed a man of the Lubitsch calibre. One of her most successful directors is possessed of a mentality little above a child's.

To the credit of Lubitsch it must be said that he was unfortunate in directing Miss Pickford. She had reached the stage where she wished to show the world that she was more than a player of children's parts. Grown opulent, she no longer wished to remain America's everyday sweetheart. She wanted to grow up. So Lubitsch was chosen to direct her in *Rosita*.

America did not accept Miss Pickford as a grownup lady

* Excerpted from *Vanity Fair*, December, 1926.
[1] It was Miss Pickford who brought Lubitsch over to direct a film with her. [Author's Note.]

. . . neither as *Rosita,* nor, later, as *Dorothy Vernon* of *Haddon Hall.*

After his failure with Miss Pickford the Hollywood public still dealt kindly with Lubitsch. It understood the circumstances. The films, as usual, were sick. They needed a tonic. Many looked toward Lubitsch.[2]

Instead of becoming the strong man . . . the modern Moses in a derby . . . Lubitsch seemed content to become a director of frothy films for sophisticated chambermaids and cinema critics.

I once said to him, "Mr. Lubitsch, why is it you are satisfied to direct light comedy when you might do another *Passion?*"

"Ah," he said, "Molière was content to do comedy."

"Yes—but Molière was something different again."

Lubitsch shrugged his shoulders.

"But Chaplin is a genius—he does comedy."

"Chaplin is merely a clever mimic," I replied, "hardly to be compared with Molière."

Lubitsch was shocked. The remark was blasphemy to him. He gesticulated.

"*Woman of Paris—Woman of Paris*—a masterpiece—such genius—such genius."

"Merely a very ordinary story," I replied.

Lubitsch stopped—I was talking a different language.

"But the treatment—the treatment," he finally gesticulated.

"Leaving Chaplin out of it, Mr. Lubitsch, you remind me of a man who is capable of writing a great novel, and is content to idle away his time with clever short stories."

His hands went upward in exasperation at this statement.

"Oh, let me alone," he cried.

Lubitsch has contended that Chaplin's *A Woman of Paris* did not insult his intelligence. Perhaps in continental Europe Mr. Lubitsch met many young ladies who, after a velvet existence in Paris, suddenly decided for no great reason to

---

[2] "Nothing more delightfully charming than Mary Pickford's new picture, *Rosita,* has been seen on the screen for some time," said *The New York Times.* "It is exquisite." "That distinguished and lovely film," said *Vanity Fair.* [Author's Note.]

spend the rest of their vapid lives among the cows and chickens.[3]

Lubitsch is also a passionate admirer of David Wark Griffith. By their gods you shall know them.

Mr. Lubitsch feels that it will be a hundred years before the screen takes its place as a great new art.

Forgetting that a boy of average intelligence can be made a director of parts as easily as he can be made a plumber, many Hollywood directors walk about as though they shook the earth. With finer artistic training, Lubitsch should not be one of these.

In films a man of genius must have a merchant as collaborator. Once in a while the merchant is a man with the soul of an artist. For instance, Jesse L. Lasky, reading Theodore Dreiser's great novel *An American Tragedy*, is an example.[4] Lasky not only read the book but reacted to it emotionally and financially, paying nearly one hundred thousand dollars for the film rights.

Lasky in buying this story immediately faces another problem. With but few exceptions directors have little capacity for emotion. Dreiser is said to have eliminated D. W. Griffith as a "sentimentalist." Lubitsch is astonishingly clever, even subtle at times. Dreiser's story would allow him a great opportunity for artistic achievement, and test any creative quality he might have.

But Lubitsch, of whom so much was expected, has recently directed a picture called *So This Is Paris*.[5]

[3] Mr. Tully errs on two points: (a) His "for no great reason" is the suicide of her true love, the news of which shatters her—certainly no trivial reason; (b) the ending he refers to was Chaplin's concession to "the popular American taste." For Europe, Chaplin's ending was harsh and reflected his true feelings about human frailty, viz., his heroine returns, after the tragic incident, to her "velvet existence," to lead a secure but loveless life. Apparently Tully was unaware of this. [Author's Note.]

[4] Mr. Lasky also rejected the screen adaptation of this novel by Sergei Eisenstein and G. Alexandrov, which had the approval of Dreiser—that's how much of an "artist's soul" Jesse Lasky had. [Author's Note.]

[5] The satire which the *New York Sun* said placed Lubitsch in a class with Lewis Carroll, Oscar Wilde, and William Congreve. [Author's Note.]

¶ *SO THIS IS PARIS* *

by Seymour Stern

Of all the delightful pieces of jiggling shadows and sophisticated nonsense, this Lubitsch hodgepodge of bare legs, un-
scrupulous hands, "symbolical" canes, and Monte Blue is by
far the best that has appeared on the screen. The story is
somewhat similar to that of *Die Fledermaus*, but there is a
bit of craziness in it that gives it a new and peculiar flavor
which Lubitsch has never before imparted to his films. For
summer fare there is nothing to equal it. It should be re-
vived every summer hereafter until the day arrives when sum-
mers are no longer hot. It is all about liars, which makes it,
at the outset, personally interesting. It is also about a sheik
who stands *nudely* before a window. Of course, Dr. Giraud is
simply a wonderful fellow—"a peach of a fellow"—but his
wife is—ah! a better peach than he, but then, you can't believe what newspapers say, because one man's foolishness
may be a greater foolishness than another man's, and the
moral to that is, when you stand in front of a window, have
your shirt on, and when you stand in back of a window, have
it on, too, otherwise this nightlife may kill you. There, in
brief, is the substance of the story, and if you don't think
that's a remarkable substance, you're infinitely mistaken. Besides this substance, the picture has the most beautiful photographic effort of any film since *The Last Laugh* (1924), a
miracle, in fact, of such astounding camera work that it will
require the combined efforts of Karl Freund and another G.
W. Bitzer to outdo it. It occurs in the ball scene, where the
dancers, of whom there are hundreds, ebb and flow, one large
group dissolving into another, and the camera, which is tilted
at every angle in the geometrical system, picking up the
rhythm of the dance by running backwards, forwards, and
sideways, provides a variety of imaginative effects—double

* From *The Greenwich Village Quill*, September, 1926.

exposure close-ups, legs running atop heads, kaleidoscopic swirls—that are nothing short of intoxicating. Whoever is responsible for it, whether Lubitsch, his cameraman, or both, has certainly proved himself a master cinematist. This is altogether Lubitsch's most advanced, though by no means his best, work. His penetrating insight into the humorous side of modern domestic life, his undeniable wit, his delicious sophistication are all there. But I have an objection.

Since he has been in America, Lubitsch has made exactly seven pictures. Of these, one, *Rosita*, was a sophisticated story of a Spanish kingdom; another, *Forbidden Paradise*, was a sophisticated story of a mythical kingdom; another, *Kiss Me Again*, was a sophisticated story of a married couple; another, *The Marriage Circle*, was a sophisticated story of two married couples; another, *Lady Windermere's Fan*, was a sophisticated story of London society; and the latest one, *So This Is Paris*, is a sophisticated story of Paris society. Heaven stop this deluge of sophisticated stories! First, because none of them measures, artistically, up to *The Marriage Circle*. Secondly, because if Herr Lubitsch could embody in a film the theoretical principles of the cinema as he did in *Deception* (*Anna Boleyn*), and could make out of a hackneyed story of the French Revolution a masterpiece of the rank of *Madame Dubarry* (*Passion*), he can repeat these performances. Thirdly, because it is unmistakably clear that Warner Brothers have stifled the man and set him in a groove. May Paramount come to the rescue!

¶ *TROUBLE IN PARADISE* *

by Dwight Macdonald

About once a year—sometimes not so often—Hollywood turns out a movie that can be accepted without innumerable

* Excerpted from *The Symposium* (Concord, New Hampshire), April–July, 1933.

reservations. In 1931 it was *Little Caesar*. Last year it was Lubitsch's *Trouble in Paradise*. That this should have been so excellent a production is more than a little strange. It is true that Lubitsch enjoys the greatest reputation of any director now active in Hollywood. But, this is based largely on his silent films. There was therefore no reason to suppose that *Trouble in Paradise* would be anything more than just another movie.

It is, with all qualifications, superb. Within the admittedly drastic limitations of its genre, it comes as close to perfection as anything I have ever seen in the movies. The opening shot of the Venetian garbage barge with its discordant gondolier strikes the note of sophisticated burlesque that is held throughout. The pace is fast, as it should be: each shot is held just long enough to make its point, and the point is never hammered in. "Lubitschisms," those touches of wit that no other director quite captures, are scattered everywhere with a prodigal hand. There is enough "camera interest" for a dozen movies. When the lovers embrace, for instance, they are pictured rapidly (1) in the flesh (2) in a mirror (3) as shadows on a satin coverlet. As always, Lubitsch makes great play with the swinging camera, but he also gets some very nice effects with rapid cutting. Sound is used with especial brilliance. There are no "songs" arbitrarily set into the narrative like plums in a pudding. Instead, the action is accompanied by a running commentary of music. Like the old movie-organ pieces (still the best solution to the problem of movie music) this makes no attempt to be "good" in itself and is quite satisfied to serve as a background for what happens on the screen. Finally the décor, by Hans Dreier, is the best "moderne" job I have yet seen on stage or screen. Most cinematic excursions into modernism are either grotesque or tasteless, but Dreier's clocks, staircases, windows, and chaise-longues are original, delicate, and even refined.

Only Lubitsch, who works out every detail on paper before he shoots a single scene, could master all these sound and cinematic devices and put them smoothly to work in a single film. Varied and brilliant as is the technique, it never becomes obtrusive. It is always used to carry on and give point to the narrative. (Which, by the way, is banal—and quite unimportant.) Consider the climax of the movie, certainly one of the classic scenes in film comedy, when Filibo suddenly remembers where he has seen the mysterious Duval before. Here the crashing chorus of mock-dramatic music, the excited jumping up and sitting down of Filibo, and the mad gyrations of the camera to follow him—all these elements come together with shattering effect. There is also the fact that Filibo is played by a master of light comedy, Edward Everett Horton. This suggests another of the film's excellences—the acting of Herbert Marshall, Charles Ruggles, and Kay Francis. But the list of virtues is endless. Enough to say that *Trouble in Paradise* almost makes one believe in Hollywood again.

¶ *COLLABORATING WITH MR. LUBITSCH* *
by Ben Hecht

Samson Raphaelson, who worked on nine scripts with Lubitsch versus the single script Hecht did, said when I showed him this facetious piece, "That's one of Ben's didoes. Lubitsch wasn't like that at all." Doubtless, it represents the impish Hecht in one of his merry-andrew moods and it may well be that Hecht's undeniable affection for Lubitsch was filtered through the same raffish "spectacles" he wore when he collaborated with Gene Fowler on *The Great Magoo* or with Charles MacArthur on *The Front Page*. At any rate, it is to be taken *con grano salis*, as they say, though parts (and these are self-evident) may be taken straight. The spectacle of Lubitsch, at a moment of high glee, doing an *entrechat* in mid air may not have been an actual fact, but it's

* Written for the Paramount Publicity Department in 1933.

an interpretation of a fact, and that's what counts. Poetic license should always be preferred to flatfooted orthodoxy, *n'est-ce pas?* [Author's Note.]

.   .   .

Mr. Lubitsch is not a very tall man. He has an interesting face—it has the dark, mocking leer of a creditor. He keeps it tilted to the right in what looks like a sarcastic manner. His eyes are extremely tragic but he has an elfin look about the mouth. He is always smoking what seems to be an expensive cigar, but isn't.

He dances frequently. He is a veritable habitué of casinos and ballrooms. He dances with grace and agility, giving one the impression of a kangaroo on a pogo stick.

In writing with Mr. Lubitsch on *Design for Living,* I was confused by what seemed to be at first glance a sort of manic-depressive psychosis on its upswing. Mr. Lubitsch, when he creates those delicate touches for which he is notorious, has a way of flinging himself around the room like an old-fashioned fancy roller skater. He pirouettes, leaps, claps his ankles together in mid air, screams at the top of his voice, and bursts into tears if contradicted.

If Mr. Lubitsch doesn't like something you suggest in the way of a line (or half a line) or a piece of business, he falls ill, takes to his bed. His elfin face fills with reproach and he lies tossing for sometimes as long as several hours, moaning, "Dull, dull, oh so dull . . . ! No good, Ben . . . terrible! Oh, how dull it is!" On such occasions he can be coaxed out of bed by questions about his early life as an actor. There were three particular reminiscences which he loved to tell, and once I could get him started on any one of them, he was on the road to recovery (his, not mine).

When Mr. Lubitsch composes scenes he always acts them out as if they were written for a calliope. He takes all the parts, regardless of the sex of the characters. Whenever I tried to act a scene out, he would sink into a chair, wrinkle his upper lip and remain sneering even after I had finished. If you sneer back at Mr. Lubitsch for anything *he* does, he takes to his bed again and is ill for a day. He is very sensitive.

The most interesting thing I recall about working with him is his modesty. He is very modest—but stubborn. I found, after working with him the first week, that when he said something I didn't like, all I had to do was keep quiet and look at him steadily and he would break down and start reviling himself. I found this side of him very amusing.

On the whole, I consider Mr. Lubitsch the best director in the movies. I felt, after our collaboration was done, that he had taught me something very vital about films. What it was, I don't remember—maybe it was how to write them. It's a pity I've forgotten, but on the other hand, Mr. Lubitsch hasn't, you may be sure.

To give you a quick concept of Mr. Lubitsch's genius as a collaborator, I will quote him just once. He was looking at me steadily as I offered what I considered a plot turn in the piece. When I finished he asked, "You think that's good?" I said I did.

"That's the kind of suggestion people send me in the mail,"said Mr. Lubitsch.[1]

[1] It is perhaps relevant to note here that following his collaboration with Lubitsch on *Design for Living*, Hecht embarked with his colleague, Charles MacArthur, as author and codirector of his own first film, the brilliant *Crime Without Passion* (1934), which would certainly have earned for him the approving smile of the master. [Author's note.]

(1933)

Re-evaluations

Following the Lubitsch Retrospective at the Berlin Film Festival in 1967, the author asked Jay Leyda and Lotte Eisner to re-evaluate the films shown, as they looked today. Added to this is a report on three of the films from David Robinson, published in *Sight and Sound*.

Der Stolz der Firma (1914)
Leyda: Wilhelm's comedy with L. as a Jewish caricature, shrewd, timid, self-pitying—this must have been just a job for him.
Eisner: Too Jewish-slapstick.

Schuhpalast Pinkus (1916)
Leyda: Not very funny, but brightly made. Wish I could see more from these farce years.
Eisner: Too Jewish-slapstick.
Robinson: Done with insolent wit.

Die Augen der Mummie Ma (1918)
Eisner: Looks funny today.

Carmen (1918)
Leyda: The only disappointment among the L. films new to me. Too glued to a footlights frontal view. Was he intimidated by Mérimée and Bizet? Deserted by his two chief virtues—[film] logic and wit. As loose as a storytelling ballet, but the hand of L. as choreographer is missing. Viewpoints and editing vague, and lots of wasted time, uncharacteristic of L. (as in the scene on the coast). But an occasional moment of filmic dialogue. Beyond Negri, no lust. Some parallel between Carmen-José and Du Barry-Armand to come.

Die Austernprinzessin (1919)

Leyda: One of the two I liked best, especially this one as a forecast of L.'s American comedies about "today's" European aristocracy. A European comedy (farce or grotesque would be more exact) about *American* aristocracy—seen from Berlin. (Imagine those hungry audiences, at the time, looking at jokes about huge quantities of food!—and at people with the power to pursue any caprice!) In New York it should be shown with one of the Chevalier films, full of lackeys and doors, and identical gags.

Eisner: Better than I thought it would be.

Robinson: Uproarious.

Die Puppe (1919)

Leyda: Everyone liked it but me, except for the first moments when L. himself arranges the scenery and his dolls. (This is a frame enlargement you should get.)

Eisner: Just ordinary.

Kölhiesel's Töchter (1920)

Leyda: Funny, especially Porten, and I ask nothing more of this "Taming of the Farm Shrew."

Eisener: This one I liked very much.

Sumurun (1920).

Leyda: The other of the two I liked best. It is exactly the brightly made, exotic spectacle you want it to be—even that embarrassing actor, L., fits into this big variety show (it has a little of everything) without hurting it.

Eisner: Looks funny today.

Anna Boleyn (1920)

Leyda: Among his most inventive, far above *Madame Dubarry*.

Die Bergkatze (1921)

Robinson: A riot of invention with an astonishingly mercurial Pola Negri at the head of a pack of brigands on the snow slopes of the Alps. Memorable particularly for the rich, zany rococo sets by Ernst Stern.

Rosita (1923)

Leyda: A big irony of history that this could have brought L.'s career so close to doom, for it is really an unusually distinguished film, with style, point, and richness (of all sorts)—perhaps too rich for Pickford fans then? The studio sets function as perfectly within the drama as in [von Gerlach's] *Vanina*. Story pattern a little too apparent—"Will he get her?" But that shouldn't have been a hindrance in 1923.

Eisner: I liked this very much. It has something of Goya and of Sternberg's *The Devil Is a Woman*.

Three Women (1924)

Leyda: The cute Berkeley students look especially strange today. Pauline Frederick, though, a fully worked out portrait. Did she ever talk about her work with L.? Hanns Sachs's famous moment (with necktie) missing from this copy—or could I have missed it?

Eisner: Did not like it very much.

Forbidden Paradise (1924)

Leyda: A really too miserable copy was shown which mangled all the ideas and pace. Must have been Negri's best United States film.

Eisner: Charming.

Lady Windermere's Fan (1925)

Eisner: Delicious.

So This Is Paris (1926)

Eisner: Did not like it very much.

The Lubitsch Retrospective at the Berlin Film Festival in 1967 was a silent one, as was the one that followed it in Paris, and many films were, of course, missing; and none of the three reporters above saw all of those. As a sample of current (1968) evaluations of at least two Lubitsch sound films may be cited these:

Desire (1936)

The New York Times, Television Department: Creamy,

tasty sophistication from Ernst Lubitsch about a jewel thief and a rich American.

Cluny Brown (1946)
The New York Times, Television Department: Delightful froth all the way, slyly lancing the British caste system. A real honey.

Some Tributes

¶ *A TRIBUTE TO LUBITSCH* *

With a Letter in Which Lubitsch Appraises
His Own Career

by Herman G. Weinberg

One summer evening in 1928 I was in the lobby of the Little
Carnegie Playhouse in New York after a showing of *The
Passion of Joan of Arc*. To arouse interest in Dreyer's great,
turbulent film, the theatre had placed some medieval manuscripts on display, and a stocky little man chewing on a cigar
had stopped to examine them. The shiny, black Napoleonic
lock on his forehead, the piercing black eyes . . . of course
. . . this demonic little gnome was none other than the
great Lubitsch! I ran over to him.

In the Russian Tea Room next door, a few minutes later,
I began praising Dreyer's film, "Pabst was right," I said at
one juncture. "Who *will* ever surpass it?"

Lubtisch had been eyeing me over his coffee.

"Are you through?" he asked.

"What do you mean?" I exclaimed. "You don't like it?"

'I don't like it?" he repeated. "*I don't like it?* Imagine
such a thing!" He lit a fresh cigar. "Of course I don't like
it! It's a wonderful *tour de force* but it'll get the cinema no-
where. One can't learn from it—it's too individual a style
of expression. It has pathologic interest as a study of hysteria—"

"But Falconetti! Have you—"

* From *Films in Review*, August–September, 1951.

"No, I *haven't* seen a performance like that," he admitted, "but it was conceived on a wrong plane."

I stared blankly.

"I mean," he continued, "I didn't believe in her. She wasn't the Joan who rallied the routed French soldiers and defeated the English. We don't get even a glimpse of that part of her. We see only a despairing Joan. Her only defiance is her pathetic sparring with the theological byplay of her inquisitors." [1]

I was about to demur when Lubitsch interrupted: "I'll show you a film tomorrow that we *all* can learn from. Meet me at eleven in the Paramount projection room. They're going to screen Pudovkin's new picture, *Storm over Asia*, for me. You'll see what I mean."

At eleven next morning I was there, and so was a group of Paramount executives. Lubitsch did a lot of joshing before the lights went out.

Then it came, still with Russian scratch titles in, the complete version of *Potomok Chingis-Khan*, all 3,092 metres of it. It was the Germans who gave it the title *Storm over Asia*, just as it was they who renamed Eisenstein's *October*, calling it *Ten Days That Shook the World*, which, of course, they got from John Reed's book. It ran about 25 percent longer than the version shown in the U.S. Two major sequences were eliminated here: the long guerilla fighting between the Mongol partisans and the British interventionists, who were referred to as "the White Army" in the U.S. version, and the complete operation for the removal of several bullets fired into Bair, the Mongol furtrader, by a British soldier prematurely ordered to shoot him.

The operation was gory indeed, and during its bloody course Lubitsch exclaimed: "*Schrecklich!* Why must he photograph the whole damn thing? He *knows* you can't show it! And who wants to see it? Is it necessary? *Menschenskind! Das ist ja aber unmöglich!*"

---

[1] This was the gist of it, not the exact words, nor will I try to reproduce his vaudeville-German accent. Joan was here certainly not the "born boss" of Shaw's version, but even Shaw could not have bettered some of the real answers she gave her inquisitors in Dreyer's film.

We were all feeling a little queasy and several Paramount executives left the projection room. The scene finally ended with Bair being sewn up and swathed like a mummy in bandages—a grotesque caricature of a man whom the British put forward as "the descendant of Genghis Khan" and set up as a puppet to rule the Mongols.

During the sequence in which the Tibetan high priest is dressing to meet the British commandant, Pudovkin cross-cuts ironically between the lama putting on his elaborate headdress and the British commandant's wife putting on her diamond tiara, between the lama putting a sacred amulet around his neck and the commandant's wife putting a pearl necklace around hers. Someone remarked: "Lubitsch touches!"

He laughed. "And very good Lubitsch touches, too, if I may say so."

And when, in the symbolic storm, the enraged Mongols, astride their wild ponies, charged the British and swept them back pell-mell like debris blown off the landscape by a tornado, Lubitsch exclaimed: "*Ach! Torrific!*"

The film's apocalyptic fury ends in a close-up of Bair crying out: "Rise, oh my brothers, in your ancient strength and free yourselves!"

"Nah?" smiled Lubitsch after the lights went up. "What do you say, now? [2] Come, let's have lunch!"

On the way out we met Chevalier. Embraces and effusions. Lubitsch was going to direct Chevalier's next picture (*The Love Parade*). With his arm around the diminutive Lubitsch, Chevalier pointed a finger heavenward and intoned, "He's going to make me act—divinely!"

At lunch, in the cool recesses of the Blue Ribbon, and over an unbroken continuity of that most seraphic of Münchner brews, Würzburger *dunkeles*, Lubitsch was in a gay mood. The comment in the projection room about "Lu-

---

[2] In 1950 the Soviets reissued *Storm Over Asia* with sound, synchronized dialogue, and music, added under the supervision of Pudovkin. In this version, the interventionists are still characterized as "the White Army," but the dishonest trader, who exploits Bair, has become an American. There is an opprobrious reference in the dialogue, now, to Mr. Churchill. [Author's note]

bitsch touches" had amused him. "I've often wondered who started that phrase," he said. "One shouldn't single out 'touches.' They're part of a whole. The camera *should* comment, insinuate, make an epigram or a *bon mot*, as well as tell a story. We're telling stories with pictures so we must try to make the pictures as expressive as we can." He finished his seidel and called out: "*Ober, nochmal dasselbe!*" He lit a fresh cigar.

He settled back in his seat and smiled. "Americans have a wrong impression how Russian propaganda films are received in Russia and Germany. The worker and peasant in Russia is not interested in seeing the same things he lived through ten years ago. He doesn't even understand them, sometimes. *Ten Days That Shook the World* was a flop in Russia. The people there are much more interested in seeing Douglas Fairbanks, the perfect optimist. And that's what they want there, optimism, as a relief from the depressing past—the war, revolution, famine—from which they are just emerging.

"As for Germany, while *Potemkin* was a tremendous success when it first showed in Berlin, the curious fact about succeeding Russian films has been that they attracted a different audience from which was probably intended by the producers.

"It is quite 'the thing' for the fashionable throng, which promenades in the morning sun along Unter den Linden and the Kurfürstendamm, to have a luxurious dinner in the evening and to follow it all by taking in a Russian propaganda picture. It is perverse! It is thrilling! But never once do you see some rich lady leave her fur coat or part of her jewels for relieving the distress of the city's poor. They are amused by these films, excited even, but never really moved. Or, if they are moved, they don't do anything about it.[3]

[3] In "The Games We Play: The Revolution Game," Margot Hentoff, writing in *The Village Voice* in September, 1967, reporting on the Fifth New York Film Festival's inaugural film, *The Battle of Algiers*, described the "fashionable" opening night's audience. "They really loved the movie, those people in Philharmonic Hall, many of them dressed in dinner clothes and holding invitations to a post-performance champagne reception. If it was the intention of the festival's program committee to *épater* the bourgeoisie with its

"To what purpose then?" he said. "Why make them in the first place if the worker ignores them just as much as the capitalist, or vice versa? It is a pity to waste so much energy in a direction which is apparently unappreciated, except by the critics, of course, for these Russians have some marvelous things to bring to motion pictures."

It was a pleasant moment, and I thought of the nights, around 1920, when Lubitsch presided over his *Stammtisch* in the back room of "Mutter" Maen's *Wirtshaus* in Berlin, arguing with the best actors, directors, writers, and painters of Germany on the art and future of the film, which then, as an art, was scarcely more than five years old. Lubitsch was then twenty-eight and had made twenty-seven films, including four major ones: *Carmen*, *The Oyster Princess*, *Madame Dubarry*, and *Die Puppe*. He was to do *Sumurun* next and *Anna Boleyn*, *Die Bergkatze*, and *The Loves of Pharaoh* the following year—finally *Die Flamme* and then the call to Hollywood. Thereafter he rode high, nor had time dulled his café irony.

"Speaking of Lubitsch touches," said L. with a wicked gleam, "you know the one about the beggar into whose hat someone dropped a gold sovereign one night? Cashing it at the bank the next day he learned it was a counterfeit, but it certainly looked impressive. He decided to pass it off on the prostitute who worked the same block. They spent the night together and next morning, reaching into his pocket to pay her, he found a hole there instead. He'd lost it. She began throwing things at him in a rage. 'Calm down, calm down!' he said. 'It was only a counterfeit, anyway!' " He shook with laughter and finally managed to say, "Real Lubitsch touch, no?"

This reminded him of a witticism of his old friend Melchior Lengyel, who wrote several of Lubitsch's later successes: "Kissing a woman's hand is never the right thing to do. It is either too much or too little."

---

choice of an opening film, then it entirely misread the temper of the bourgeoisie. It doesn't *épater*, these days. It just has fun. Has there ever before been such a time when the oppressors themselves sit and applaud their own symbolic murder?" [Author's Note.]

Lubitsch guffawed anew. "I ask you—isn't that as good as Oscar Wilde—or Lubitsch?"

He was irrepressible that afternoon. The great success of *The Patriot* was just behind him. Before that had been the equally successful *Student Prince*, and before that six dazzling comedies in a row: *So This Is Paris, Lady Windermere's Fan, Kiss Me Again, Forbidden Paradise, Three Women,* and *The Marriage Circle*—social satires that swept away the conventional bric-a-brac that cluttered up the American screen. They started a whole school of direction, and they created a laconic new cinema language. But Lubitsch was now on the threshold of sound. Would he be as original and inventive in the new medium?

The Love Parade was the happy answer, followed by *Monte Carlo*. The latter was put together with marvelous precision. When the Blue Empress clattered along the rails to the singing of "Beyond the Blue Horizon," we did not perceive at first its cunning craftsmanship and Lubitsch's unerring cutting, so enchanted were we with the lilt and bounce of the thing.

What was Lubitsch not able to do? He could make a silent film of an Oscar Wilde comedy *(Lady Windermere's Fan)*, without a single Wildean epigram, but with so much *panache* that Alfred Kerr, "the George Jean Nathan of Berlin," described it as being in the "purest *Burgtheater* style." He could make a comedy about a mother and a daughter in love with the same man *(Three Women)* and insert in it sad and bitter insights into the tragedy for a woman of encroaching age. He could think of having Miriam Hopkins, as the bored princess in *The Smiling Lieutenant*, play checkers desultorily on the floor of her bedroom with her suitor-prince (Maurice Chevalier) until the prince, noticing her suppressed irritation, flings the checkerboard onto the bed with a questioning smile, which she returns gratefully. And he could also think of moving his camera (in *The Man I Killed*) past row after row of pews to show officers kneeling at prayer in church, their sabres gleaming and jutting arrogantly out into the aisle.

Everybody has favorite "Lubitsch touches." In *The Mar-*

riage Circle, Marie Prevost is smoldering with desire for Monte Blue, husband of her best girl friend. A chill breeze springs up, fluttering her scarf. Monte, always the gallant, wraps it more snugly around her, but she flings it contemptuously to the ground. She's not cold, she's warm! In *One Hour with You*, Genevieve Tobin lures Maurice Chevalier onto a terrace in her campaign to get him to divorce his wife and marry her. (He is also the husband of her best girl friend.) After a fervent embrace and long kiss, his bow tie is disarranged. He doesn't know how to tie it and pleads with her to do it and thus efface the telltale marks of their tryst. She ties it and kisses him again. Then pulls the tie asunder again and blithely walks back into the house.

But perhaps the greatest Lubitsch touch of all was the laconic razz Charles Laughton gave to his boss in *If I Had a Million* after he suddenly came into a million dollars. It released a suppressed desire of countless millions the world over. And it showed that though Lubitsch was a success in the talkies, he didn't need dialogue to achieve his best effects.

Fundamentally, the "Lubitsch touch" was that hardy perennial, "the gag," with a difference. It did not rely on slapstick or violence, trickery or extravagance, as most gags do. And it was never inserted into a film for its own sake. "Lubitsch touches" were always an integral part of the story, were comments on the story, insinuating things that were best indicated deftly. They were the flowering of an authentic cinema language, and in him derived from a humorous skepticism about the human animal. They were usually biologic, because sex made Lubitsch laugh harder than anything else. (It is said that Aretino died during a fit of laughter over a ribald story told him about his sister.)

Lubitsch was the director's director. Preston Sturges paid him a charming passing tribute in *Sullivan's Travels*,[4] a film that owes much of its irrepressible mockery to the "Attila of Hollywood," as Ted Shane, that most debonair of *The New Yorker* film critics, once called Lubitsch.

[4] Veronica Lake, as a would-be star, replied to Joel McCrea, a director who asks what he can do for her, "Introduce me to Lubitsch." Piqued at being by-passed by her, he asks dead-pan, "Who's Lubitsch?"

Much of what Lubitsch introduced has been absorbed into the technique of almost every first class director.[5] The first directors to be influenced by him were Monta Bell, Paul Bern, Frank Tuttle, Richard Rosson, Lewis Milestone, Erle Kenton (in his delightful parody of Lubitsch's style, *Other Women's Husbands*), and Roy del Ruth (in the equally delightful *Wolf's Clothing*). And, most of all, Mal St. Clair and H. d'Abbadie d'Arrast, of fondest memory.

What made Lubitsch what he was? I think the answer can be found in his background. A third of him was that very special brand of Berlin humor that mixes sarcasm with contempt; another third was the mellow, laughing, futile cynicism of the Central European café humor; and the final third was his Jewish irony, which leavened all his work and made it so palatable. Without it he might have sometimes antagonized us, or have been content merely to titillate us. He did much more than that. He left us with a wistful smile at the absurd *comédie humaine*.

About four months before his death I received from him a remarkable letter in which he summed up his life's work. It is the only known document where Lubitsch evaluates his whole career himself. I can think of no more fitting conclusion to this tribute than this modest statement from so protean a figure in the cinema. In it is the modesty without false modesty, the pride without arrogance, of a life lived according to its best precepts.

. . .

The letter was in reply to the text of the monograph, *An Index to the Films of Ernst Lubitsch*, which Theodore Huff had prepared for the British Film Institute at my behest, and which I edited and sent to Lubitsch for his approval.

[5] "He can be said to have invented the "jump cut," so beloved by Godard and other of the "new wave" directors. Indeed, as Ivor Montague points out, he was the first great innovator of parts of action, not merely for speeding the action but as a witty expression, a sort of visual epigram." (*Film World*, Penguin Books, London, 1964.)

July 10, 1947

Dear Mr. Weinberg:

Enclosed I am sending you a copy of a letter which I sent to Mr. Theodore Huff. I should like to repeat that I think Mr. Huff's criticism is sincere and very good, but there are some points on which I might differ, but that is only natural. The purpose of this letter is not to contradict his criticism, but to point out as impartially as possible (if that is possible at all) what in my opinion are the most important phases of my career.

In speaking of the pictures which I have made in the past, I naturally judge them from memory and the effect they had at the time they were produced, and not by present standards.

The well-known actor, the late Victor Arnold who is mentioned in your Index, was my teacher. He had a great influence on my entire career and my future. Not only did he introduce me to Max Reinhardt, but he also was responsible for my first success in pictures in getting me the part of the apprentice in *Die Firma Heiratet*.

Although being starred in the next picture, *Der Stolz der Firma*, and despite its success, my picture career came to a standstill. I was typed, and no one seemed to write any part which would have fitted me. After two successes, I found myself completely left out of pictures, and as I was unwilling to give up I found it necessary that I had to create parts for myself. Together with an actor friend of mine, the late Erich Schoenfelder, I wrote a series of one-reelers which I sold to the Union Company. I directed and starred in them. And that is how I became a director. If my acting career had progressed more smoothly I wonder if I ever would have become a director.

After having completed this series of one-reel comedies, I decided to switch to feature pictures again. Like every comedian, I longed to play a straight leading man, a sort of 'bon vivant' role. So together with my collaborators I wrote a screenplay, called *Als Ich Tot War* (*When I Was Dead*). This picture was a complete failure as the audiences were unwilling to accept me as a straight leading man.

I decided to switch back again to the kind of parts which had brought me my first success in the picture *Schuhpalast Pinkus*. This picture was a great success, and I made a new contract with the Union Company for a series of that kind of pictures. I like to mention that at that time these pictures were considered feature pictures and were the main attraction.

It was during this period that I discovered Ossi Oswalda, and gave her the leading part in one of my pictures. She became so successful that I decided to star her in her own pictures and just direct her. Eventually I became more and more interested in directing than in acting, and after making my first dramatic film with Pola Negri and Jannings I completely lost interest in being an actor. Only in 1919, I believe, when I acted in *Sumurun*, or *One Arabian Night* as it was called in America, did I appear before the camera again. My last stage appearance was in 1918 in a revue, *Die Welt Geht Unter* at the Apollo Theatre in Berlin.

I would say that the three most outstanding comedies I made as a director in Germany were *Die Austernprinzessin*, *Die Puppe*, and *Kölhiesel's Töchter*. *Die Austernprinzessin* was my first comedy which showed something of a definite style. I remember a piece of business which caused a lot of comment at the time. A poor man had to wait in the magnificent entrance hall of the home of a multi-millionaire. The parquet floor of the multimillionaire's home was of a most complicated design. The poor man in order to overcome his impatience and his humiliation after having waited for hours walked along the outlines of the very intricate pattern on the floor. It is very difficult to describe this nuance and I don't know if I succeeded, but it was the first time I turned from comedy to satire.

In a completely different style was *Die Puppe*. It was, like *Die Austernprinzessin*, a great success from every angle. It was pure fantasy; most of the sets were made of cardboard, some even out of paper. Even to this day I still consider it one of the most imaginative pictures I ever made.

However, the most popular of all the comedies I made in Germany was *Kölhiesel's Töchter*. It was *The Taming of the Shrew* transferred to the Bavarian mountains. It was typical German. This picture has since been remade three or four times.

Of the historical and costume period of my pictures, I would say that *Carmen*, *Madame Du Barry* (*Passion*), and *Anna Boleyn* (*Deception*) were the three outstanding pictures. The importance of these pictures, in my opinion, was the fact that they differed completely from the Italian school, then very much *en vogue*, which had a kind of grand-opera-like quality. I tried to de-operatize my pictures and to humanize my historical characters—I treated the intimate nuances just as important as the mass movements, and tried to blend them both together. In this connection I might mention *Sumurun* (*Arabian Nights*) which was a playful fantasy, based on the Max Reinhardt production. It was successful, but not up to the standard of the three aforementioned pictures.

The picture *Die Bergkatze* was a complete failure, and yet this picture had more inventiveness and satirical pictorial wit than many of my other pictures. Released shortly after the war, I found the German audiences in no mood to accept a picture which satirized militarism and war.

There were two other pictures during my German period which I believe did not get the right evaluation, *Rausch* and *Die Flamme* (*Montmartre*). As an antidote against the great big historical canvases, I felt the necessity of making some small intimate *Kammerspiele*. Both pictures were very successful. Naturally the acting of Asta Nielsen, Alfred Abel, and Carl Meinhard and the rest of the cast in *Rausch* was outstanding and was recognized at the time as an example of a *Kammerspiel* tone.

The same applied to *Montmartre* with Pola Negri. The version which was released in America had a different finish and was cut to pieces and did not give the slightest idea of the dramatic value and the impact this picture had in its original version.

In my silent period in Germany as well as in America I tried to use less and less subtitles. It was my aim to tell the story through pictorial nuances and the facial expressions of my actors. There were very often long scenes in which people were talking without being interrupted by subtitles. The lip movement was used as a kind of pantomime. Not that I wanted the audience to become lip readers, but I tried to time the speech in such a way that the audience could listen with their eyes.

About my American period you are naturally fully informed, and therefore I can be much briefer. I again should like to point out what in my opinion were the most essential pictures of my American period.

Of the silent days I would like to name *The Marriage Circle*, *Lady Windermere's Fan*, and *The Patriot*, and also *Kiss Me Again*.

The talking-picture period is too well known to you and Mr. Huff for me to go into it at length, and I will right away jump to the period which in the Index is described as my "downhill" period.

It might be true that my career is moving downward, and I will not try to dispute it. Nevertheless, I would like to point out that during that very period I have made four outstanding pictures, three of which were in the opinion of many people the three best pictures of my entire career: *Trouble in Paradise*, *Ninotchka*, and *Shop Around the Corner*.

As for pure style I think I have done nothing better or as good as *Trouble in Paradise*.

As to satire, I believe I probably was never sharper than in *Ninotchka*, and I feel that I succeeded in the very difficult task of blending a political satire with a romantic story.

As for human comedy, I think I never was as good as in *Shop*

Around the Corner. Never did I make a picture in which the atmosphere and the characters were truer than in this picture. The picture, produced in twenty-six days at a very modest cost, was not a sensational, but a good success.

Heaven Can Wait—I consider it one of my major productions, because I tried to break away in several respects from the established moving picture formula. I encountered partly great resistance before I made this picture because it had no message and made no point whatsoever. The hero was a man only interested in good living with no aim of accomplishing anything, or of doing anything noble. Being asked by the studio why I wanted to make such a pointless picture, I answered that I hoped to introduce to a motion picture audience a number of people, and if the audience should find them likable—that would be sufficient for its success. And as it turned out, I was fortunately right. Besides, I showed the happy marriage in a truer light than it is usually done in moving pictures where a happy marriage is only too often portrayed as a very dull and unexciting by-the-fireplace affair.

To Be or Not to Be has caused a lot of controversy and in my opinion has been unjustly attacked. This picture never made fun of Poles, it only satirized actors and the Nazi spirit and the foul Nazi humor. Despite being farcical, it was a truer picture of Naziism than was shown in most novels, magazine stories, and pictures which dealt with the same subject. In those stories the Germans were pictured as a people who were beleaguered by the Nazi gang and tried to fight this menace through the underground whenever they could. I never believed in that and it is now definitely proven that this so-called underground-spirit among the German people never existed.

In the last few years my activities were unfortunately greatly curtailed due to long and repeated illnesses, but I hope to start *The Lady in Ermine* in the near future, my first musical picture in fifteen years.

I agree with Mr. Huff whole-heartedly that I made sometimes pictures which were not up to my standard, but then it can only be said about a mediocrity that all his works live up to his standard.

Attached you will find a list of corrected data. I should like to make the same suggestion to you that I made to Mr. Huff: if you do not agree with my comments, throw them in the waste basket. But I would very much appreciate it if you would let me know which corrections, if any, you are going to make and when the Index is going to be published in England.

Sincerely yours,
Ernst Lubitsch

¶ *ERNST LUBITSCH* *

A SYMPOSIUM

Maurice Chevalier

I made four pictures with Ernst Lubitsch: *Love Parade, Smiling Lieutenant, One Hour with You,* and *The Merry Widow.*

Our way of working together was always very friendly and appreciative of the other fellow.

In my particular case I think there is no other way to make pictures than to obey the director I have accepted. Kind of placing my reputation on his knees.

But with Ernst, he was big enough to let me suggest a little something now and then, and in that case he would shoot the scene his way and my way. He was the one to decide after what was best.

I understood him in one twinkle. I knew what he was after.

I caressed a dream to make one more with him. A story called *Papa* from a French play. He liked it, but I was not old enough at that time to play a *Papa.*

Now, I am.

But Ernst is no more young or old. He is just gone. Bless his soul.

He taught me a lot. I did my best to satisfy him.

He stays in my heart as one of my "greats."

Charles Brackett and Billy Wilder

To write for Ernst Lubitsch was an education, a stimulus, a privilege, but it was no cinch.

Though he never took credit, he was a writer, too, in the full intimacy of collaboration. One had to understand the

* Excerpted from *The Screen Writer,* Vol. 3, No. 8 (Hollywood), January 1948, pp. 15–19.

kind of stylized film he wanted to make, and supply it with material. And always he was there, saying, "Is this the best we can do? Does it ring the bell? When it's right, it rings the bell."

He composed his pictures by segments rather than all in one piece. And he was apt to approach each portion with the terrifying statement, "This scene must be *hilahrious*." Thereupon, all minds involved focused on making the scene *hilahrious* and were held to that task with a kind of pneumatic-drill steadiness until, by George, the scene became *hilahrious*.

We remember how, when the pressure was heaviest, when the mere presence of so much mental effort in the room had become oppressive, he would retreat for long periods to that only refuge of collaborators—the bathroom—and come forth with a solution so often that we accused him of keeping a ghost writer hidden in the plumbing.

After the scene was drilled out, the individual lines had to be attacked by the same method. There was a scene in the first picture we did with him, in which Claudette Colbert was supposed to say something withering to Gary Cooper and dive off a raft into the Mediterranean. Always when he came to that line Ernst would go to the same corner of the room where we worked. "Then Claudette says . . . . .?" he would enunciate, leaving a proper hollow space and a gigantic question mark, "and makes a graceful dive." His hands would point and he'd dip forward into the corner. Then he would turn back to us, his eyes imploring us, not for just a mediocre joke, not for a fine, showy joke, even, but for *the* line—the inevitable withering remark which must be waiting somewhere in space. Incidentally, none of the lines we found was ever *it*, and as a tribute to the tremendous drive of personality, may we say that, as we remembered him, standing, diving into the baseboard, our minds again went searching for it, with supreme futility.

On the other hand, when an idea was mentioned which really fertilized his brain, what he could do with it: toss it into the air, make it catch the light one way, then another, spin it out, compress it, try it against this setting, against that, get the nth ultimate out of it.

The greatest disservice one could do him was to be enchanted beyond all reason by his interpretation of some idea too fantastic for celluloid. For instance, in that particular picture, his conception of a mad detective, a detective obsessed with a passion for his own disguises. The hero had hired the fellow to get evidence against his wife and was afraid she might suspect he had done so. Ernst's acting out of the detective reassuring the husband on that score remains with us:

"Sir, believe me, she suspects nothing. Nothing. Yesterday little did she notice a nun at the corner, telling her beads"—(a look of piercing, maniacal craftiness from the black eyes), "nor, this morning, did she pay any attention to a certain little girl playing marbles in front of the post office."

It was irresistible. One lost track completely of the fact that this figure was to be portrayed by a flesh-and-blood actor, instead of being recounted by a cigar-puffing magician. One rolled on the floor: "That's it! That's it!"

And then the eyes would grow distressed. "I'm not sure. Does it ring the bell? When it's right, it rings the bell. Is this the best we can do?"

Jeanette MacDonald

Ernst had, not a German, but an American sense of humor. The most American sense of humor I know of. It made for nice understanding with his fellow workers. But I always think of him first as a fighter. A fighter for what he believed in. He'd fight with you and for you anywhere in the world. He was a man of terrific force and vitality. And that was the only thing sad—to see him lose it toward the end. The vitality was still there inside—but he was afraid to let it go. Even when he laughed, it was no longer robust—it was like he had been warned not to laugh too hard. This Thanksgiving he was holding forth at my dinner table, and he was more like his old self than he had been in a long time. He was quite happy, and very serious in his opinions of the investigations in Washington.

He was always thinking of practical jokes—more than

anyone I know, he enjoyed them. There always had to be a big audience around for the denouement. Making *The Merry Widow*, I was under contract to Metro the time they signed Evelyn Laye, the fine British actress, to do musicals, also. I hadn't learned of it yet, but Ernst saw it in the *Hollywood Reporter* headlined: "Evelyn Laye Signed by Metro for Musicals." That morning, I had a big emotional scene where I was supposed to be singing while crying, and I started singing, sobbing and breaking my heart all over the set. During the scene I was supposed to go over to a mantelpiece. When I got to the mantelpiece, and was about to put my head down sobbing, there, propped on cardboard right under my eyes, was the headline from the *Reporter*. When I saw it, I stopped singing then and there. I could only stand gaping at that headline—then look blankly around the set. Ernst was laughing to burst.

To me, great people are always simple and Ernst was the simplest man I ever knew. He had no flaw in his greatness, no chichi, nor false vanity. On the set, he had the greatness of his art, but no "artiness." I have known so many directors who idealized him and styled some part of his work in their own careers. And to me, he was the greatest cutter in the business. Only Thanksgiving night he was talking of the lack of knowledge of cutting among some current directors. He cut as he worked on the set—that is, he shot just what he wanted. He visualized in the script the precise way he wanted it to work on the screen and I never knew him to be in trouble on a picture. He whipped his troubles in script. His scripts were almost invariably his pictures.

He never came here nor did I ever go to his house, but what he played the piano and he always ended playing Viennese waltzes. He was limited in his piano accomplishments, and could only play in a couple of keys—but his own satisfaction with his playing made it lovely. I have seen him sit down and play before some of the greatest pianists in the world with no compunction whatsoever and on the sets, frequently push them aside and say—"No, no, I want it to be like this . . ." and somehow even without the technical knowledge, he made them understand and the music became part of him and the picture.

Hans Kräly

I was to learn later that the young man tenaciously smoking a cigar was Ernst Lubitsch. The year was 1913. The place was Berlin. They were shooting a full-length comedy called *Die Firma Heiratet*, an old Union Film Corporation picture, starring Victor Arnold. Lubitsch played the part of an apprentice in a wholesale house, and I played the part of a clerk. His small part was soon to bring Lubitsch to stardom, although at the time I never imagined that he and I were to work for many years together.

A few months later I was up to both ears writing a series of one-reel comedies for the German comedian Albert Paulig. Lubitsch, in the interim, had started to make one-reelers also. He approached me one day and asked if we could do a picture together. I agreed, although as writer the firm could only pay me 25 marks (approximately $6) for the entire script. Lubitsch admitted that the sum was rather unhandsome, but promised to sweeten the proposition by appointing me his assistant director, at the same time by giving me a small bit to play in the picture.

From that time on we worked together for 17 years.

In those days casting was done in the café houses around the Friedrichstrasse. To kill two birds with one stone, Lubitsch suggested that we do our work in the cafés. We would outline a story one day, and write it the next. Two completed one-reel pictures per month was the average. But the actors soon caught on to what we were up to and formed the habit of dropping by our table to ask if we had parts for them. Lubitsch, who had a magnificent gift for concentration, was disturbed by these interruptions. By nature he was somewhat shy and reluctant to hurt anyone's feelings. So he solved the difficulty by fleeing from one obscure café to another, always one jump ahead of the actors.

After thirty to forty of these improvised productions, Lubitsch persuaded his producer, Paul Davidson, to let him launch into three-reelers. The first of these, *Schuhpalast Pinkus*, was to achieve a signal success.

It wasn't long before Davidson told me that he had decided to have Lubitsch direct a drama. It was an important decision. Lubitsch had been so successful with comedy that I was dismayed at the idea. But Paul Davidson said, "Don't look at me that way. He can do it! I know it!" I was to discover that my judgment had been wrong. The drama that Lubitsch was to direct was *Der Augen der Mummie Ma,* starring Emil Jannings and Pola Negri. It was to prove the first film drama that the German press took seriously.

From then on in rapid succession came such pictures as *Die Puppe, Die Bergkatze, Kölhiesel's Töchter, Rausch, Carmen, Sumurun, Dubarry, Anna Boleyn, Die Flamme, Das Weib des Pharao,* and others.

Of these films those which will be remembered in this country under their English titles are *Passion, Deception, Gypsy Love, One Arabian Night,* and *The Loves of Pharaoh.*

In my personal remembrances of Lubitsch I shall never forget the pleasure it was to work with him. No script ever took us longer than six weeks. And the day's work was rarely more than a few hours. I confess that the number of cigars that went up in smoke was terrific. But although our actual periods of work were short, Lubitsch was so highly concentrated in his work that after a few hours he was exhausted. It was then that he invariably suggested that perhaps I was tired!

Of course by this time we no longer worked in café houses but hid away in mountain lodges.

An added pleasure to myself as writer was that every word of the final script was translated into action on the screen. Lubitsch never made changes once he began to direct. Consequently he resented improvised last-minute suggestions from actors.

Another pleasant memory was Lubitsch's constant sense of humor. He loved to play practical jokes on his friends. Emil Jannings, for example, had a horror of coffins. In *Dubarry* there was a scene in which a coffin was to be carried through the palace. Lubitsch pretended that the coffin was to be opened by Dubarry for a last fond farewell. Jannings quickly visualized the drama of such a touching situation and allowed Lubitsch to persuade him to lie in the coffin and have the lid fastened down. But once he had Jannings locked in the coffin, Lubitsch promptly called off the day's shooting. The studio was soon deserted except for Lubitsch who was spying on the coffin from behind the set. Nothing happened. When Lubitsch hastily opened the coffin he found Jannings as pale as a corpse, and furious at the trap into which he had been inveigled.

Although not religious in the conventional sense, nevertheless, Lubitsch never undertook an important action in his life, nor started a day's directing, without pausing for half a minute for a short silent prayer. Few people knew of this. He never spoke of it.

Passion and *Deception* led Lubitsch to Hollywood, under contract to Mary Pickford, to direct *Rosita*.

I remember the morning he left for America. When the ship sailed from Bremerhaven, carrying Lubitsch—the hope and pride of the German film industry—a small group of us were on the dock to wish him bon voyage and wave farewell.

His father was nearly in tears at the thought of his son going to California to a world of Indians, mountain lions, rattlesnakes, and countless other wild animals.

But Ernst Lubitsch was not to be lost in a wilderness. He was to gain new triumphs.

Samson Raphaelson

Lubitsch loved ideas more than anything in the world, except his daughter Nicola. It didn't matter what kind of ideas. He could become equally impassioned over an exit speech for a character in the current script, the relative merits of Horowitz and Heifetz, the aesthetics of modern painting, or whether now is the time to buy real estate. And his passion was usually much stronger than that of anyone else around him, so he was likely to dominate in a group. Yet I never saw, even in this territory of egotists, anyone who didn't light up with pleasure in Lubitsch's company. We got that pleasure, not from his brilliancy or his rightness—he was far from infallible, and his wit, being human, had its lesser moments —but from the purity and childlike delight of his lifelong love affair with ideas.

An idea mattered to him more, for instance, than where his forkful of food happened to be traveling at a given moment. This director, who had an unerring eye for style, from the surface of clothes and manners down to the most subtle intonation of an aristocrat's heart, was, in his personal life, inclined to reach for the handiest pair of trousers and coat whether they clashed or not, to shout like a king or a peasant (but never like a gentleman) and go through life unaware of many refinements and shadings, with that clumsiness which is the passport of an honest man. He had no time for manners, but the grace within him was unmistakable, and everyone kindled to it, errand boy and mogul, mechanic and artist. Garbo smiled, indeed, in his presence, and so did Sinclair Lewis and Thomas Mann. He was born with the happy gift of revealing himself instantly and to all.

As an artist he was sophisticated, as a man almost naive. As an artist shrewd, as a man simple. As an artist, economical, precise, exacting; as a man, he was always forgetting his reading glasses, his cigars, manuscripts, and half the time it was an effort for him to remember his own telephone number.

However great the cinema historians will eventually estimate him, he was bigger as a person.

I doubt if a greater craftsman ever lived. I was enchanted with Charles Brackett's picture of Lubitsch arriving beyond the Pearly Gates, meeting the other show people, Molière, Congreve, Shakespeare. Even if they had never heard of him, I know that in ten minutes he became one of them. I am sure that, as time goes on and they become better acquainted, many of them will feel—as the mortal writers who really knew Lubitsch feel—that here is one who profoundly respects and understands the art of writing.

He was genuinely modest. He never sought fame or coveted prizes. He was incapable of employing the art of personal publicity. You could never wound him by speaking critically of his work. And somehow he never wounded his fellow workers with his innocent forthrightness. If he once accepted you, it was because he believed in you. Thus he could say, "Oh, that's lousy!" and at the same time you felt his rich appreciation of what you hoped were your hidden virtues.

A superb actor, he was totally incapable of acting in his human relations. He did not have one manner for the great and another for the lowly, one style for the drawing room and another for the bar. He was as free from guile and pretense as children are supposed to be, and this made him endlessly various and charming.

I am sorry I was never able to say all this to him while he was alive.

Steffie Trondle

I had never met Ernst Lubitsch before and I would not have recognized the little man with the broad jovial smile and the twinkling eyes who entered the office one morning if it had not been for his trademark—the big, black cigar. Little did I realize then that it would be my privilege to be associated with him for nearly twenty years.

Ernst Lubitsch, the man with those wonderfully intelligent eyes, was an artist who wanted perfection in everything he did. His mind was so quick that often it was difficult to follow him. I recall how years ago a writer had been waiting for weeks for an appointment to tell him a story idea. When he came out of Mr. Lubitsch's office the man was upset. "Here I am waiting for weeks for an appointment, and after listening to me for five minutes he turns around and tells me the story."

A conscientious and serious worker himself, he expected the same from all those who worked with him. He was always ready to excuse mistakes, but had no tolerance with anyone neglecting his duty. Few men in the industry ever had a more thorough knowledge of every phase of production than he. At a conference with the music department preparatory to *The Love Parade*, his first musical picture, I remember one of the men saying that they worked all night trying to figure out how one of the numbers could be handled. Mr. Lubitsch jumped up: "But gentlemen, that is so easy," and in a few minutes he explained to them how it should and could be done. It was this great knowledge and sureness that earned him the admiration and respect of all those who had the good fortune to work with him.

Surprising as it may seem, the master of sophistication was really a little boy at heart who loved to play tricks on others. I remember one morning at the time he was working with Messrs. Brackett and Wilder and Reisch on *Ninotchka*. I was late in getting to the office (as usual!) and they were already inside when I came. In the center of my desk I noticed a book. I took one glance at the rather lurid title and the picture of a scantily draped woman, shrugged my shoulders—and that was all. A minute later the door opened from the inside; Mr. Lubitsch stuck his head out and asked: "What's the matter, are you sick?" Then I learned that the four big men, like little boys had scrambled around to set the cap inside the book before I arrived and had been standing behind the door listening, expecting me to pick up the book and scream as the cap would go off. Mr. Lubitsch was a very disappointed man!

During the same picture the three writers had argued with him for hours, trying to convince him that he was wrong on one particular point in the story. Finally, he called me in and asked me what my reaction would be. With four pairs of eyes staring at me, I tried to think. And I shall never forget the look on Mr. Lubitsch's face when I finally answered—he was speechless. My reactions coincided with those of the writers. I had let him down.

For all his greatness, Ernst Lubitsch was a very simple man as far as he himself was concerned, and deeply appreciative of any kindness shown him. A box of cigars, or the cookies the little Hungarian lady would bake for him would please him no end. Like a little boy he would leave in the evening taking his present home with him. Despite all the lavishness in his pictures, he was a very simple and modest man as far as he himself was concerned. Last summer after having urged him for weeks to get some new clothes, he came to the office and said: "I was at the tailor and do you know what he has done?" (I had visions that the whole suit had been botched up.) "He made me *two* suits! And what could I do . . . I like them." I told him he hadn't had a new suit for three or four years and that the tailor probably decided he needed two new ones.

Much has been said and written about Ernst Lubitsch, the

artist. But how much more there is to be said about Ernst Lubitsch, the man, and his enduring friendship and loyalty. A friend in need could always count on help from him. And as to his generosity there was just no end. "Only one package a month . . . oh no, the man should get at least two packages a month," he said to me only the other day. And that was only one of the many, many similar cases. Before the rise of Hitler, a trip to Berlin, to be able to meet at the Bühnen-klub with all his old friends and former colleagues, that was the ideal vacation for Ernst Lubitsch.

But the most touching side in the man was his deep devotion to his small daughter Nicola, and his letters to her. The master of sophistication telling the little girl about her kitten and her dolls—how they missed her. No, Ernst Lubitsch was not a sentimentalist, but a little man with a great, big heart, whose memory will always be cherished by all who knew him.

¶ A TRIBUTE TO LUBITSCH 1892–1947 *

by Walter Reisch, Lewis Milestone, William Wyler, Andrew Marton, Henry Koster, Frank Capra, King Vidor, Alfred Hitchcock, H. C. Potter

Ernst Lubitsch, the Director whose "touch" became a legend, enjoyed and still enjoys a place so rare in the memory of his peers and his pals, some refuse to concede his passing. "My friend Ernst Lubitsch did not die twenty years ago," Director Lewis Milestone told *Action!* recently. "The author of the 'Lubitsch Touch' will live on as long as comedy lives on."

After a European career as an actor and director, Lubitsch

* *Action!*, The Magazine of the Directors Guild of America (Hollywood), November–December, 1967.

was brought to the U.S. in 1923 to direct Mary Pickford in
Rosita. He stayed to become the Director's Director.

He was a dark, restless, hyperactive little man who drove
himself relentlessly, seemed to derive energy and comfort
from the huge black cigar inevitably clenched between his
teeth.

Nearly every Sunday afternoon Ernst Lubitsch called on
his next door neighbor, writer-director Walter Reisch, and
it was Mr. Reisch who proposed this salute. Expressing his
own thoughts about Lubitsch and "the touch," Reisch wrote,
"The most important thing about his style is the well-known
fact that he was the inventor of elegant boudoir comedy—
films full of matrimonial escapades, marriage-go-rounds, frivolous affairs. Sex and more sex was the motive for almost
everything his characters did, but so adroitly did he handle
his *tours de amour,* he never had a minute of censorship
trouble in three decades of picture making. There was not
one of his films in which a wife or a husband did not get
into a risqué situation. There was double entendre on every
page of his dialogue. Still, there was never any nudity or sex
violence, or smut or pornography, or art house close-ups.
The Lubitsch touch was a synonym for impeccable taste
without losing one iota of piquancy. Eroticism with Lubitsch
was charm; adultery was not a syndrome but capricious
frivolity. Nobody phrased it better than the late Ronald
Colman: 'When you enter a movie house in the middle of
the second reel and haven't seen the credits, you still know
at once that a Lubitsch picture is on the screen.' He had
a handwriting of his own, a style he invented.

"Bedroom doors always played leads in Lubitsch films
without getting any billing. At the storehouse for discarded
sets on the Paramount lot, they still show you doors that
were specially built for scenes with that touch—innumerable
doors that closed behind neglected wives, opened for lovers,
were locked by pouting mistresses and slammed by cuckolded
husbands. Endless is the roster of names that played gallivant-
ing husbands and those foolish wives and merry and not so
merry widows and femmes fatales. Lubitsch was the great
puppeteer who made them all dance to his baton, to his
touch."

Seeking to fathom the man and his touch, *Action!* queried several of Lubitsch's peers and pals, received a set of replies achieving a rare and revealing salute.

Said William Wyler, "Ernst Lubitsch was truly the *auteur* of his films. He created a style of sophisticated comedy peculiarly his own, as well as a new style of musical, both unknown before his time. His films bore the recognizable and indelible stamp of the gay, clever, witty, mischievous master, whose delightful personality matched his work. I am proud to have known him as a friend and teacher. Lubitsch's films were truly Lubitsch's, possessive credit intended."

From Paris, Andrew Marton wired: "Regarding Ernst Lubitsch, more than anything else I miss his kind encouragement, which came out of his special kindness toward humanity. This is the attitude that gave birth to the famous Lubitsch touch which was never bitter, never malicious, or sarcastic, but always kind like he was."

Commented Henry Koster, "There was no subtle innuendo, no sophisticated twist until Ernst Lubitsch came along and the period of pie throwing and pants splitting came to an end. He was one of the truly great who raised the movies up to the highest level. Today, after twenty years, we miss him as much as when we lost him—even more so."

Frank Capra, a celebrated director of poignant comedy in his own right, pointed out, "Ernst Lubitsch was the complete architect of motion pictures. His stamp was on every frame of film—from conception to delivery. For high-style, romantic comedies and spicy musicals he set a standard that has not been equaled. The Lubitsch 'touch' was unique."

"Ernst Lubitsch inaugurated expressionism in the directing of moving pictures with his Lubitsch touch," King Vidor said. "I was able to walk into a projection booth, look through the small glass aperture at the screen and detect that it was a Lubitsch film within a few seconds time. This is how he infused every foot of film he directed with his charming and witty personality."

Alfred Hitchcock recalls, "I first saw Lubitsch performing at the London Coliseum in a wordless play called *Sumurun* in February, 1911. He was playing the part of a clown. Naturally, one had no idea of what this clown was to become.

Then of course, I met him in the great days of *Loves of Pharoah*, etc. And then, his greatest contribution, to me, to the cinema, was his making of *The Marriage Circle*. Ernst Lubitsch, like his great colleagues Murnau, Lang, and Robison, was a man of 'pure Cinema.' "

Director H. C. Potter summed up his hearty and heartfelt thoughts: "With Ernst you always felt you were living in the midst of a Schnitzler play, say *The Affairs of Anatol*, which you hoped would never end. He looked on life with a gay irreverance that was completely irresistible.

"The Lubitsch Touch? Take *If I Had a Million* (in which Paramount gave six directors freedom to conjure up what might happen if you suddenly came into $1,000,000). Ernst's version, without one *word* of dialogue:

"Charles Laughton, lowly clerk in Goliath Corporation, receives telegram announcing bonanza. Deadpan, he slowly closes huge ledger, removes 'sleeve protectors,' rises, starts walking. Camera trucks with him (waist figure, profile, no expression). He plods through two huge roomsful of detail-ridden clerks like himself. The deliberate walk continues (camera steadily trucking) through an appalling succession of offices filled with Lowly Vice-Presidents, Middle Vice-Presidents, Major Vice-Presidents.

"Without slackening or increasing the deliberate pace which, from the start, has maintained the same clock-like, monotonous beat, he goes through an imposing doorway and passes Outer Secretaries, Inner Secretaries. He breasts the Innermost Sanctum door with the inexorability of a Sherman tank.

"The Mogul, behind a huge desk, looks up at him, "Mr. Brown?" says Laughton. "Yes," replies the Mogul. Laughton then makes the first and only violent movement in the entire episode. He purses his lips, sticks out his tongue, and emits a blasting Bronx cheer. Blackout.

"That was Ernst."

¶ LUBITSCH AND EISENSTEIN *

by H. H. Wollenberg

There appears a certain, though superficial, parallel between Lubitsch and Eisenstein. In both cases, there is a distinct change from their earlier to their later productions. Just as Eisenstein turned from the topical to the historical, so Lubitsch, who had made his great entry with monumental period films like *Carmen, Madame Dubarry, Sumurun, Anna Boleyn, The Loves of Pharaoh,* stuck to sophisticated comedy ever since sound had conquered the screen.

Lubitsch achieved the reputation of the leading director of the early Twenties on account of the international success of *Madame Dubarry,* a success which had its climax when, in 1923, he was called by filmdom's First Lady, Mary Pickford, to Hollywood, to make a film with and for her. Eisenstein, too, owed a great deal to foreign response. The then People's Commissar of the Soviet Union, A. V. Lunacharsky himself, wrote about *Potemkin*: "In Russia, the full revolutionary force and the novel technique of this brilliant film fragment were not immediately appreciated. It was *only from the German echo* that we were able to realize what Eisenstein had achieved."

As different in type, origin, outlook, and purpose as the two men were, one feels that they had one most important thing in common: both were creative, and the fact that they both died early is, one feels, more than a merely incidental and superficial parallel. As we have seen, the creative artist of the film is liable to struggle harder, and to consume his energies sooner, than any other artist. For the realization of his visions, his efforts in self-expression, are tied up with financial premises. The painter, the composer, the poet, the writer may after all freely choose their subject. Can the artist of the film . . .? Whether he depends on a board of directors or on a state bureaucracy—he is certainly not a free

* Excerpted from *Sight and Sound,* Spring 1948.

agent, and there are certain limitations even for such prominent men as Eisenstein and Lubitsch.

Lubitsch had found the formula for coming to terms with Hollywood on the basis of box office at the least possible concessions to his sophisticated taste and artistic manner. No complaining articles of his have ever appeared. However, was he quite as happy as he seemed in all his splendor? We know one remark of his, which is characteristic of his wit: "We, in Hollywood, acquire the finest novels in order to smell their leather bindings." This one sentence betrays that he lived and worked in Hollywood not without seeing its shortcomings with open eyes. However, Lubitsch was no revolutionary. As far back as in 1930, a Berlin film critic commented on Lubitsch's famous cigar that, "unfortunately, it was not smoked in Moscow instead of Hollywood." Looking back now that the cigar has gone out for good—I wonder if the critic was really right. . . .

¶ HOLLYWOOD—"LA GRANDE EPOQUE" *

by S. N. Behrman

In its great days when the Industry was the fifth largest in America, before the cannibalism of the machines undermined its monopoly, Hollywood enlisted the services of the most extraordinary group of artists ever gathered in one place in the history of the world. Its product whiled away the hours for begrimed miners in Merthyr Tydfil and for bored maharajahs in their palaces in India. It entertained the world.

. . .

With the influx of the refugees in the thirties, Hollywood became a kind of Athens. It was as crowded with artists as

* Excerpted from *The New York Times*, July 17, 1966.

Renaissance Florence. The modest living room of Salka Viertel's house in Mabery Road was surely, in those days, the most fascinating salon in America. You would meet there Thomas and Heinrich Mann, Otto Klemperer, Bruno Walter, Leopold Stokowski, Arnold Schoenberg, the Franz Werfels, Miss Garbo, Max Reinhardt, Aldous Huxley, Fritzi Masary, Sam Hoffenstein. The latter's *Poems in Praise of Practically Nothing* was found by the bedside of Chief Justice Holmes when he died. These names are only a sprinkling, a full list would read like an Almanach de Gotha of the arts. It was a Golden Era. It had never happened before. It will never happen again.

It was an extraordinary community; it was an enthralling time. In all the world there was not a more aristocratic acting skill than Miss Garbo's. There were the Chaplin films. There were the Marx Brothers films. There were the Harold Lloyd and the Douglas Fairbanks films. There were the Lubitsch films. Ernst Lubitsch was the only director in Hollywood who had his own signature.[1] There was no one there then as witty, as personal. You knew it was a Lubitsch film before it started. Under the credit titles of *The Merry Widow* you saw a dedicated geographer, with a hand glass, peering at a map of southeastern Europe, trying vainly to locate the country which Prince Danilo deserts for the blandishments of Paris. He gives up in despair.

Lubitsch himself was a remarkable man as well as a unique director. He was gay, full of fun, impassioned, serious. I shall never forget one night at a Hollywood gathering when some cynic pooh-poohed the idea of the Warner Brothers inviting Max Reinhardt to make *A Midsummer Night's Dream*. Lubitsch poured vitriol over the skeptic, said it was too bad if Hollywood, swimming in riches, could not afford to take a chance on the most imaginative and daring director in the world, to invite him to film a masterpiece which he had already produced, with fabulous effect, on the stage. It

---

[1] This wasn't exactly true, there were others who also produced "signed" works, like Stroheim, Sternberg, Mal St. Clair, Harry d'Arrast, Preston Sturges, Capra, Ford—not to mention Griffith and Chaplin. But Lubitsch was certainly "archetypical" of the *genre*. [Author's Note.]

was a terrible day for very many people when Ernst Lubitsch died. I shall miss him till the day comes when I will no longer miss anybody.

Charles Chaplin

He could do more to show the grace and humor of sex in a nonlustful way than any other director I've ever heard of.

From *My Autobiography*

Greta Garbo

He was the only great director out there. *Ninotchka* was the only time I had a great director in Hollywood.

Cited by Mercedes de Acosta in *Here Lies the Heart*

Joseph Mankiewicz

I worshiped him. I admired his work enormously. He went head and shoulders beyond everyone in the field of sophisticated high comedy.

Orson Welles

Lubitsch was a giant . . . his talent and originality were stupefying.

From an interview with Orson Welles published in *Cahiers du Cinéma* (Paris), April 1965.

Jean Renoir

To maintain the admirable balance of nature, God provides to the defeated nations the gift of Art. It is what happened to Germany after the defeat of 1918. Berlin, before Hitler, was blooming with talents. In this short Renaissance, the Jews, not only of Germany but also of the surrounding countries, brought to this capital a certain spirit which was probably the best expression of the time. Lubitsch was a great example of this ironic approach to the big problems of life. His films were loaded with a kind of wit which was specifically the essence of the intellectual Berlin in those days. This man was so strong that when he was asked by Hollywood to work there, he not only didn't lose his Berlin style but he converted the Hollywood industry to his own way of expression. Hollywood is still influenced by Lubitsch, that means indirectly by the Berlin of my youth.

From a Letter to the Author, July 22, 1967.

René Clair

The historians of the cinema will doubtless say there was not one but two Lubitsches: one before and the other after the appearance of A Woman of Paris. This masterpiece of Chaplin created a style which inspired Lubitsch, the imprint of which can be found in his best comedies.

Such a statement, however, does not diminish his merit. One needn't blush because one had teachers. Only the ignorant believe that they are completely exempt from any influence. From Lady Windermere's Fan and Trouble in Paradise to To Be or Not to Be, what genial invention and science of comedy! One would wish that in his turn Lubitsch had disciples today. Our time needs laughter. As Aldous Huxley said, humor is extremely important; it is the modern manifestation of humility.

From a letter to the Author, September 11, 1967.

S. N. Behrman

I knew Lubitsch and loved him. You have a wonderful subject, and no one I know deserves a book more than he, and your title is just right.

From a letter to the Author, September 5, 1968.

Melvyn Douglas

He was an imaginative, perceptive, mischievous and an altogether brilliant director. He was also one of my dearest friends in Hollywood. To this day, I miss him professionally and personally.

From a letter to the Author, March 9, 1968.

Douglas Fairbanks, Jr.

He never forgot that dialogue should complement, not replace, what is essentially a visual medium. He accomplished his purpose in a style so recognizably his own that the phrase, "the Lubitsch touch," used to describe a humorously oblique and sophisticated directorial device, became famous.

It was a joy to work with him (I was in his last picture) and he was certainly one of the three or four most influential shapers of the art of the cinema.

From a letter to the Author, March, 1968.

Jack Benny

He was the greatest director in the motion picture industry. He was also very easy to work with as he always played a scene first and just by watching him you knew exactly what to do. The Lubitsch touch was something no other director had and the nice thing about being in one of his pictures was that you knew while you were making it that it just *couldn't* be bad.

In a letter to the Author, dated May 9, 1968.

¶ CHEZ ERNST *

by Jean-Georges Auriol

Translated by Ingrid Burke

The rococo drawing rooms of Ernst Lubitsch. How he would have rejoiced had he seen how everyone relished the sumptuous fare served in them. One could be sure to dine perfectly at "Ernst's," and the epicure was sure to find the same favorite sauces and garnishes.

The service was always meticulous at "Ernst's," the proprietor correcting with a murmur the manner of one of his staff if his usual urbanity were about to slip into mere obsequiousness or his good humor into impertinence. A man could take his mistress to supper at "Ernst's" and see his wife there without the slightest chance of a scandal. Ernst could transform such a difficulty, or even possible sensation, into a slightly audacious farce. And Lubitsch's subtle handling of such a situation would cause some celebrities who were enjoying themselves in his establishment to say, "Ernst (the French usually called him Ernst), why on earth didn't you take up a diplomatic career? You would have made a first-class Ambassador."

Ernst would smile gratefully, without speaking at first, so that the gentleman would be overcome by his own compliment, which always seemed insolent in retrospect; then he would offer some champagne from his private stock to the Countess (or the Ambassador's wife or whoever it might be) delighted to be able to steal with his glowing look an answering one which said, "What a major-domo he would be for me!" and "I could even sleep with him . . .!" So it is for her that he explains finally, in order not to offend such illustrious clients: "To each his calling. I am only an artist . . ." — letting it be understood: If I were not who I am,

* Excerpted from the American edition of *Cahiers du Cinéma*, No. 9, March 1967. First published in *La Revue du Cinéma*, September 1948.

nor where I am, how would you spend your evenings when you are in Vienna, Budapest, or even in Paris? . . . in short, somewhere in a still preserved corner of old Europe, in some glittering establishment whose walls are covered with photographs of all the Royal Families of the era.

He was a great middle-class liberal, in fact, a self-made man—stout, nervous, jovial, although perhaps less stout than anything else. Born into the lower middle class, he despised neither peasant nor working man nor the petty clerk that he had himself once been; he understood only that everyone should dress in his Sunday best to come to see his films before going off to dance at a family party or as fortune decreed, in pairs. Lubitsch came just in time to portray the brilliance of a society threatened with disappearance because it was no longer cared for, and hence, no longer defended. He adored it, and because of him we can sigh for the return of that world which seems to us flamboyant and artificial, although attractive, comfortable, and gracious. The world which he portrays in such shimmering colors which are not necessarily more false than the severe dust-gray of our ruined age; a world that we can always study in his comedies with the satisfaction of finding its real inhabitants, whether they be absurd, enviable, or charming.

For charm, in the hazy and delightful sense which this word has when used conversationally, was one of Lubitsch's secrets. This little Berliner with strongly marked, almost Oriental, features, whose eyes flashed darkly and as animatedly as did all his movements, was basically self-centered and sensual, but he commanded obedience because he was kindly, always ready to help others, and to show satisfaction and even admiration when required: he was all the more impulsive and enthusiastic as nobody had ever outwitted him. He knew so well how to surround himself with the right friends that it was believed that he himself brought good luck.

Lubitsch's first little theater was his father's shop, where he learned to observe and criticize mankind, at least on the surface, and to make fun of what he regarded as grown-up child's play. On leaving school he studied acting with the classical actor Victor Arnold, who persuaded him to enter the

Deutsches Theater where Max Reinhardt gave him comic roles in his ballet pantomimes. It was again through Arnold that he was able to make his debut at the Ufa as early as 1913.

The third person to have a beneficial influence on his career was Pola Negri. Was it he who made the fortune of this dreamy Polish woman, endowed her with the passionate temperament of an Italian diva, with her mass of brown hair, her feverish eyes, and, moreover, something peasantlike and voracious in her narrow face with its radiant lips? Or perhaps, as this village girl, who became a modern Venus, claims it was she who "discovered" him. Undoubtedly they brought each other good fortune. Hollywood met them separately, having first been astonished by the sensational production of *Dubarry*, but they were reunited shortly afterward, and Pola profited from following the trail which Ernst had blazed in America. This trail of success was marked out for temples of love which were to be occupied by heroines of differing types, but they were always Continental: for Lubitsch's women were never "Yankee."

When the American producers had persuaded him to come, and then encouraged him to stay in their studios, Ernst did not know how best to serve them, but they knew that he was indispensable for creating a new product. Thus did Louis XIV invite the Dutch clothmakers to France, installing them and making them French citizens, as Francis I had earlier attracted great Italian artists to France.

Perhaps Lubitsch was bewitched by America, as were many Europeans after the First World War, but it is clear that he went there with the clear idea of enlarging his horizons. One can guess at the many conversations with his script writer Hans Kräly, and with other friends whom he took to Hollywood, or who followed him there. There had to be an American cinema slightly different from that which even the Americans thought best, for on the one hand Americans consider those virtues for which we envy them bad, and on the other hand they praise many of our vices, owing, undoubtedly, to the optical effects on the mind resulting from removal from environment—effects which explain, for instance, the seemingly inordinate success of *The Baker's Wife* in the United States while most Americans smile indulgently at our admiration for Chaplin, Stroheim, Langdon, Welles, and other artists who seem mediocre or even failures to them.

In support of the belief that there are "few people of any great quality among film producers" and that "for the cinema a genius must double as a businessman," Jim Tully points out that Lubitsch was not anxious to film Theodore Dreiser's *American Tragedy* and preferred to direct a film entitled *So This Is Paris*.

I doubt whether Lubitsch could have digested the harshness of the "Yankee jungle," because he decided at an early age to banish harshness from his work. He could not stare for long into the unfathomable depths which Stroheim scanned without feeling dizzy. He had resolved to chase all bitterness from the eyes of his spectators.

This Jewish connoisseur was sufficiently Christian to be able to thank God for being able to live in a world where one could find happiness by means of a little goodwill.

Capra, the idealist, is reproached often enough for his "simplistic ethics" and for the fact that he enjoins love of living more with seriousness than humor. But it would be childish, unjust, and even barbarous to reproach this Arabian story teller by comparing him to the Western Lubitsch who makes his public laugh so frivolously. To assume this attitude, a judge would have to pronounce judgment from high on a steel platform, whose composition would remain a secret at present. One must remember, however, the comical fall of Chaplin's two dictators who rashly wanted to raise themselves in their shabby mechanical chairs at the barber's.

I am one of the audience, and I want to know: who is there now to give us light musical comedy and other crisp desserts on fantastical dreams? But I am also a filmmaker, and my answer is that Preston Sturges's inflammable oil wells have not quite dried up, and there are several pretenders to the throne of the Great Entertainer: a Mitchell Leisen may have certain rights to a crown which is rather too heavy for him, and a George Cukor or a Billy Wilder, who certainly possess charm, are attracted by other titles. There remains Mankiewicz . . .

How can a child who cries at the end of the summer holidays be comforted? He can be told that another summer will come, which will be equally wonderful. But he cries even more at this, not knowing how to explain that he won't be the same child again. Certainly Lubitsch's public is as sentimental as this child; and it knows quite well that *Ernst's* is closed on account of death. This particular restaurant will never be open again.

¶ AVE ATQUE VALE *
by Billy Wilder

I still remember the day of the funeral. After the ceremony, William Wyler and I walked silently to our car. Finally I said, just to say something to break the silence, "No more Lubitsch." To which Wyler replied, "Worse than that—no more Lubitsch films."

How right we were. For twenty years since then we all tried to find the secret of the "Lubitsch touch." Nothing doing. Oh, if we were lucky, we sometimes managed a few feet of film here and there in our work that momentarily sparkled like Lubitsch. *Like* Lubitsch, not *real* Lubitsch.

His art is lost. That most elegant of screen magicians took his secret with him.

* *Action!*, Magazine of the Screen Directors Guild of America (Hollywood), November, 1967.

A Reminiscence
by Nicola Lubitsch *

> There's rosemary, that's for
> remembrance: pray you, love,
> remember.
>
> —HAMLET

He was the most wonderful father anyone ever had, and he
loved me more than anything in the world.

* From a Letter to the Author, Winter, 1968.

L'Envoi

Degas once found himself in the merry company of some friends who were contributing their epitaphs to posterity. The usually dour artist permitted himself a faint smile when he was asked to contribute his own. "Just say," he replied, *"He liked to draw."*

It would come as close to the quintessence of Lubitsch, as I think it is possible to come so laconically, to echo the sentiments of Degas by saying, *"He liked to make films."*

Annotated Filmography

¶ THE GERMAN PERIOD

From 1909 to 1911, Lubitsch served as an apprentice at the Berlin
Bioscope Studios, as bit-part actor, property man, lighting assistant,
etc., following which he was introduced to Max Reinhardt by his
drama teacher and mentor, the popular Berlin comedian Victor
Arnold. His debut as an actor was at the Deutsches Theater in
Reinhardt's production of *Hamlet*, as one of the gravediggers. Subsequently he appeared (chiefly in old men's roles, which he liked to
do) in plays by Sudermann, Shaw, Wilde, etc. He originated the
role of the hunchback in Reinhardt's stage production of *Sumurun*,
which he was one day to play again in a film under his own direction. But his real love was films and he soon found himself working
there as a comic actor. Most of the films of his German period were
produced under the aegis of Paul Davidson, head of Union-Film in
Berlin.

Of all the big German directors of the so-called Golden Age, only
Lubitsch never worked for Erich Pommer, that mentor of so many
directorial lights of Ufa. Lubitsch left Germany in 1922 before
Davidson's Union-Film and Ufa merged with Pommer's own company, Decla(Deutsche Eclair)-Bioskop, out of all which emerged
the great monolith, Ufa.

1912

The Miracle

> A film made of the London production of Karl Vollmoeller's
> stage spectacle, directed by Max Reinhardt. Lubitsch, then on
> tour with Reinhardt's troupe, was in the cast. Setting: A con-
> vent and elsewhere in Spain.

Venezianische Nächte (Venetian Nights). Ma.-Lu.-Film.

> Written and directed by Max Reinhardt. Photography: Karl

Freund. With Ernst Matray, Victor Varconi, Eric Stein, Ernst Lubitsch. Setting: Venice.

An early attempt to put the "glamour" of Venice on the screen. Max Reinhardt's first film, *The Miracle*, having been a filmed play.

1913

Meyer auf der Alm (Meyer on the Alps). Union-Film, released by Universal Film-Verleigh. (1 reel)

Starring Ernst Lubitsch, his screen debut as a comic actor. With Sophie Pagay. Setting: Swiss Alps.

A popular song of the period was "Was macht der kleine Meyer auf dem grossen Himalaya?"

Georges Sadoul, in his *Dictionnaire des Cinéastes* (Paris) 1965, refers to a film that year, *Le Club des Invisibles*, produced by Decla-Pommer in Vienna.

Bedingung: Kein Anhang (Condition: No Dependants). Deutsche Bioskop. (2 reels)

Directed by Stellan Rye. Scenario: Luise Heilborn-Korbitz. Photography: Guido Seeber. With Hans Wassermann, Albert Paulig, Emil Albes, Ernst Lubitsch, Siddie Sinnen, Helene Voss.

1914

Fräulein Piccolo (Miss Piccolo). Luna-Film. (3 reels) (30 min.)

Directed by Franz Hofer. Photography: Gotthardt Wolf. Settings: Fritz Kränke. With Dorrit Weixler, Franz Schwaiger, Martin Wolff, Max Lehmann, Alice Hechy, Helene Voss, Karl Harbacher, Ernst Lubitsch. Setting: Provincial Germany.

An officer during maneuvers is billeted at an inn where he falls in love with the innkeeper's daughter, acting as maid there. After considerable contretemps, including an attempt by a drunken lout (played by Lubitsch) to get her to his room, all ends happily and the girl gets her lieutenant.

Die Firma Heiratet (The Firm Marries). Union-Film, released January 23, 1914. (1 reel)

Directed by Carl Wilhelm. Scenario by Walter Turzsinsky and Jacques Burg. With Victor Arnold, Ernst Lubitsch (as "Kom-

mis Moritz" Abramowski), Albert Paulig, Alfred Kühne, Resel
Orla, Hans Kräly (later to become Lubitsch's ace scenarist).
Setting: Berlin. Lubitsch's first big success as an actor. It was
quite possibly the first film with Lubitsch to be shown in
America, released here as *The Perfect Thirty-six*. (Later remade
as a German sound film.)

Der Stolz der Firma (The Pride of the Firm). Projektions A. G.-
Union-Film, released July 31, 1914. (3 reels) (45 min.)
    Directed by Carl Wilhelm. Scenario by Walter Turzsinsky and
Jacques Burg. Starring Ernst Lubitsch (as Siegmund Lach-
mann), Marthe Kriwitsch, Victor Arnold, Albert Paulig, Alfred
Kühne. Setting: Berlin,
    This was regarded as a feature in this length.

Fräulein Seifenschaum (Miss Soapsuds). Projektions A. G.-Union-
Film. (1 reel)
    Written and directed by Ernst Lubitsch, his first directorial
effort. Sets by Kurt Richter. Starring Lubitsch. Setting: Berlin.

Meyer als Soldat (Soldier Meyer). Union-Film.
    Starring Ernst Lubitsch. Setting: Berlin.

Rund um die Ehe (Ring Around Marriage).
    Starring Ernst Lubitsch. (One might hazard a guess that this
was an early forerunner of *The Marriage Circle*.) Further details lacking.

Hans Trutz in Schlaraffenland (Hans Trutz in Never-Never Land).
Projektions A. G.-Union-Film. (4 reels)
    Directed by Paul Wegener. Scenario by Wegener. Photography
by Frederik Fuglsang. Sets by Rochus Gliese. With Ernst
Lubitsch (playing a playful devil). The date for this has not
been exactly established but it was around this time, though
possibly 1917. Starring Paul Wegener, Lyda Salmonova, Fritz
Rasp.
    The story dated back to the fifteenth century. (The "Never-
Never Land" of the title refers to a fairytale country where
everyone lived affluently and joyously without working.) Hans
Sachs, the famous shoemaker-poet of Richard Wagner's *Die
Meistersinger von Nürnberg* (there was a real Hans Sachs),
once wrote a play about this Utopia, *Schlaraffenland*, and
Breughel's painting of the same name is, of course, well known.

1915

Arme Marie! (Poor Marie!). Vitascope-Union-Film released May 14, 1915.
> Directed by Max Mack. Scenario by Walter Turzsinsky and Robert Wiene (who four years later was to direct the epochal *Cabinet of Dr. Caligari*). Photography by Hermann Böttger.
> With Felix Basch, Friedrich Zelnick (who was later to direct *The Weavers*, by Gerhart Hauptmann), Ernst Lubitsch, Hanni Weisse. Subtitled *Ein Warenhausroman* (A Department Store Romance). Setting: Berlin.

Robert und Bertram (Robert and Bertram). Projektions A. G.-Union-Film. (3 reels)
> Directed by Max Mack. Photography by Max Lutze. With Eugen Burg, Ferdinand Bonn, Wilhelm Diegelmann, Ernst Lubitsch.

Blinde Kuh (Blind Man's Buff). Union-Film, released May 28, 1915.
> Directed by Ernst Lubitsch. With Resel Orla and Lubitsch.

Auf Eis Geführt (A Trip on the Ice). Union-Film, released May 28, 1915.
> Directed by Ernst Lubitsch. Scenario by Hans Kräly. With Albert Paulig and Lubitsch.

Zucker und Zimt (Sugar and Spice). Matray–Lubitsch Film. (2 reels)
> Directed by Ernst Matray and Ernst Lubitsch. Scenario by Ernst Matray, Ernst Lubitsch, and Greta Schröder-Matray. Assistant director: Richard Lowenbein. With Ernst Matray, Ernst Lubitsch, Helene Voss, Alice Scheel-Hechy, Paul Ludwig Stein, Victor Colani.

. . .

There also exists a reference to a film either by or with Lubitsch (perhaps both) called *Komtesse Doddy*. Pola Negri and Harry Liedtke were costarred. If so, it marks the first appearance of these three in a film together, a circumstance which was to be repeated five years later so notably in *Sumurun*. One film lexicon cites Georg Jacoby as the director, but this is not corroborated elsewhere.

1916

Dr. Satansohn (Dr. Satanson).
> Directed by Edmund Edel. Scenario by Edmund Edel. With Ernst Lubitsch, Erich Schönfelder, Hans Felix, Yo Larte, Marga Köhler.

Leutnant auf Befehl (Lieutenant by Command). Projektions A. G.-Union-Film.
> Directed by Ernst Lubitsch. With Ossi Oswalda, Ernst Lubitsch, Victor Janson, Erich Schönfelder.

Wo Ist Mein Schatz? (Where Is My Treasure?). Union-Film, released February 25, 1916.
> Directed by Ernst Lubitsch and starring Lubitsch.

Als Ich Tot War (When I Was Dead).
> Written and directed by Ernst Lubitsch. Lubitsch played a "bon vivant" in a straight role in this feature, but audiences wouldn't accept him in a non-comic role and he returned to short comedies.

Der Schwarze Moritz (Black Moritz). Union-Film, released June 2, 1916.
> Directed by Ernst Lubitsch. Scenario by Louis Taufstein and Eugen Berg. Music by Martin Knopf. Lubitsch's first "musical film." With Lubitsch (in blackface), Erna Albert, Margareta Kupfer. Setting: Berlin. (Stroheim once also appeared in blackface, in a French film, *Tempête sur Paris*, 1939.)

Schuhpalast Pinkus (Shoe Salon Pinkus). Projektions A. G.-Union-Film, released June 9, 1916.
> Directed by Ernst Lubitsch. Scenario by Hans Kräly (his first notable collaboration with Lubitsch, a collaboration subsequently to flower into many of Lubitsch's most famous films) and Erich Schönfelder. Sets by Kurt Richter. With Lubitsch (as Solomon Pinkus), Else Kenter, Guido Herzfeld, Ossi Oswalda. Setting: Berlin.
>
> Lubitsch's first big success as a director.

Der Gemischte Frauenchor (The Mixed Ladies Chorus). Union-Film, released July 21, 1916.
> Directed by and starring Ernst Lubitsch.

Der G.M.B.H. Tenor (The Tenor, Inc.). Union-Film, released December 22, 1916.

> Directed by Ernst Lubitsch. Photography by Theodor Sparkuhl. Costarring Lubitsch and Ossi Oswalda, who was later to become a popular star of the day under Lubitsch and others, especially in the former's *Die Puppe*. Also: Victor Janson.

. . .

> Around this period there appear references to two other possible Lubitsch films, *Die Ehe der Luise Rohrbach* (The Marriage of Luise Rohrbach) and *Fräulein Julie* (Miss Julie) from the Strindberg play. The former costarred Henny Porten and Emil Jannings, but Oscar Messter in his *Mein Weg ins Film* cites Rudolph Biebrach as the director. As to *Fräulein Julie*, Julius Urgiss is credited with the scenario and Asta Nielsen and Alfred Abel are listed as the costars. Divergent sources cite both Leopold Jessner (very possible, since he later did Wedekind's *Erdgeist* in a film, *Lou Lou*) and Felix Basch. However, further corroboration for both films, in any case, is lacking. (The date for this *Fräulein Julie* may even be as late as 1921.)

1917

Ossis Tagebuch (Ossi's Diary). Projektions A. G.-Union-Film, released October 5, 1917.

> Directed by Ernst Lubitsch. Scenario by Lubitsch and Erich Schönfelder. Starring Ossi Oswalda and with Hermann Thimig. Lubitsch's first directorial effort in which he did not also appear as an actor.

Der Blusenkönig (The Blouse King). Union-Film, released November 2, 1917.

> Directed by Ernst Lubitsch, with Lubitsch and Käthe Dorsch. Setting: Berlin.

Wenn Vier Dasselbe Machen (When Four Do Likewise). Union-Film, released November 16, 1917.

> Directed by Ernst Lubitsch. Scenario by Lubitsch and Erich Schönfelder. With Ossi Oswalda, Emil Jannings (the precursor of what was to become one of the cinema's most notable teams: Jannings–Lubitsch), Fritz Schulz. Setting: Berlin.

Ein Fideles Gefängnis (The Merry Jail). Union-Film, released November 30, 1917.

Directed by Ernst Lubitsch. Based on the Johann Strauss operetta, *Die Fledermaus*. With Harry Liedtke, Ossi Oswalda, Erich Schönfelder, Paul Biensfeldt, Käthe Dorsch, Emil Jannings, and Lubitsch (as Frosch the jailer). (Nine years later, in Hollywood, Lubitsch will rework the *Fledermaus* plot from its French original, *Réveillon* by Meilhac and Halévy, for *So This Is Paris*.) Setting: Vienna, pre-World War I.

· · ·

That year Lubitsch signs a new contract with Union-Film.

1918

Prinz Sami (Prince Sami). Union-Film, released January 11, 1918. Directed by Ernst Lubitsch. With Ossi Oswalda and Lubitsch. An oriental burlesque.

Der Rodelkavalier (The Tobaggan Cavalier). Union-Film, released March, 1918.
Directed by Ernst Lubitsch. With Ossi Oswalda, Harry Liedtke, Lubitsch, and Ferry Silka (good old Ferry Silka—what ever became of him?)

Ich Möchte Kein Mann Sein (I Don't Want to Be a Man). Pagu-Ufa Film. (3 reels) (Possibly 1919)
Directed by Ernst Lubitsch from a scenario by Hans Kräly and Lubitsch (now it starts, that epochal collaboration). Photography by Theodor Sparkuhl. Sets by Kurt Richter. With Ossi Oswalda, Ferry Silka, Margareta Kupfer, Kurt Goetz, Victor Janson.
A print of this rare film is in the archives of the George Eastman House in Rochester, thanks to the sleuthing of James Card, its curator of films.

Der Fall Rosentopf (The Rosentopf Case). Union-Film, released September 24, 1918.
Directed by Ernst Lubitsch and costarring Lubitsch and Ossi Oswalda, with Gertrude Hesterberg.

· · ·

All the above listed films, with the exceptions as noted, were for the most part one-reel films and, again with exceptions as noted, comedies.

Die Augen der Mummie Ma (The Eyes of the Mummy Ma). Pro-
jektions A. G.-Union, released by Ufa, October 3, 1918. (Released in the U.S. by Paramount, August 2, 1922.) (55 min.)
  Directed by Ernst Lubitsch (his first feature). Scenario by
  Hans Kräly and Emil Rameau. Photography by Alfred Hansen.
  Sets by Kurt Richter. Setting: Various and Egypt.
  ʾWith Pola Negri (Mara, a temple dancer), Harry Liedtke
  (Wendland, a painter), Emil Jannings (Radu, an Egyptian
  religious fanatic), Max Laurence (Duke of Hohenfels).
  This was Pola Negri's first feature film with Lubitsch as
  director. Also, the first feature which the celebrated trio,
  Lubitsch–Negri–Jannings, did together. Finally, it was the first
  Lubitsch feature film to be shown in America, though, curiously, without his credit as director on the screen. Negri, who
  was to follow Lubitsch to America, was the important "name"
  on this one in the U.S.

Das Mädel vom Ballet (The Ballet Girl). Union-Film, released December 6, 1918. (3 reels)
  Directed by Ernst Lubitsch. With Ossi Oswalda, Harry Liedtke.

. . .

A project to do a film called *Mania* with Pola Negri, sets to be
designed by Paul Leni. Unrealized.

Carmen (released in the U.S. as *Gypsy Blood*). Union-Ufa Produc-
tion, released December 17, 1918. (Released in the U.S. by First
National, May 8, 1921.) (60 min.)
  Directed by Ernst Lubitsch. Scenario by Hans Kräly and Nor-
  bert Falk from the story by Prosper Mérimée. Photography by
  Alfred Hansen. Sets by Karl Machus and Kurt Richter. Setting:
  Early nineteenth-century Spain.
  The story is told in flashback as a tale told by a traveler over
  a campfire at night.[2] The "frame" scenes of the campfire were
  in hand-tinted color.
  With Pola Negri (Carmen), Harry Liedtke (Don José
  Navarro), Magnus Stifter (Escamillo), and Fritz Richard,
  Leopold von Ledebur, Grete Diercks, Wilhelm Diegelmann,
  Heinrich Peer, Paul Biensfeldt, Margarete Kupfer, Sophie Pa-
  gay, Paul Conradi, Max Kronert, Victor Janson, Albert Venohr.

[2] It will be recalled that in Mérimée's story, the tale is also told
"in flashback," by the story's narrator, Don José, to a friend who
visits him in prison. Only Lubitsch, of all those who have tackled
this story, retained the flashback.

The film that put Lubitsch and Negri at the top of the motion-picture profession in Europe. It was not shown in American until after *Passion* (*Madame Dubarry*) and *Deception* (*Anna Boleyn*), however, by which time both their reputations were made here.

Carmen has been one of the hardy perennials of the cinema garden. Although the cinema as an art form was only three years old in 1918 (if we date its beginning in 1915, the year of Griffith's *The Birth of a Nation*), there had already been nine previous filmings of Prosper Mérimée's story, including De Mille's with Geraldine Farrar, and Theda Bara's for Fox, both in 1915. Later versions include those with Viviane Romance and Rita Hayworth as the "rose-between-the-teeth" lady who was to become, at least for the screen, the classic prototype of the *femme fatale*. Curiously, it has never been filmed by the Spaniards themselves, the Raquel Meller version by Jacques Feyder, though filmed in Spain, being essentially a French work. Could it be that its psychology was, *au fond*, not Spanish but French?

Perhaps there is a giveaway, a clue to this, in Christian Jacque's *Carmen* wherein Viviane Romance, in the title role, says to her nasty bandit-paramour, "Some day they're going to hang you and I'll cut you down and use a piece of that rope to make me a belt to bring me luck!" This is a French superstition, not a Spanish one.

There must have been something very basic in Prosper Mérimée's story to have appealed over the years (it was written in 1847) in so many diverse ways: the opera by Bizet, the burlesque by Chaplin (1915), the Moscow Art Theatre's highly stylized production, *Carmencita and the Soldier*, the all-Negro theatrical and film productions of *Carmen Jones*, and even the recent facetious *Carmen Baby*.

A curious new version of the opera *Carmen* was staged by Jean-Louis Barrault at the Metropolitan Opera House in New York City in late 1967, which was described by the critics as an unintentional burlesque.

If there had been no *Carmen* by Mérimée to show them the way, would there have been a *Thaïs* by Anatole France or a *Woman and Puppet* by Pierre Louÿs?

. . .

For 1918 a film attributed to Lubitsch, *Führmann Henschel*, has been cited by Patrick Brion, Mario Verdone, Jean Mitry, Maurice Bessy, Roberto Chiti, and Bernard Eisenschitz, then revoked by him, but not cited by the Deutsche Kinemathek nor by Theodore Huff, among film lexicographers. No further corroboration has been found. It is listed as a Union-Film (its title translates as *The Coachman Henschel*) and was adapted from a story of Gerhart Hauptmann by Hans Kräly. (A clue: did Kräly ever work for directors other than Lubitsch, once they established themselves as such a salutary team?) Photography was by Theodor Sparkuhl. Emil Jannings was starred as an aging coachman who is driven to suicide by the lack of understanding and vulgarity of his second wife, his former housekeeper. It seems to have been a forerunner of such later *Kammerspiel* (small chamber works, as in music) psychological character studies as *Nju* and *The Last Laugh*, also with Jannings, as well as *Scherben* (Fragments) and *Sylvesterabend* (New Year's Eve) by Lupu Pick. (It is also not cited by Curt Riess in *Das Gab's Nur Einmal*, nor by Lotte Eisner, that supreme authority on the German cinema.) Its definitive status as a Lubitsch film remains to be established.

Marionetten (Marionettes).
> Directed by Ernst Lubitsch. Photographed by Greenbaum. With Ernst Matray. (Further details lacking.)

1919

Meier aus Berlin (Meyer of Berlin). Union-Film, released January 17, 1919.
> Directed by Ernst Lubitsch, starring Lubitsch, Ossi Oswalda, Erich Schönfelder. Setting: Berlin.

Meine Frau, die Film Schauspielerin (My Wife, the Film Star). Union-Film, released January 24, 1919. (1200 meters)
> Directed by Ernst Lubitsch. Scenario by Hans Kräly and Lubitsch. Photography by Theodor Sparkuhl. Sets by Kurt Richter. Starring Ossi Oswalda, Paul Biensfeldt, Victor Janson, Hans Kräly, Julius Dewald, Max Kronert. Setting: Berlin.

Schwabenmädle (The Girl from Swabia). Union-Film, released February 21, 1919. (3 reels)
> Directed by Ernst Lubitsch. With Ossi Oswalda and Carl Auen. Setting: Swabia, Germany.

Die Austernprinzessin (The Oyster Princess). Union-Film, released by Ufa June 25, 1919. (70 min.)

Directed by Ernst Lubitsch. Scenario by Hans Kräly and Lubitsch. Photography by Theodor Sparkuhl. Sets by Ernst Stern, Emil Hasler, Karl Machus.[3] Technical advisor: Erich Waschneck. Setting: Pre-World War I Central Europe.

With Ossi Oswalda (daughter of the American Oyster King), Harry Liedtke (Prince Nuki), Victor Janson (Mr. Quaker, the Oyster King), Julius Falkenstein, Kurt Bois, Hans Junkermann, Max Kronert, Albert Paulig.

This feature comedy opened Ufa's first big theatre, the Marmorenhaus. An original score by a twenty-piece orchestra accompanied the film. It was the first satirical long film by Lubitsch, a *genre* he was subsequently to make uniquely his own.

Rausch (Intoxication). Argus-Film, released August 1, 1919. (5 reels)

Directed by Ernst Lubitsch. Scenario by Hans Kräly. From the play *There Are Crimes and Crimes* by Strindberg. Photography by Karl Freund. Sets by Rochus Gliese.

With Asta Nielsen, Alfred Abel, Karl Meinhard, Grete Dierke, Marga Köhler, Frida Richard, Sophie Pagay, Rudolph Klein-Rohden, Heinz Stieda. Setting: Sweden, turn of the century.

Der Lustige Ehemann (The Merry Husband). Pagu-Ufa. (3 reels)

Directed by Leo Lasko. Scenario by Ernst Lubitsch, after an idea by Richard Wilde. Photography by Theodor Sparkuhl. With Victor Janson (in a dual role), Irmgard Bern, Marga Köhler, Heddy Jendry, Wally Koch.

Madame Dubarry (released in the U.S. as *Passion*). Union-Ufa, released September 19, 1919. (Released in the U.S. by First National, December 12, 1920, though possibly October 10 of that year.) The film opened the new Ufa-Palast Am Zoo Theater in Berlin. (Musical score for the American premiere at the Capitol Theatre in New York by David Mendoza and William Axt.) (85 min.)

Directed by Ernst Lubitsch. Scenario by Fred Orbing, Hans Kräly. Photography by Theodor Sparkuhl. Sets by Karl Machus and Kurt Richter. Costumes by Ali Hubert. Technical advisor: Kurt Waschneck. Setting: Paris, eighteenth century.

[3] The Twenty-sixth Venice Film Festival brochure cites Kurt Richter as the sole designer, as does the Lubitsch Retrospective brochure, Berlin, 1967.

Pola Negri (Jeanette Bécu, later Mme. Dubarry); Emil Jannings (Louis XV), Harry Liedtke (Armand de Foix), Eduard von Winterstein (Jean Dubarry), Reinhold Schünzel (Duc de Choiseul), Elsa Berna (Duchesse de Grammont), Frederich Immler (Duc de Richelieu), Gustave Czimeg (Duc d'Aiguillon), Carl Platen (Guillaume Dubarry), Bernhard Goetzke, Magnus Stifter, Paul Biensfeldt, Willy Kaiser, Alexander Ekert, Robert Sortsch-Pla, Marga Köhler.

One of the milestones in the history of the screen and the film which not only established the German film industry as a world contender and inaugurated the glory of Ufa, but which consolidated the reputation of Lubitsch as the foremost European director of the period. With this work Lubitsch became the great "humanizer of history." The first important foreign film shown in the U.S.

(*The Cabinet of Dr. Caligari*, another early epochal German film of 1919 did not première in the U.S. till the spring of the following year, April 10, 1921, under the sponsorship of Samuel Goldwyn.)

. . .

An unrealized project to do *Medea* with Pola Negri after the trilogy, *The Golden Fleece*, by Grillparzer.

Die Puppe (The Doll). Projektions A. G.-Union-Ufa, released December 14, 1919. (60 min.)

Directed by Ernst Lubitsch. Scenario by Hans Kräly and Lubitsch after the operetta by A. E. Wilner, inspired by themes from E. T. A. Hoffmann. Photography by Theodor Sparkuhl. Sets and costumes by Kurt Richter. Technical advisor: Kurt Waschneck. Setting: Central Europe, Pre-World War I.

Ossi Oswalda (the "doll," daughter of Hilarius), Hermann Thimig (Lancelot von Chanterelle, apprentice to Hilarius), Victor Janson (Hilarius, maker of mechanical dolls), Max Kronert (Baron von Chanterelle), Marga Köhler (wife of Hilarius), Gerhard Ritterband (apprentice), Jakob Tiedtke (Prior of the Abbey), Josephine Dora (Nurse), Paul Morgan, Herr Lapitzki, Hedy Searle, Arthur Weinschenk.

Not released in the U.S. until 1928, after initial censor trouble over some anticlerical scenes. Lubitsch appears himself as the "stage manager" in a prologue, arranging the opening set in miniature before the story proper begins. An original "touch," being the only time in screen annals a director did this in his film. Lubitsch regarded it as one of his most inventive films.

1920

Kölhiesels Töchter (Kölhiesel's Daughters). Messter-Union-Ufa, released March 9, 1920. (70 min.)

Directed by Ernst Lubitsch. Scenario by Hans Kräly and Lubitsch, from a story by Friedrich Raff and Julius Urgiss. Photography by Theodor Sparkuhl. Sets by Hans Winter. Costumes by Jan Baluschek. Setting: Bavaria, Germany, Pre-World War I.

With Henny Porten in the dual role of the pretty Gretl and the homely Liesl, and Emil Jannings as Peer Xavero, a dumb ox of a farmhand, vender of Bavarian beer. Also in the cast: Jakob Tiedtke (as Mathias Kölhiesel) and Gustav von Wagenheim (Paul).

This broad Bavarian comedy was so popular that it was subsequently remade twice in Germany as sound films, in 1930 and 1943.

Romeo und Julia im Schnee (Romeo and Juliet in the Snow). Maxim-Film/Ufa, released March 28, 1920. (3 reels)

Directed by Ernst Lubitsch. Scenario by Hans Kräly and Lubitsch. Photography by Theodor Sparkuhl.

With Lotte Neumann, Julius Falkenstein, Jakob Tiedtke, Gustav von Wagenheim, Marga Köhler, Ernest Rückert, Josephine Dora, Paul Biensfeldt, Hermann Picha, Paul Passarge.

Lubitsch's last short comedy.

Sumurun (released in the U.S. as *One Arabian Night*). Premiere at the Ufa-Palast Am Zoo, Berlin. Decla-Bioskop, released by Union-Ufa, September 1, 1920. (Released in the U.S. by First National, October 2, 1921.) (90 min.)

"Ein orientalisches Spiel" from *The Arabian Nights*, after the stage pantomime of Friedrich Freska and Victor Holländer produced by Max Reinhardt. Adapted to the screen by Hans Kräly and Lubitsch. Directed by Ernst Lubitsch. Photography by Theodor Sparkuhl. Sets by Kurt Richter and Erno Metzner. Costumes by Ali Hubert. Technical advisor: Kurt Waschneck. Musical score by Victor Holländer. Setting: Basra, in the Caliphate of Baghdad, ninth century.

Ernst Lubitsch (Yeggar, a hunchback clown, director of a traveling show), Pola Negri (Yannaia, a dancer in the show, enamored of by Yeggar), Paul Wegener (a rich old sheik),

Jenny Hasselquist (Zuleika, known by her name of endearment, Sumurun, the sheik's favorite), Aud Egede Nissen (Haidee, her maid), Harry Liedtke (Nur-al-Djin, a merchant), Carl Clewing (the sheik's son), Margarete Kupfer (the old woman), Jakob Tiedtke (head eunuch of the sheik's harem), Max Kronert (Muffti, first servant of Nur-al-Djin), Paul Graetz (Puffti, second servant of Nur-al-Djin), Paul Biensfeldt (slave dealer).

Lubitsch and Negri had previously appeared in their respective roles in the Reinhardt stage production of what was originally an elaborate pantomime-ballet. With this film, Lubitsch became known as "the Max Reinhardt of the cinema."

There were some 65 feet of censor cuts. The original length of the film was 2400 meters, reduced after the censor cuts to 2379 meters. A contemporary of Lubitsch and another of the earliest German screen pioneers, F. W. Murnau, had earlier that year done *Der Bucklige und die Tänzerin* (The Hunchback and the Dancer), but this was a modern story.

Josef von Sternberg was to declare Lubitsch's playing of the hunchback in *Sumurun* "wonderful."

. . .

An unrealized project to do *Salome* with Pola Negri, with settings by Ernst Stern.

A sketch written by Hans Kräly and Lubitsch especially for Ossi Oswalda, incorporated into her film *Die Wohnungsnot* (The Housing Shortage).

Anna Boleyn (released in the U.S. as *Deception*). Union-Ufa, released December 14, 1920. (Released in the U.S. by Paramount, April 17, 1921; premiere in U.S. at Capitol Theatre, New York.)

Directed by Ernst Lubitsch. Scenario by Fred Orbing, Hans Kräly. Photography by Theodor Sparkuhl. Sets by Kurt Richter and Poelzig. Costumes by Ali Hubert. Musical score for the American premiere, Hugo Riesenfeld. Setting: England, sixteenth century, Tudor period.

Henny Porten (Anne Boleyn), Emil Jannings (Henry VIII), Aud Egede Nissen (Jane Seymour), Paul Hartmann (Henry Norris), Ludwig Hartau, Ferdinand von Alten, Paul Biensfeldt, Wilhelm Diegelmann, Friedrich Kühne, Maria Reisenhofer, Hedwig Pauli, Hilde Müller, Karl Platen, Erling Hanson, Sophie Pagay, Josef Klein.

Lubitsch's most inventive film up to that time.

1921

Die Bergkatze (The Mountain Cat/The Wildcat). Union-Ufa, released April 14, 1921. Premiere at the Ufa-Palast Am Zoo, Berlin. (100 min.)

Directed by Ernst Lubitsch. Scenario by Hans Kräly and Lubitsch. Photography by Theodor Sparkuhl. Sets by Ernst Stern. Costumes by Ernst Stern and Emil Hasler.

Pola Negri (Rischka, the "wildcat"), Victor Janson (Commander of Fort Tossenstein), Paul Heidemann (Lt. Alexis), Wilhelm Diegelmann (Claudius, Rischka's father, brigand chief), Hermann Thimig (Pepo, a timid brigand), Edith Meller (Lilli, daughter of the fort commander), Marga Köhler (wife of the fort commander), Paul Graetz (Zorfano), Max Kronert (Masillio), Erwin Kopp (Tripo), Paul Biensfeldt (Dafko). Setting: Mountains of Central Europe, nineteenth century.

This antimilitarist satire was a favorite of H. L. Mencken.

. . .

Mario Verdone, Leonardo Autera, Roberto Paolella, and Roberto Chiti cite a film, *Vendetta*, as a work of Lubitsch this year, for Union-Film, but it is not corroborated by Jean Mitry, Antonio Barbero, and Theodore Huff. Allegedly costarring Negri, Jannings, and Liedtke. Its definitive status as a Lubitsch film remains to be established. Curt Riess cites it as being before *Die Augen der Mummie Ma*.

1922

Following upon a long-term contract entered into between Lubitsch and the Hamilton Theatrical Corporation of New York, he started his first picture under that contract, *Das Weib des Pharao*, a spectacle with an ancient Egyptian setting.

Das Weib des Pharao (The Wife of Pharaoh). (Released in the U.S. as *The Loves of Pharaoh*.) Efa (Europäische Film Allianz)-Ufa, and Ernst Lubitsch Film, GMBH, released March 14, 1922. (Released in the U.S. by Paramount, February 1, 1922.) Berlin premiere: December 8, 1921. (6 reels)

Directed by Ernst Lubitsch. Scenario by Norbert Falk and Hans Kräly. Photography by Theodor Sparkuhl and Alfred Hansen. Sets by Erno Metzner, Ernst Stern, and Kurt Richter.

Costumes by Ali Hubert. Technical and architectural consultant: Max Gronau. Musical score by Eduard Künneke. Setting: Egypt of the ancient pharaohs.

Musical score in the U.S. by Hugo Riesenfeld.

Emil Jannings (Pharaoh Amenes), Harry Liedtke (Ramphis), Dagny Servaes (Theonis), Paul Wegener (Samlak, King of Ethiopia), Lyda Salmonova (Makeda, his daughter), Albert Basserman (Sotis, the architect), Friedrich Kühne (High Priest), Paul Biensfeldt (Menon, counselor to the pharaoh), Mady Christians, Tina Dietrich.

The most spectacular film produced in Europe up to that time, and technically the most advanced of the spectacles. (Lang's *Siegfried* did not appear until 1923.)

(Again the pioneer, Murnau, antedated Lubitsch's *Pharaoh* film with the Egyptian sequence of his episodic *Satanas* three years before, in 1919, but the first film which may have inspired Lubitsch to do an ancient Egyptian subject was *Der Schädel der Pharaonentochter* (The Skull of Pharaoh's Daughter), directed by one Otz Tollen, also starring Jannings as the pharaoh, made the year before, in 1921. It was again a film of episodes set in five different ages and told chronologically, like *Satanas* and Dreyer's *Leaves from Satan's Diary* [1920]. The parallel and polyphonic treatment of Griffith's episodic *Intolerance*, however, still remains unique as a more sophisticated employment of the cinema medium, especially considering its date, 1916, when the cinema, with the exception of Griffith's own *The Birth of a Nation* the year before, was decidedly a wilderness.)

. . .

On December 22, 1921 Lubitsch arrived in the United States for his first visit, bringing with him a print of his *Pharaoh* film. He came also to study American production methods, for the rising star of Hollywood in the world cinema firmament was even that early already a comet that could no longer be ignored. Theodore Huff reminds us that Lubitsch was present at the opening of Griffith's *Orphans of the Storm* at the Apollo Theatre on West 42nd Street, New York, January 3, 1922. That June, he returned to Germany for another picture under his Hamilton Theatrical Corporation contract.

Die Flamme (The Flame). (Released in the U.S. as *Montmartre*.) Efa-Ufa, and Ernst Lubitsch Film, GMBH, released September 16, 1923. (Released in the U.S. by Paramount, July 1, 1924, after the release of his first two American films, *Rosita* and *The Marriage Circle*.)

Directed by Ernst Lubitsch. Adapted from the play, *Die Flamme* by Hans Müller. Scenario by Hans Kräly and Rudolph Kurtz (who later was to write a classic book on German film Expressionism). Photography by Theodor Sparkuhl and Alfred Hansen. Sets by Ernst Stern and Kurt Richter. Setting: Paris, late nineteenth century.

Pola Negri (Yvette), Hermann Thimig (Leduc, a musician), Alfred Abel (a *flaneur*, his friend), Hilda Wörner (Louise), Max Adalbert, Frida Richard, Jakob Tiedtke.

The one Lubitsch film that was badly mutilated for its American release. The last German film by Lubitsch. It was made with two endings, like Chaplin's *A Woman of Paris* and Pabst's *Pandora's Box*, the original unhappy one for Europe and a happy end for America. In each case, the happy ending was false to the points of their respective themes.

.   .   .

Rumors were bruited about at the time of a new work by Lubitsch to be called *Carnival in Toledo* but nothing materialized, nor did a project on the life of Johann Strauss.

.   .   .

Lubitsch, having been invited by Mary Pickford to direct her in a film, came again to the United States in December, 1922, with his secretary and personal assistant, Heinrich (later Henry) Blanke, bringing with him the treatment (that he had done with Edward Knoblock) of a film to be called *Marguerite and Faust*, based on Goethe's tragedy, which Miss Pickford rejected. Already "America's Sweetheart," she wished to "graduate" from hoydenish roles into something more grown-up. Perhaps finding Marguerite's fate too depressing, she chose *Dorothy Vernon of Haddon Hall*, set against a background of the court of Queen Elizabeth at the time of the Tudors. Lubitsch groaned when he read the scenario. Finally, they compromised on a script that Lubitsch had "up his sleeve" all along against such a contingency—*Rosita*. At Lubitsch's suggestion, Miss Pickford engaged the Danish director, Sven Gade, to do the sets. (Gade, director of Asta Nielsen's *Hamlet*, had come to the U.S. from Denmark to stage *Johannes Kreisler* for the theatrical producer, Arch Selwyn.) For her leading man, Miss Pickford wanted an engaging young man already making a name for himself in Paris—Maurice Chevalier. She didn't get him.

. . .

"Meanwhile, back at the ranch . . ."—which is to say back in Germany—Lubitsch's departure for America was followed by the merger of Paul Davidson's Union-Film with Alfred Hugenberg's Ufa. This in turn was followed by the merger of Union-Ufa with Erich Pommer's Decla(Deutsche Eclair)-Bioskop. Out of these amalgamations emerged the monolith Ufa, which was to become, under the aegis of Erich Pommer as production chief, the biggest and best studio complex not only in Germany but in all of Europe. (Lubitsch, however, was the only big German director who never worked at Ufa or under Pommer.)

¶ THE AMERICAN PERIOD

1923

Rosita. United Artists and the Mary Pickford Co. Premiere at the Lyric Theatre, New York, September 3, 1923. (85 min.)
     Directed by Ernst Lubitsch. From the play *Don Caesar de Bazan* by Adolphe D'Ennery and P. S. P. Dumanoir. Adapted by Edward Knoblock. Scenario by Edward Knoblock and Hans Kräly. Photography by Charles Rosher. Sets by Sven Gade. First assistant to Lubitsch: Jimmy Townsend. Setting: Toledo, Spain, nineteenth century.
     Mary Pickford (Rosita, a street singer), Holbrook Blinn (the King), Irene Rich (the Queen), George Walsh (Don Diego), Charles Belcher (Prime Minister), Frank Leigh (Prison Commandant), Mathilde Comont (Rosita's mother), George Periolat (Rosita's father), Bert Sprotte (jailer), Snitz Edwards (little jailer), Mme. de Bodamere (servant), Phillipe de Lacey and Donald McAlpin (brothers of Rosita), Mario Carillo (majordomo), Doreen Turner (Rosita's sister), Charles Farrell.
     By a coincidence, the same play served Herbert Brenon as a film for Pola Negri, who had followed Lubitsch to America. It was *The Spanish Dancer*, made that same year.

. . .

Following *Rosita*, rumors circulated that Lubitsch would next direct Pickford in *Romeo and Juliet* as her second film with him in his three-picture contract with her. It didn't happen. She went on to make *Dorothy Vernon of Haddon Hall* with Marshall Neilan. Lubitsch then thought of doing Sacha Guitry's *Deburau* which had concluded a successful run on Broadway on the stage the year before. At the same time, he was approached by Douglas Fairbanks to direct him in Doug's forthcoming pirate picture. Said Lubitsch to Fairbanks, "If I ever direct a picture with you, when you're jumping from roof to roof I'll give you something to do on those roofs!" (The Fairbanks project turned out to be *The Black Pirate*, one of the first color films, directed by Albert Parker.)

· · ·

There was a small company, almost a fledgling one, run by four brothers—Harry, Albert, Sam, and Jack Warner—whose biggest epic up to that time had been the 1918 war-propaganda film, *My Four Years in Germany*, from the book by the then American Ambassador to the court of Kaiser Wilhelm II, James W. Gerard. ("America won't fight!" says the Kaiser. "So America won't fight, eh?" answers Gerard in a meaningful close-up.) For the most part, however, they made, in the immortal phrase of Ben Hecht, "pictures about horses, for horses" (and about dogs, for dogs, alas, some of which were directed by a then recent graduate of Mack Sennett's slapstick conservatory, Malcolm St. Clair, who was to become our home-grown Lubitsch beginning with *Are Parents People?* for Paramount in 1925). After completing *Rosita*, Lubitsch saw Chaplin's epochal *A Woman of Paris*, which was to change the whole course of screen direction in one area—the comedy of manners, which, up to that time, had been the special province of Cecil B. De Mille, especially an opus called *Forbidden Fruit*, which surprised Lubitsch by its glints of sharp observation. But if Lubitsch was surprised by this De Mille work, he was absolutely *bouleversé* by the Chaplin film. And although the "Lubitsch touch" was already evident in *Die Flamme* and even before, it was now beginning to flower as never before in the Hollywood gardens, more specifically on the Warner Brothers back lot and the hothouse garden of their studio. For it was this little company that signed Lubitsch, after *Rosita*, to a five-picture contract, which was to put Warner Brothers on the cinematic map the way Stroheim put Universal on the same map three years before with the mordantly sophisticated *Foolish Wives*.

1924

The Marriage Circle. Warner Brothers, released February 3, 1924.
Premiere, Strand Theatre, New York. (8 reels)

Directed by Ernst Lubitsch. From the play *Only a Dream*, by
Lothar Schmidt (Goldschmidt).[4] Adaptation and scenario by
Paul Bern. Assistant directors: James Flood and Henry Blanke.
Photography by Charles Van Enger. Setting: Vienna, pre-
World War I.

Florence Vidor (Charlotte Braun), Monte Blue (Dr. Franz
Braun), Marie Prevost (Mizzi Stock), Adolphe Menjou (Professor Josef Stock), Creighton Hale (Dr. Gustave Müller),
Harry Myers (private detective), Dale Fuller (fresh from her
harrowing role as the mad Maria Macapa in Stroheim's *Greed*,
as the neurotic patient), Esther Ralston.

Inspired by Chaplin's *A Woman of Paris*, Lubitsch's own
epochal first American comedy of manners in turn was to in-
spire a whole school of filmmakers here, including Malcolm St.
Clair, H. d'Abbadie d'Arrast (who had been Chaplin's assistant
on *A Woman of Paris* and *The Gold Rush*), Frank Tuttle,
Richard Rosson, Monta Bell, Erle Kenton, Roy Del Ruth,
Frank Capra, Rouben Mamoulian, Preston Sturges, the early
Lewis Milestone, etc.

The Marriage Circle was a favorite film of George Jean
Nathan, that arch *ciné*-misanthrope, and of Chaplin and
Kurosawa. In 1927, Lubitsch told Robert E. Sherwood that it
was his own favorite of all his films. It remains also the favorite
Lubitsch film of Alfred Hitchcock.

Following the completion of *The Marriage Circle*, Lubitsch
again picked up the idea to do *Deburau*, as his second film for
Warners. And again he was deflected from this project, this
time by an altogether different subject.

Three Women. Warner Brothers, released October 5, 1924. (75
min.)

Directed by Ernst Lubitsch. Story by Lubitsch and Hans Kräly,
adapted from Yolanthe Marees's *The Lilie*. Scenario by Hans
Kräly. Photography by Charles Van Enger. Setting: America,
early twenties.

Pauline Fredrick (Mrs. Mabel Wilton), May McAvoy
(Jeanne, her daughter), Marie Prevost (Harriet), Lew Cody

[4] Lothar Schmidt translated the letters of Ninon de L'Enclos.

(Edmund Lamont), Willard Louis (John Howard), Pierre Gendron (Fred Colman), Mary Carr (his mother), Raymond McKee (Harvey Craig).

A rich but aging widow, her young and innocent daughter, and a rake's mistress are the three women of the title, all "romanced" (in Hollywood parlance) by the same rake and each for a different purpose. A harsh and incisive probing of feminine psychology.

Forbidden Paradise. Paramount, released November 16, 1924. Premiere at the Rialto Theatre, New York. (60 min.)

Directed by Ernst Lubitsch. From the play, *The Czarina*, by Lajos Biro and Melchior Lengyel. Scenario by Hans Kräly and Agnes Christine Johnston. Photography by Charles Van Enger. Sets by Hans Dreier (who was a decade later to collaborate on the sets for another film on Catherine II of Russia in Sternberg's *The Scarlet Empress*). Setting: a mythical Slavic kingdom of pre-World War I.

Pola Negri (Catherine, the Czarina), Adolphe Menjou (court chamberlain), Rod La Rocque (Capt. Alexis Czerny), Pauline Starke (Anna, lady-in-waiting to the Czarina and fiancée of Capt. Alexis), Fred Malatesta (French ambassador), Nick de Ruiz (the rebellious general), Carrie D'Aumery, Clark Gable as an extra.

Loosely inspired by the amorous intrigues of Catherine II ("the Great") of Russia, the film was a modernied adaptation of a Broadway stage success, *The Czarina*, starring Doris Keane. Although ostensibly set in eighteenth-century Russia, Lubitsch introduced such raffish updatings as the Czarina's bobbed hair, a motor car, and checkbooks, in his aim to make this a satire on all queens, on the frailty of all women, in all times.

Voted one of the ten best films of 1925 and termed by Paul Rotha in 1949 "Lubitsch's most brilliant film."

1925

Kiss Me Again. Warner Brothers, released August 2, 1925. Premiere at the Piccadilly Theatre, New York. (7 reels)

Directed by Ernst Lubitsch. From the play, *Divorçons* (Let's Get Divorced) by Victorien Sardou and Émile de Najac. Scenario by Hans Kräly. Photography by Charles Van Enger. Setting: Paris of the twenties.

Marie Prevost (Loulou Fleury), Monte Blue (Gaston Fleury,

her husband), John Roche (Maurice Ferrière, a concert pianist, enamored of Loulou), Willard Louis (Dubois, a divorce lawyer), Clara Bow (Grizette, Dubois's secretary).

A favorite film of Robert Flaherty and Edmund Wilson. Voted one of the ten best films of 1925.

Lady Windermere's Fan. Warner Brothers, released December 27, 1925. Premiere at the Piccadilly Theatre, New York. (80 min.)
    Directed by Ernst Lubitsch. Adapted from the play of Oscar Wilde by Julien Josephson. Photography by Charles Van Enger. Setting: London of the early twenties.
    Irene Rich (Mrs. Erlynne), May McAvoy (Lady Windermere), Bert Lytell (Lord Windermere), Ronald Colman (Lord Darlington), Edward Martindel (Lord Augustus), Helen Dunbar, Carrie d'Aumery, Billie Bennett (three gossipy duchesses).
    A *tour de force*, capturing the Wildean spirit without the use of a single Wildean epigram. Lubitsch said they had no place in a silent film and substituted visual epigrams for the spoken Wilde wit.
    Alfred Kerr, the famous Berlin dramatic critic, called it a work "in the purest Burgtheater style," and it was a favorite film of Edmund Wilson. Voted one of the ten best films of 1925. (Three Lubitsch films made that list that year—an unparalleled feat.)

1926

In July 1926, it was reported that Mary Pickford and Douglas Fairbanks would costar in a film under the dual direction of Max Reinhardt and Lubitsch. It didn't happen. Instead, Lubitsch made . . .

So This Is Paris. Warner Brothers, released August 15, 1926. Premiere at the Cameo Theatre, New York, sponsored by Symon Gould of the Film Arts Guild.
    Directed by Ernst Lubitsch. Scenario and adaptation by Hans Kräly from the play, *Réveillon,* by Henri Meilhac and Ludovic Halévy. Photography by John Mescall. Setting: Paris of the twenties. (60 min.)
    Monte Blue (Dr. Giraud), Patsy Ruth Miller (Suzanne Giraud, his wife), Lilyan Tashman (Georgette Lalle, an "old flame" of Dr. Giraud), André de Beranger (Monsieur Lalle, her husband), Myrna Loy (the maid), Sidney D'Albrook (the cop).

The source of this comedy was the same as for Johann Strauss's operetta *Die Fledermaus*.

"In one sequence," went a report at the time, "Lubitsch has pictured a host of dance-crazed revelers performing the Charleston. Like an animated cubist painting, his camera has caught the pulsing pandemonium of the scene and the tempo of his dissolving scenes has the swing of a futuristic rhapsody. The kaleidoscopic sequence discloses a blazingly illuminated ballroom where hundreds are hitting the highspots with the Charleston. It glows, it fades. The grinning wide-mouth face of the Negro jazzbo appears, dims. Now are seen misty, tipsily lifted glasses, faint swift-swept fiddle bows, laughing or leering faces, twinkling toes, rattling drums—all intermingling, tantalizing, exhilarating, a chaos of impressions."

Voted one of the ten best films of 1926.

Lubitsch then left for Germany, his first return since his American screen debut, to film exteriors and backgrounds for his next picture, *Old Heidelberg*, later titled *The Student Prince*.

1927

The Student Prince. Metro-Goldwyn-Mayer, released September 21, 1927. Premiere at the Capitol Theatre, New York.

Directed by Ernst Lubitsch. Adapted from the play, *Old Heidelberg*, by W. Meyer-Förster and the operetta, *The Student Prince*, by Dorothy Donnelly and Sigmund Romberg. Scenario by Hans Kräly. Photography by John Mescall. Settings by Cedric Gibbons and Richard Day (who had previously designed for Stroheim *Foolish Wives*, *The Merry Widow*, and *The Wedding March* in collaboration with E.v.S.). Costumes by Ali Hubert. Assistant: Eric Locke. Editor: Andrew Marton. Titles by Marian Ainslee (who collaborated with Stroheim on the titles for *Foolish Wives*) and Ruth Cummings. An Irving Thalberg production. Musical score by David Mendoza and William Axt (who had arranged the musical scores for Stroheim's *The Merry Widow* and King Vidor's *The Big Parade*). Setting: pre-World War I Heidelberg, Germany. (10 reels)

Ramon Novarro (Prince Karl Heinrich), Norma Shearer (Kätchen), Jean Hersholt (who had played the harrowing role of Marcus Scholer in Stroheim's *Greed*, now as the genial Dr. Juttner, tutor to the Prince), Gustave von Seyffertitz (who was to become a favorite player for Sternberg, as King Karl VII), Phillipe De Lacey (Prince Karl as a child), Edgar Nor-torn (Lutz), Bobby Mack (Kellermann), Edward Connelly (Court Marshall), Otis Harlan (Old Ruder), John S. Peters (a student), Edythe Chapman, Lionel Belmore, Lincoln Steadman, George K. Arthur.

(This had been made once before in Hollywood in 1915 as *Old Heidelberg* by Triangle, supervised by D. W. Griffith, starring Dorothy Gish and Wallace Reid. Stroheim was technical advisor on sets and costumes.)

Reportedly "doctored" after Lubitsch completed his original version, the love scenes were retaken by John Stahl at Louis B. Mayer's request. Lubitsch was also unhappy with the casting, the two stars having been imposed on him by MGM (Miss Shearer being the wife of the producer and Novarro being far too Latin for his role). But Lubitsch's imprint remained.

. . .

A year before, in October, 1926, Lubitsch had signed a contract with Paramount to prepare for the reuniting of Jannings, whom Paramount was about to import, and his erstwhile successful director in Germany.

. . .

After completing *The Student Prince*, Lubitsch mentioned to Josef von Sternberg an idea for a film based on a true occurrence, in which a former Czarist general, cast up by the Russian Revolution on these shores, a refugee and an exile, had drifted, like so many others, to Hollywood where he found work as an extra playing his once real-life role. The film became one of Sternberg's greatest successes, *The Last Command*, starring Emil Jannings, released in January, 1928.

Lubitsch followed *The Last Command* with a Russian subject of his own that same year, also with Jannings, their first reunion since *Das Weib des Pharao* in Berlin six years before.

1928

The Patriot. Paramount, released August 17, 1928. Premiere at the Rialto Theatre, New York. (12 reels)

Directed by Ernst Lubitsch. Adapted by Hans Kräly from the novel by Alfred Neumann, the stage adaptation by Ashley Dukes, and from *Paul I* by Dimitri Merejkowski. Photographed by Bert Glennon. Sets by Hans Dreier. Costumes by Ali Hubert. Titles by Julian Johnson. Music (synchronized score) by Domenico Savino and Gerard Garbonaro. Setting: Russia, 1796–1801.

Emil Jannings (Czar Paul I, son of Catherine the Great and the mad Peter I), Lewis Stone (Count Pahlen, "the patriot"), Florence Vidor (Countess Anna Ostermann), Neil Hamilton (Crown Prince Alexander), Harry Cording (Stefan), Vera Voronina (Mlle. Lapoukhine, the Czar's mistress).

Lubitsch may have been inspired to tackle this subject following the success of Alfred Neumann's dramatization in Berlin in a production directed by Leopold Jessner at the Lessing Theatre. Fritz Kortner played the mad Czar, with Paul Wegener as Pahlen, in a memorable performance. Gilbert Miller had produced it in New York the season before the film opened with no success.

Having been completed on the eve of the advent of the sound film, *The Patriot* (like others of the last big silent films) was not only given a synchronized musical score but had sound effects grafted onto it, and occasional voices at climactic moments, such as Jannings's cry, "Pahlen! Pahlen!" calling for his best friend when he realizes an attempt is being made to assassinate him (engineered by Pahlen, of course, as his patriotic deed for Russia). Originally, all voice sounds were assigned to subtitles and Lubitsch was not responsible for the added sound. It was Lubitsch's swan song with Jannings.

Voted one of the ten best films of 1928. (Sternberg did not care for it and had a temporary falling out with Lubitsch over it. Six years later, he was to do a similar subject about the mad Czar Peter III and his consort, Catherine, in *The Scarlet Empress*.)

1929

Eternal Love. United Artists, released May 12, 1929. (9 reels)

Directed by Ernst Lubitsch. From the novel *Der König der Bernina* by Jakob Christoph Beer. Adaptation and scenario by Hans Kräly. Photography by Oliver Marsh. Titles by Katherine Hilliker and H. H. Caldwell. Editor: Andrew Marton. Music (synchronized) by Hugo Riesenfeld. A Joseph M. Schenck production; John W. Considine, associate producer. Setting: Switzerland, early nineteenth century, during the Napoleonic invasion of Austria.

John Barrymore (Marcus Paltram), Camilla Horn (fresh from playing Marguerite in Murnau's *Faust*, as Ciglia), Victor Varconi (Lorenz Gruber), Mona Rico (Pia), Hobart Bosworth (Pastor Tass), Bodil Rosing (housekeeper), Evelyn Selbie (Pia's mother).

"Lost" in the flurry that accompanied the changeover in the public's interest from the silent film to the sound film, it appears also to have been an unsympathetic vehicle for all concerned, including the director, though even here there were occasional "Lubitsch touches." It was Lubitsch's last silent feature and his last with Hans Kräly, his longtime scenarist. Some sound effects were added.

. . .

Lubitsch was to have directed another silent film, *The Tempest*, with John Barrymore, whom he regarded highly, from a story with a Russian locale by Erich von Stroheim, for Joseph M. Schenck, also for United Artists. He demurred, however, and the directorial reins went to an emigré White Russian who had previously worked in Paris, Vyatcheslav Tourjansky, following which Lewis Milestone took over, and following him, Sam Taylor. Lubitsch was right; he could "smell" the "jinx" on this one. The film that resulted was so (to put it politely) "undistinguished" that Stroheim insisted his name be removed as author of the original story.

Anne Nichols's hit play, *Abie's Irish Rose*, was suggested to Lubitsch as his first sound film but he rejected it as not being for him.

The Love Parade. Paramount, released November 19, 1929. (12 reels)

Directed by Ernst Lubitsch. From the play, *The Prince Consort*, by Leon Xanrof and Jules Chancel. Adaptation and screenplay by Ernest Vajda and Guy Bolton. Photography by Victor Milner. Settings by Hans Dreier. Music by Victor Schertzinger (who was, himself, a director) with lyrics by Clifford Grey. Setting: A mythical kingdom—Sylvania—on the order of Monaco, pre-World War I. Songs: "Ooh La, La," "Paris, Stay the Same," "Dream Lover," "My Love Parade," "Let's Be Common," "Grenadiers' Song," "Nobody's Using It Now," "The Queen Is Always Right."

Maurice Chevalier (Count Alfred Renard), Jeanette MacDonald (Queen Louise of Sylvania), Lupino Lane (Jacques, valet to Count Alfred), Lillian Roth (Lulu, maid to Queen Louise), Edgar Norton (master of ceremonies), Lionel Belmore (Prime Minister), Albert Roccardi (Foreign Minister), Carleton Stockdale (Admiral), Eugene Pallette (Minister of War), E. H. Calvert (Sylvanian Ambassador), Yola d'Avril (Paulette, mistress of Count Alfred), André Sheron (her jealous "hoos-

bond"), Margaret Fealy (first lady-in-waiting to Queen
Louise), Virginia Bruce (second lady-in-waiting), Russell
Powell (Afghan Ambassador), Winter Hall (bishop), Ben
Turpin (lackey), Anton Vaverka, Albert de Winton, Wilhelm
von Hardenburg, Josephine Hall, Rosalind Charles, Helene
Friend, Jean Harlow (as an extra in the theatre audience).

Lubitsch's first sound film and a milestone in the development of that genre, being, indeed, as Theodore Huff pointed
out, "the first truly cinematic screen musical in America." He
could have included Europe, as René Clair's epochal *Sous les
Toits de Paris* did not appear in Paris until the following year.
But for 1929, the three most notable of all the very first sound
films were *The Love Parade*, Mamoulian's *Applause*, and King
Vidor's *Hallelujah*. (Chaplin was still making silent films, and
The Blue Angel and *Morocco* by Sternberg, also notable among
the earliest sound films, did not appear until 1930.)

1930

Paramount on Parade. Paramount, released April 19, 1930. (102
min.)
A revue, choreographed by David Bennett, designed by John
Wenger, supervised by Elsie Janis, with twelve Paramount directors participating, including Ernst Lubitsch. Photography by
Harry Fishbeck and Victor Milner.
Lubitsch sequences: "The Origin of the Apache Dance," "A
Park in Paris," and "Sweeping the Clouds Away," all starring
Maurice Chevalier, with Evelyn Brent costarring in the first.
Featuring the songs, "All I Want Is Just One Girl" (Whiting–
Robin) and "Sweeping the Clouds Away" (Sam Coslow).

Monte Carlo. Paramount, released August 27, 1930. (90 min.)
Directed by Ernst Lubitsch. From the play, *The Blue Coast*,
by Hans Müller, and episodes from *Monsieur Beaucaire*, by
Booth Tarkington and Evelyn Sutherland. Screenplay by Ernest
Vajda. Additional dialogue by Vincent Lawrence. Photographed
by Victor Milner. Sets by Hans Dreier. Music by Richard Whiting and Frank Harling. Lyrics by Leo Robin. Setting: Monte
Carlo, the twenties.
Songs: "Give Me a Moment Please," "Always," "Beyond
the Blue Horizon," "This Is Something New to Me," "Women,
Just Women," "I'm a Simple-Hearted Man," "You'll Love Me
and Like It," "Whatever It Is, It's Grand."
Jack Buchanan (Count Rudolph Fallière), Jeanette Mac-

Donald (Countess Vera von Conti), Zasu Pitts (back to the comic roles after being rescued from them by Stroheim in *Greed* and *The Wedding March*, two of the most beautiful performances ever given by an actress in the annals of the screen, now as Maria, maid to the Countess), Tyler Brooke (Armand), Claude Allister (Prince Otto von Seibenheim), Lionel Belmore (Duke Gustave von Seibenheim, his father), John Roche (Paul, a ladies' hairdresser), Albert Conti (master of ceremonies), Billy Bevan (train conductor), Donald Novis ("Monsieur Beaucaire"), Helen Garden ("Lady Mary"), David Percy (herald), Erik Bey (Lord Winterset), Sidney Bracey (hunchback at casino), Edgar Norton, Geraldine Dvorak.

Famous for the "Blue Express" train sequence and its accompanying song, "Beyond the Blue Horizon," orchestrating flying rails, whirring train wheels, the chorus of peasants in the passing fields, and Jeanette MacDonald's singing through the speeding train window into an exhilarating grandslam ending as the train hurtles its way "beyond the blue horizon" to happiness for the romantic couple. The "Lubitsch touch" was also a virtuoso one, as witness the impressionistic Charleston Ball sequence in *So This Is Paris* and this high-spirited exercise in cinema *panache*. The last vestiges of the operetta stage had now disappeared and Lubitsch had achieved absolute fluidity of camera movement as in his best silent films, while sound has now been deftly integrated with the image.

Lubitsch was then offered Dreiser's *An American Tragedy* by Paramount after they had rejected Eisenstein's scenario for it. He declined and Sternberg finally did it.

1931

The Smiling Lieutenant. Paramount, released March 22, 1931. Premiere at the Criterion Theatre, New York. (102 min.)

Directed by Ernst Lubitsch. Based on the operetta *A Waltz Dream*, by Leopold Jacobson and Felix Dormann, with music by Oscar Strauss, and the novel *Nux, der Prinzgemahl*, by Hans Müller. Adaptation and screenplay by Ernest Vajda, Samson Raphaelson, and Lubitsch. Photographed by George Folsey. Sets by Hans Dreier. Music by Oscar Strauss. Lyrics by Clifford Grey. Setting: Vienna, pre-World War I.

Maurice Chevalier (Niki), Claudette Colbert (Franzi), Miriam Hopkins (Princess Anna), George Barbier (King Adolf, her father), Charles Ruggles (Max), Hugh O'Connell (orderly), Robert Strange (Adjutant von Rockoff), Janet Reade

(Lily), Lon MacSunday (Emperor), Elizabeth Patterson (Baroness von Schwedel), Harry Bradley (Count von Halden), Werner Saxtorph (Josef), Karl Stall (master of ceremonies), Granville Bates (bill collector).

Lubitsch had originally been assigned by Ufa to direct the silent version of this operetta based on a 1907 novel, *Nux, the Prince Consort*, by Hans Müller, and the Jacobson–Dormann libretto. After Lubitsch's departure for America, the project was reassigned to Ludwig Berger, with the success we know. (MGM released it in the U.S. as *The Waltz Dream*.) (The "model" may have been Prince Albert, prince consort to Queen Victoria.) Now that sound had come in, Lubitsch picked up the project he had dropped a decade before to take fullest advantage of the Strauss music on the sound track. Compared with the evanescent charm of Berger's silent version, *The Smiling Lieutenant* was a brash "Americanization," but with a buoyant gusto and exuberance that had become so characteristic of the "Americanized" Lubitsch himself.

1932

The Man I Killed. (Later released as *Broken Lullaby*.) Paramount, released January 19, 1932. Premiere at the Criterion Theatre, New York. (77 min.)

Directed by Ernst Lubitsch. From the play *L'Homme Que J'ai Tué*, by Maurice Rostand and the American adaptation by Reginald Berkeley. Screenplay by Ernest Vajda, Samson Raphaelson. Photography by Victor Milner. Sets by Hans Dreier. Setting: Germany, Post-World War I.

Lionel Barrymore (Dr. Hölderlin), Nancy Carroll (Elsa), Phillips Holmes (Paul), Tom Douglas (Walter Hölderlin), Zasu Pitts (Anna), Lucien Littlefield (Schultz), Louise Carter (Frau Hölderlin), Frank Sheridan (priest), George Bickel (Bresslauer), Emma Dunn (Frau Müller), Tully Marshall (gravedigger), Lillian Elliott (Frau Bresslauer), Marvin Stephens (Fritz), Reginald Pasch (his father), Joan Standing (flowershop girl), Rodney McKennon (war veteran), Torben Meyer (waiter at inn).

A pacifist tract, Lubitsch's only dramatic sound film. One of Jean Mitry's two favorite Lubitsch films.

One Hour with You. Paramount, released March 22, 1932. (9 reels)

Directed by Ernst Lubitsch. Dialogue director, George Cukor. From the play, *Only a Dream*, by Lothar Schmidt. Screenplay by Samson Raphaelson. Photography by Victor Milner. Sets by Hans Dreier. Music by Oscar Strauss and Richard Whiting. Lyrics by Leo Robin. Setting: Paris, early thirties.

Songs: "Mitzi," "What Would You Do?" "One Hour With You," "What a Little Thing Like a Wedding Ring Can Do," "We Will Always Be Sweethearts," "Three Times a Day."

Maurice Chevalier (Dr. André Bertier), Jeanette MacDonald (Colette Bertier), Genevieve Tobin (Mitzi Olivier), Roland Young (Professor Olivier), Charles Ruggles (Adolphe), George Barbier (Police Commissioner), Josephine Dunn (Mlle. Martel), Richard Carle (detective), Charles Judels (policeman), Barbara Leonard (Mitzi's maid).

A musical remake of *The Marriage Circle*. A French version was also made with Chevalier and MacDonald.

Trouble in Paradise. Paramount, released November 8, 1932. Premiere at the Rivoli Theatre, New York. (83 min.)

Directed and produced by Ernst Lubitsch. From the play, *The Honest Finder*, by Laszlo Aladar. Screenplay by Samson Raphaelson. Photography by Victor Milner. Sets by Hans Dreier. Music by W. Frank Harling. Setting: Venice, Paris, early thirties.

Miriam Hopkins (Lily), Kay Francis (Marianne), Herbert Marshall (Gaston Monescu), Charles Ruggles (The Major), Edward Everett Horton (François), C. Aubrey Smith (Giron), Robert Greig (Jacques, the butler).

This masterpiece of sardonic humor was Lubitsch's own favorite. (Also Jean Mitry's.)

If I Had a Million. Paramount, released December 2, 1932. (88 min.)

Seven variations on a theme by seven directors. From a story by Robert Dell Andrews, *Windfall*. The seven directors were: Lubitsch, Norman Taurog, Stephen S. Roberts, Norman McLeod, James Cruze, William A. Seiter, H. Bruce Humberstone. Production supervision: Ernst Lubitsch. Setting of Lubitsch sequence: America, early thirties.

The Lubitsch sequence was written by himself and starred Charles Laughton. With one character, three words, and a sound effect (a "razzberry"), Lubitsch achieved not only the shortest but also the most hilarious episode of the seven. This razz had to be reshot for England into something less "obscene." Although the directors of the sequences were not individually identified, everyone guessed correctly which was Lubitsch's.

1933

Early in 1933, Lubitsch appeared in a bit part, as himself, in *Mr. Broadway*, a comedy starring Ed Sullivan and other show people, directed by Johnnie Walker and Edgar G. Ulmer. (Source: Bernard Eisenschitz.)

Design for Living. Paramount, released November 19, 1933. (90 min.)

Directed by Ernst Lubitsch. From the play by Noël Coward. Adaptation and screenplay by Ben Hecht. Photography by Victor Milner. Sets by Hans Dreier. Music by Nathaniel Finston. Setting: America, early thirties.

Fredric March (Tom), Gary Cooper (George), Miriam Hopkins (Gilda), Edward Everett Horton (Max), Franklin Pangborn (Mr. Douglas), Isabel Jewel (lisping stenographer), Harry Dunkinson, Helena Phillips, James Donlin, Vernon Steele, Thomas Braidon, Jane Darwell, Armand Kaliz, Adrienne D'Ambricourt, Wyndham Standing, Nora Cecil, George Savidan, Cosmo Bellew, Barry Vinton, Emile Chautard (first film teacher of Josef von Sternberg), Mrs. Treboal.

A misguided attempt by Ben Hecht to duplicate the feat accomplished by Lubitsch in transferring *Lady Windermere's Fan* to the screen without a line of Wilde's dialogue. Hecht boasted he retained but one line of Coward's ("For the good of our immortal souls!"), substituting farcical gags. He was, of course, constrained by the Hays Office (the film industry's own self-regulatory moral code) from utilizing Coward's amoral text to an important extent. Anyway, this *ménage à trois*, about "three people who love each other very much" (Coward's description of his play), was better served on the stage when Alfred Lunt, Lynn Fontanne, and Coward himself played it. The Hollywood players, for all their physical charm, were no match for these virtuosi.

1934

The Merry Widow. Metro-Goldwyn-Mayer, released October 11, 1934. (110 min.)

Directed by Ernst Lubitsch. Produced by Irving Thalberg.

Based on the operetta by Victor Leon and Leo Stein, music by Franz Lehár. Screenplay by Ernest Vajda and Samson Raphaelson. Photography by Oliver Marsh. Sets by Cedric Gibbons, Gabriel Scognamillo, Fredric Hope, and Edwin B. Willis. Wardrobe by Ali Hubert and Adrian. Choreography by Albertina Rasch. Music by Franz Lehár, adapted and arranged by Herbert Stothart. Lyrics by Lorenz Hart, and Gus Kahn. Setting: A mythical kingdom—Illyria—remotely derived from Pre-World War I Montenegro, the original setting.

Maurice Chevalier (Prince Danilo), Jeanette MacDonald (Sonia), Edward Everett Horton (Ambassador), Una Merkel (Queen Dolores), George Barbier (King Achmed), Ruth Channing (Lolo), Sterling Holloway (orderly), Donald Meek (valet), Hermann Bing (Zizipoff), Henry Armetta (the Turk), Minna Gombell (who had appeared as the prostitute in Stroheim's unreleased *Walking Down Broadway* the year before, as Marcelle), Akim Tamiroff, Shirley Ross, Barbara Leonard, George Davis, Dorothy Nelson, Eleanor Hunt, Erik Rhodes.

Jeanette MacDonald was chosen when Grace Moore, originally assigned the title role, refused second billing to Chevalier. A French version with Chevalier and MacDonald was also made.

.   .   .

Because *The Merry Widow* was the last film Lubitsch made with Maurice Chevalier, one film should be noted here that both wanted to make together, which, somehow, never got made. (Even Adolphe Menjou stated that he, too, hoped Lubitsch would make it with him.) The project was derived from a boulevard farce by De Flers and Caillavet, who, along with Georges Feydeau, Marivaux, Labiche, Sardou, de Najac, Halévy, and that merry company of French *fin-de-siècle* playwrights, were convulsing Parisian theatre audiences with ribald laughter. The play was *Papa* and—but let Chevalier describe it himself, as he did in a letter to me dated July 12, 1967: "I always regretted not having made that picture with Ernst Lubitsch, as I always considered him the greatest director I have worked with. It was a story about a father (*Papa*) who, trying to arrange a quarrel with the sweetheart of his son, became so convincing that the girl fell head over heels in love with him." An adaptation by Zoë Akins for the American stage played successfully on Broadway in 1919.

.   .   .

In 1935, Lubitsch became production chief of Paramount and, during the course of Sternberg's filming of the latter's last film with Marlene Dietrich at that studio, changed its title (for box-office reasons) from *Caprice Espagnole* (Sternberg's title) to *The Devil Is a Woman*.

.   .   .

1936

In April, 1936, Lubitsch went abroad, first to Paris, then to Vienna, finally to Moscow. In Vienna he met Walter Reisch, the brilliant young Viennese scenarist of *Maskerade, Episode, Unfinished Symphony*, and imparted to him a long-held, but secret, wish—his desire to do a sumptuous film in color of Richard Strauss's comic opera *Der Rosenkavalier*. This never materialized. (See *An Interview with Walter Reisch* in this book for details.)

Desire. Paramount, released April 11, 1936. (89 min.)
    Supervised by Ernst Lubitsch in his new role as production chief of Paramount. Directed by Frank Borzage. A remake of the German film *Die Schönen Tage von Aranjuez*, and its French version, *Adieu les Beaux Jours*, both starring Brigitte Helm in the Dietrich role. Derived from a play by Hans Szekely and R. A. Stemmle. Director of the original film versions: Johannes Meyer. Supervisor of the French version: Serge de Poligny. American adaptation and screenplay by Edwin Justus Mayer, Waldemar Young, and Samuel Hoffenstein. Photography by Charles Lang and Victor Milner. Sets by Hans Dreier, Robert Usher. Music by Frederick Holländer (whose songs for *The Blue Angel* had so helped bring Dietrich to fame). Lyrics by Leo Robin. Setting: Spain, mid-thirties.
    Marlene Dietrich (Madcleine de Beaupré), Gary Cooper (Tom Bradley), John Halliday (Carlos Margoli), William Frawley (Mr. Gibson), Ernest Cossart (Aristide Duval), Akim Tamiroff (police official), Alan Mowbray (Dr. Edouard Pauquet), Effie Tilbury (Aunt Olga), Enrique Acosta (Pedro), Alice Feliz (Pepi), Stanley Andrew (customs inspector).
    The American version retained the Spanish locale of the original.

.   .   .

In his new role as producer instead of director, Lubitsch next suggested a remake of Paramount's silent 1926 *Hotel Imperial*, starring Pola Negri, which Mauritz Stiller and Erich Pommer had so successfully produced from Lajos Biro's *Hotel Stadt*

Lemberg, about the effect the war had on a small, nondescript wayside hotel in Galicia during the Austro–Russian fighting in the early months of World War I. Henry Hathaway was to have directed, with Marlene Dietrich and Charles Boyer playing the Pola Negri and James Hall roles.

It was to be called *I Loved a Soldier*. When William Le Baron suddenly replaced Lubitsch as production chief of Paramount, Margaret Sullavan replaced Dietrich, but following an accident sustained by Miss Sullavan the film was abandoned. Two years later, using the same sets but with a new script, and starring Isa Miranda, the picture was finally remade as *Hotel Imperial*. It was no match for the silent Stiller version.

1937

Angel. Paramount, released November 3, 1937.

Directed by Ernst Lubitsch. Based on a play by Melchior Lengyel. Adapted by Guy Bolton and Russell Medcraft. Screenplay by Samson Raphaelson. Photography by Charles Lang. Sets by Hans Dreier, Robert Usher, and A. E. Freudman. Music by Frederick Holländer. Lyrics by Leo Robin. Setting: London, Paris, mid-thirties.

Marlene Dietrich (Lady Maria Barker), Herbert Marshall (Sir Frederick Barker), Melvyn Douglas (Anthony Halton), Edward Everett Horton (Graham), Ernest Cossart (Walton), Laura Hope Crewes (Grand Duchess Anna Dmitrievna), Ivan Lebedeff, Herbert Mundin, Dennie Moore, Lionel Pape, Phyllis Coghlan, Leonard Carey, Eric Wilton, Gerald Hamer, Herbert Evans, Michael Visaroff, Olf Hytten, Duci Kerekjarto (the gypsy violinist), Sam Harris.

. . .

That year, the Academy of Motion Picture Arts awarded Lubitsch a special "Oscar" for his "twenty-five years' contribution to the motion pictures," dating it from his first work as an actor at Union-Film in Berlin in 1913.

1938

Bluebeard's Eighth Wife. Paramount, released March 23, 1938. (80 min.)

Produced and directed by Ernst Lubitsch. From the play by Alfred Savoir and its American adaptation by Charlton Andrews. Screenplay by Charles Brackett and Billy Wilder. Photography by Leo Tover. Sets by Hans Dreier, Robert Usher, and A. E. Freudman. Gowns by Travis Banton. Music by Werner Heymann. Setting: France, mid-thirties.

Claudette Colbert (Nicole de Loiselle), Gary Cooper (Michael Brandon), Edward Everett Horton (Marquis de Loiselle), David Niven (Albert De Regnier), Elizabeth Patterson (Aunt Hedwige), Hermann Bing [5] (Monsieur Pepinard), Warren Hymer (Kid Mulligan), Franklin Pangborn (assistant hotel manager), Armand Cortes, Rolfe Sedan, Lawrence Grant, Lionel Pape, Tyler Brooke, Tom Ricketts, Barlowe Borland, Charles Halton—and Sacha Guitry emerging from a hotel in a Cannes background shot.

Savoir's farce had previously served as a starring vehicle on the stage for Ina Claire in 1921 and on the screen for Gloria Swanson in 1923. (It was Lubitsch's last film for Paramount.)

. . .

That year, Lubitsch was made an Officer of the Legion of Honor by the French Government.

. . .

During Lubitsch's tenure as production chief of Paramount, he once planned to redo the story *La Chienne*, by Georges de la Fouchardière, which had served Jean Renoir so well for the harsh and unrelenting film he made of it in 1931. Out of a sordid tale of a prostitute who enters into a casual liaison with an unhappily married *petit bourgeois* who kills her when she mocks him, flees, and becomes a bum, while her pimp is guillotined for the crime, Renoir fashioned a realistic social analysis of certain aspects of Montmartre life. (It might also have been called "The Pleasures and Miseries of the Poor.") Paramount hesitantly bought the remake rights for Lubitsch at his request, but the several writers assigned to the adaptation were unable to come up with a screenplay acceptable to the studio. Fritz Lang then acquired the rights for his newly formed Diana Productions and with the aid of Dudley Nichols's adaptation

[5] Hermann Bing, who had come to the U.S. with Murnau, as his assistant, and who managed to get only bit parts in Hollywood, as in Lubitsch's *The Merry Widow* and *Bluebeard's Eighth Wife*, Sternberg's *The King Steps Out*, and Julien Duvivier's *The Great Waltz*, always playing the same comic role, a German caricature complete with a vaudeville German accent and a sputtering, frenzied delivery, eventually was unable even to obtain such bit parts and, after having had no work for two years, shot himself.

made his own version, *Scarlet Street*, with Joan Bennett, Edward G. Robinson, and Dan Duryea in the roles originally played by Janie Mareze, Michel Simon, and Georges Flamant. The Lang version was no match for the Renoir original. Doubtless, censorship militated against Lang's valiant attempt to do so "un-Hollywood" a story as the devastating *La Chienne*.

It is intriguing to speculate on what Lubitsch might have succeeded in doing, through his subtlety, with so cruel a subject. But the revelation here is that behind the "flippant" delineator of sophisticated comedy there always lurked the serious dramaturgist to whom life was interesting, as Goethe had said, wherever one touched it.

Five cinema "chess moves" followed next, manipulated by the studio overlords, in which Lubitsch was removed from the direction of *The Women*, based on the Claire Booth Luce play, and George Cukor was removed from the direction of *Gone With the Wind*. Lubitsch was then assigned to a picture with Garbo, while Cukor took over *The Women*, and Victor Fleming replaced Cukor on *Gone With the Wind*.

1939

As far back as 1932, Lubitsch had wanted to make a film with Garbo but only now was he able to achieve it. For Garbo it was a real "lifesaver," after the ill-fated *Conquest*, in which she had played the Countess Walewska to Charles Boyer's Napoleon. Shooting started May 31, 1939, and was completed in fifty-eight days. It was:

Ninotchka. Metro-Goldwyn-Mayer. Premiere at Grauman's Chinese Theatre, Hollywood, October 6, 1939, and released nationally November 3, 1939. (110 min.)

Directed by Ernst Lubitsch. From a story by Melchior Lengyel. Adaptation and screenplay by Charles Brackett, Billy Wilder, and Walter Reisch. Photography by William Daniels (who had served as co-photographer on Stroheim's *Foolish Wives, Merry-Go-Round* and *Greed*). Sets by Cedric Gibbons, Randall Duell, Edwin B. Willis. Gowns by Adrian. Music by Werner Heymann. Setting: Paris, Moscow, early twenties.

Greta Garbo (Ninotchka), Melvyn Douglas (Leon), Ina Claire (Grand Duchess Swana), Bela Lugosi (Razinin); Committee from the Soviet Board of Trade: Sig Ruman (Iranoff), Felix Bressart (Buljanoff), Alexander Granach (Kopalski); Gregory Gaye (Rakonin), Rolfe Sedan (hotel manager), Ed-

win Maxwell (Mercier), Richard Carle (Gaston), George To-
bias (Commissar of Visa Bureau), Paul Ellis, Peggy Moran,
Dorothy Adams.

"Garbo laughs!" announced the publicity blurbs, but Garbo
had already laughed in *Queen Christina* for Mamoulian. For
all that, this good-humored satire on Communists vs. Capitalists was Garbo's favorite among all her American films, a
favorite of the director himself, and voted "One of the ten
Best Films of 1939." "Lubitsch Rides Again!" they said. Certainly he was high in the saddle and at the top of his most
scintillating form again. Not since *Trouble in Paradise* had he
achieved this peak.

So popular was it that it was remade twice, as *Silk Stock-
ings*—on the stage as a musical and then as a screen musical
by Rouben Mamoulian.

1940

The Shop Around the Corner. Metro-Goldwyn-Mayer, released January 25 (28?), 1940. (97 min.)
Produced and directed by Ernst Lubitsch. From a play by Nikolaus Laszlo. Screenplay by Samson Raphaelson. Photography
by William Daniels. Sets by Cedric Gibbons, Wade B. Rubot-
tom, Edwin B. Willis. Music by Werner Heymann.

Margaret Sullavan (Klara Novak), James Stewart (Alfred
Kralik), Frank Morgan (Hugo Matuschek), Joseph Schildkraut
(Ferenc Vadas), Sara Haden (Flora), Felix Bressart (Piro-
vitch), William Tracy (Pepi Katona), Inez Courtney (Ilona),
Sarah Edwards (lady customer), Edwin Maxwell (Doctor),
Charles Halton (detective), Charles Smith (Rudy). Setting:
Budapest, late thirties.

.   .   .

Lubitsch then planned to form his own production company,
but it didn't work out.

1941

That Uncertain Feeling. United Artists, released May 1, 1941. (84
min.)
Directed by Ernst Lubitsch. From the play *Divorçons*, by Vic-
torien Sardou and Émile de Najac. Adaptation by Walter
Reisch. Screenplay by Donald Ogden Stewart. Photography by
George Barnes. Sets by Alex Golitzen. Music by Werner

Heymann. Gowns by Irene. Assistants: Horace Hough, Lee Sholen.

Merle Oberon (Jill Baker), Melvyn Douglas (Larry Baker), Burgess Meredith (Sebastien), Alan Mowbray (Dr. Vengard), Olive Blakeney (Margie Stalling), and Harry Davenport, Eve Arden, Sig Ruman, Richard Carle, Mary Currier, Jean Fenwick. Setting: New York, late thirties.

A remake of *Kiss Me Again*, with the story updated and transplanted from Paris to New York. Need we add that it was no match for the original?

1942

To Be or Not to Be. United Artists, released March 6, 1942. (99 min.)

Produced by Ernst Lubitsch and Alexander Korda. Directed by Ernst Lubitsch. From a story by Lubitsch and Melchior Lengyel. Screenplay by Edwin Justus Mayer. Photography by Rudolph Maté (the great cinematographer of Dreyer's *Passion of Joan of Arc*). Sets by Vincent Korda, Julia Heron. Gowns by Irene. Music by Werner Heymann.

Carole Lombard (Maria Tura), Jack Benny (Josef Tura), Robert Stack (Lt. Stanislaws Sobinski), Felix Bressart (Greenberg), Lionel Atwill (Ravitch), Stanley Ridges (Professor Siletsky), Sig Ruman (Col. Ehrhardt), Tom Dugan (Bronski), Charles Halton (Dobosh), George Lynn (actor-adjutant), Henry Victor (Capt. Schultz), Maude Edburne (Anna), Armand Wright, Erno Verebes, Halliwell Hobbes, Miles Mander, Leslie Dennison, Frank Reicher, Peter Caldwell, Wolfgang Zilzer, Olaf Hytten, Charles Irwin, Leland Hodgson, Alec Craig, James Finlayson, Edgar Licho, Robert O. Davis, Roland Varno, Helmut Dantine, Otto Reischew, Maurice Murphy, Gene Rizzi, Paul Barrett, John Kellogg. Setting: Warsaw, early forties, during the Nazi occupation.

Lubitsch's one "controversial" film, because of one line of dialogue (discussed elsewhere in this book). The last screen appearance of Carole Lombard. Shortly afterward, she was killed in a plane crash.

1943

At the beginning of 1943, Lubitsch signed a producer-director contract with Twentieth-Century Fox.

Heaven Can Wait. Twenty-Century Fox, released August 11, 1943, (112 min.)

Produced and directed by Ernst Lubitsch. From the play *Birthdays*, by Laszlo Bus-Fekéte. Adaptation and screenplay by Samson Raphaelson. Photographed by Edward Cronjager. Sets by James Basevi, Leland Fuller, Thomas Little, Walter M. Scott. Wardrobe by René Hubert. Music by Alfred Newman. Setting: Hell, New York, and Kansas, late nineteenth century.

Gene Tierney (Martha), Don Ameche (Henry Van Cleve), Charles Coburn (Hugo Van Cleve), Marjorie Main (Mrs. Strabel), Laird Cregar (His Excellency), Spring Byington (Bertha Van Cleve), Allyn Joslyn (Albert Van Cleve), Eugene Pallette (E. F. Strabel), Signe Hasso (Mademoiselle), Louis Calhern (Randolph Van Cleve), Helene Reynolds, Aubrey Mather, Michael Ames, Clarence Muse, Scotty Beckett, Dickie Moore, Dickie Jones, Trudy Marshall, Florence Bates, Clara Blandick, Anita Bolster, Nino Pepitone, Claire Du Brey, Maureen Rodin-Ryan, Alfred Haller, Frank Orth, Grace Hampton, Charles Halton, Claire James, Rose-Anne Murray, Marian Rosamond, Adele Jurgens, Ruth Brady.

Lubitsch's first film in color. ("I liked the way Lubitsch used color in *Heaven Can Wait*," said D. W. Griffith.)

Next on the Lubitsch agenda was to be a film based on H. I. Phillips's satire on the WACS, *All Out Arlene*, kidding the idea of female military personnel. Not realized.

. . .

In late 1944, Lubitsch was stricken with illness during the production of *A Royal Scandal* (1945), a remake of his early success, *Forbidden Paradise*. Tallulah Bankhead and Charles Coburn were starred in the original Pola Negri and Adolphe Menjou roles. The adaptation this time was by Edwin Justus Mayer and Bruno Frank *sans* the participation of Lubitsch as co-writer, as he always was on his films, whether credited or not. The direction was confided to Otto Preminger. Although Lubitsch initiated the project, and was listed as the producer, the result was not a Lubitsch film. (He played a bit part in it.)

He recovered and was well enough to do a stint as an actor in a bit part in Gregory Ratoff's comedy *Where Do We Go From Here?* (1945) for Fox, in which he reputedly played a sailor who mutinies against Christopher Columbus on board the *Santa Maria* (source for this oddity: Bernard Eisenschitz.)

Under his Fox contract,[6] Lubitsch became again the nominal producer of a new film, *Dragonwyck* (1946), directed by Joseph Mankiewicz from the novel by Anya Seton, starring Gene Tierney, Vincent Price, and Walter Huston. There was nothing of Lubitsch in it.

By the Spring of 1946 he felt up to tackling the full direction of a film again.

1946

Cluny Brown. Twentieth-Century Fox, released June 1, 1946. (100 min.)

Produced and directed by Ernst Lubitsch. From the novel by Margery Sharp. Adaptation and screenplay by Samuel Hoffenstein and Elizabeth Reinhardt. Photography by Joseph La Shelle. Sets by Lyle Wheeler, J. Russell Spencer, Thomas Little, Paul Fox. Wardrobe by Bonnie Cashin. Music by Cyril Mockridge and Emil Newman. Setting: Rural England, late forties.

Charles Boyer (Adam Belinski), Jennifer Jones (Cluny Brown), Peter Lawford (Andrew Carmel), Helen Walker (Betty Cream), Reginald Gardiner (Hilary Ames), Reginald Owen (Sir Henry Carmel), C. Aubrey Smith (Col. Duff Graham), Richard Haydn (Wilson), Margaret Bannerman, Sara Allgood, Ernest Cossart, Florence Bates, Una O'Connor, Queenie Leonard, Billy Bevan, Michael Dyne, Christopher Severn, Rex Evans, Ottola Nesmith, Harold de Becker, Jean Prescott, Al Winters, Clive Morgan, Charles Coleman, George Kirby, Whit Bissell, Betty Rae Brown, Mira McKinney, Philip Morris, Betty Fairfax, Norman Ainsley, Buster Slaven.

Back to the good old fooling, as before . . .

.   .   .

Out of friendship for Douglas Fairbanks, Jr., Lubitsch read a script young Fairbanks and Robert Thoeren wrote from a story by Justin Huntly McCarthy. The script was called *The Fighting O'Flynn*, a picaresque tale set in Ireland. The director made a number of suggestions which, according to Fairbanks, benefited the film when it was subsequently produced.

.   .   .

[6] Lubitsch had by this time worked for five of the seven major American studios, excepting only Universal and Columbia.

Cluny Brown was to be Lubitsch's last film. After eight days of shooting his next one, *That Lady in Ermine* (1948), from an operetta, *This Is the Moment*, by Rudolph Schanzer and E. Welisch, adapted by Samson Raphaelson, also for Fox, and starring Betty Grable and Douglas Fairbanks, Jr., Lubitsch was stricken with a relapse of his previous illness. It was his sixth heart attack. Direction was again taken over by Otto Preminger.

On November 30, 1947, Ernst Lubitsch died.

Selected Chronological Bibliography

Any bibliography must of necessity be a limited one. However carefully selected and representative, there are bound to be omissions even when endeavoring to draw upon works in half a dozen languages as this one does. But no bibliography of Ernst Lubitsch would be complete in even a partially representative form without mention of the excellent writings on him by Richard Watts, Jr., and John S. Cohen, Jr., which appeared during 1925–1928 in the columns of *The New York Herald Tribune* and *The New York Sun*. These the interested reader will find scattered through the three volumes of *Weinberg Scrap-Books of Film Reviews* in the archives of the Film Department of The Museum of Modern Art in New York, together with those of Ted Shane of *The New Yorker* and Robert E. Sherwood of the old *Life*—these four having contributed among the most illuminating and earliest appreciations of the very special style that set "The Sultan of Satire" apart from his colleagues.

Passion (Madame Dubarry), in *Exceptional Photoplays*. National Board of Review (New York) November, 1920.
Sumurun: Ein Roman aus dem Morgenlande, by Richard Riess. A novelization of the film. Erich Reiss Verlag (Berlin) 1920.

Sumurun, in *The Nation* (New York) October 5, 1921.
Carmen, in *Exceptional Photoplays*. National Board of Review (New York) May, 1921.
Sumurun, in *Exceptional Photoplays*. National Board of Review (New York) October, 1921.

"The Film Wizard of Europe," by Herbert Howe. *Photoplay* (New York) December, 1922.
"Ernst Lubitsch—German Director," by Peter Milne. *Motion Picture Directory*, Falk Publishing Co. (London) 1922.
Loves of Pharaoh, in *Exceptional Photoplays*. National Board of Review (New York) January, 1922.
"Interview with Lubitsch," in *The New York World*, January 7, 1922.

"An Interview with Ernst Lubitsch," by Sumner Smith. *Moving Picture World*, January 7, 1922.

"Avec Ernst Lubitsch," in *Deux Ans dans les Studios Américaines*, by Robert Florey. Éditions Pascal (Paris) 1923. "Lubitsch travail avec Mary Pickford," *ibid*.

Rosita, in *Exceptional Photoplays*. National Board of Review (New York) October, 1923.

Forbidden Paradise, in *Film Daily* (New York) November 30, 1924.

Three Women (reviewed by Robert E. Sherwood), in *Life* (New York) October, 1924.

"Wie mein erster Grossfilm endstand," by Ernst Lubitsch in *Lichtbild Bühne* (Berlin) 1924.

"Conserving the Director," in *Exceptional Photoplays*. National Board of Review (New York) December, 1924. *Rosita* and *The Marriage Circle*, *ibid*.

Montmartre (Die Flamme), in *Exceptional Photoplays*. National Board of Review (New York) February, 1924.

Rosita and *Loves of Pharaoh*, in *Representative Photoplays Analyzed*, by O'Dell Scott. Hollywood, 1924.

"Status of the Directors," in *Motion Picture Classic* (New York) November, 1925.

Kiss Me Again (reviewed by Ted Shane), in *The New Yorker* (New York), August 1, 1925.

Lady Windermere's Fan (reviewed by Ted Shane), in *The New Yorker* (New York), December 12, 1925.

"Motion Pictures and the Masses," by E. Pathop in *Exceptional Photoplays*. National Board of Review (New York) February, 1925.

Let's Go to the Movies, by Iris Barry. Payson & Clark (New York) 1926.

Let's Go to the Pictures, by Iris Barry. Chatto & Windus (London) 1926.

The Marriage Circle, in *The Film Society Programme Notes* (London) January 17, 1926.

"Masters of the Motion Pictures," by Matthew Josephson. *Motion Picture Classic* (New York) August, 1926.

Lady Windermere's Fan (reviewed by Robert Herring), in *The London Mercury* (London) July, 1926.

Lady Windermere's Fan, in *National Board of Review Magazine* (New York) March, 1926.

Other Women's Husbands (reviewed by Ted Shane), in *The New Yorker* (New York) May 1, 1926.

"Ernst Lubitsch," by Jim Tully. *Vanity Fair* (New York) December, 1926.

"Lubitsch and Negri at Ufa," in *Pola Negri, Ihre Debut, Ihre Filme, Ihre Erlebnisse*, by Robert Florey. Verlag: Die Grosse Kinostars (Berlin) 1927. *ibid.*, Paris, 1927.

"Ernst Lubitsch Looks at Life and the Cinema," by Robert Grosvenor. *Cinema Art* (London) October, 1927.

"Hollywood, das Filmparadies," by Ernst Lubitsch. *Lichtbild Bühne* (Berlin) 1927.

The Student Prince, in *National Board of Review Magazine* (New York) October, 1927.

Эрнст Любич *(Ernst Lubitsch)*, by Vladimir Nedoborovo. (Moscow) 1927.

The Patriot, in *The National Board of Review Magazine* (New York) September, 1928.

The Patriot (reviewed by Gilbert Seldes), in *The New Yorker* (New York) September 15, 1928.

Three Women in "Psychology of the Films," by Dr. Hanns Sachs. *Close-Up* (Terrieet, Switzerland) November, 1928.

Weinberg Scrap-Books of Film Reviews, compiled by Herman G. Weinberg. Vol. 1—1925/26, Vol. 2—1927, Vol. 3—1928. Archives of the Museum of Modern Art Film Department (Card Index: 80.78, W–431) (New York) 1925–28.

"The Musical Talkie," by Iris Barry. *Museum of Modern Art Film Library Program Notes*, Series IV, Program 7 (New York) 1929.

The Patriot (reviewed by Celia Simpson), in *The Spectator* (London) January 5, 1929.

"Lubitsch Views the Movies," by Herman G. Weinberg. *Movie Makers Magazine* (New York) September, 1929.

"The Thrilling Installment," by Hugh Castle. *Close-Up* (Territet, Switzerland) August, 1930.

"Dans les coulisses d'un grand film," by Ali Hubert. *La Revue du Cinéma* (Paris) May, 1930.

Hollywood: Legende und Wirklichkeit, by Ali Hubert. (Foreword by Emil Jannings.) Verlag: E. A. Seemann (Leipzig) 1930.

"Lubitsch au travail," by Ali Hubert. *La Revue du Cinéma*. No. 10 (Paris) 1930.

Monte Carlo (reviewed by Alexander Bakshy), in *The Nation* (New York) October 1, 1930.

The Love Parade, in *National Board of Review Magazine* (New York) January, 1930.

Monte Carlo (reviewed by Creighton Peet), in *The Outlook and Independent* (New York) September 17, 1930.

"Motion Picture Comedy," by Harry Alan Potamkin in *New World Monthly* (New York) February, 1930.

"Ernst Lubitsch," in *La Revue du Cinéma*, Nos. 7 & 12 (Paris) 1930.

The Film Till Now, by Paul Rotha. Jonathan Cape & Harrison Smith (London) 1930.

A History of the Movies, by Benjamin Hampton. Covici–Friede (New York) 1931.

Rosita and *Monte Carlo* in *Cinema,* by C. A. Lejeune. Maclehose (London) 1931.

"Ernst Lubitsch," by Michael Orme. *Illustrated London News* (London) January 31, 1931.

"The Style of Ernst Lubitsch," by Kenneth White. *Hound & Horn* (Concord, N.H.) January–March, 1931.

Know Your Movies, by Welford Beaton. Howard Hill (Hollywood) 1932.

The Smiling Lieutenant, in *The Devil's Camera,* by R. G. Burnett and E. D. Martell. Subtitled: "The Menace of a Film-Ridden World." Chapter on *The Smiling Lieutenant* called: "To the Ultimate Sanity of the White Race." The Epworth Press (London) 1932.

Broken Lullaby (The Man I Killed), in *National Board of Review Magazine* (New York) February, 1932. *ibid.* (reviewed by Margaret Marshall), in *The Nation* (New York) February 17, 1932. *ibid., Theatre Guild Magazine* (New York) March, 1932.

"Field Generals of the Film," by Harry Alan Potamkin. *Vanity Fair* (New York) March, 1932.

"Ernst Lubitsch" (incl. *Rosita Carmen, Sumurun, Passion, Montmartre*) in *Time* (New York) February 1, 1932.

If I Had a Million (reviewed by Campbell Nairne), in *Cinema Quarterly* (Edinburgh) Spring, 1933.

"The Film of *Design for Living,*" by Alistaire Cooke in *The London Observer* (London) September 24, 1933.

"Film Directing," by Ernst Lubitsch in *The World Film Encyclopedia* (London) 1933.

"What Constitutes Good Pictures?" by John McAndrew in *National Board of Review Magazine* (New York) February, 1933.

"Notes on Hollywood Directors," by Dwight Macdonald in *The Symposium* (Concord, N.H.) April–July, 1933.

Design for Living (reviewed by Forsyth Hardy), in *Cinema Quarterly,* Vol. 2, No. 3 (Edinburgh) Spring, 1934.

The Merry Widow (reviewed by William Troy), in *The Nation* (New York) November, 1934.

The Merry Widow (reviewed by Otis Ferguson), in *The New Republic* (New York) November 21, 1934.

"Lucio D'Ambra, precurseur de Lubitsch," by Corrado Pavolini in *Scenario,* No. 1 (Paris) 1934.

"The Lubitsch Touch," in *Cue* (New York) July 27, 1935.

"La pantomima moderna," by Ernst Lubitsch. *Lo schermo*, No. 1 (Rome) 1935.

"The Versatility of Mr. Lubitsch," in *The Living Age* (Boston) June, 1936.

"Gli attori che ho diretto in America," by Ernst Lubitsch. *Cinema*, No. 28 (Milan) August, 1937. *ibid.*, *Premier Plan*, No. 32 (Lyon) March, 1964.
"Lubitsch Demands Beauties," by Ernst Lubitsch. *New York World-Telegram*, October, 1937.

History of the Cinema, by Maurice Bardèche and Robert Brassilach. Translated and edited by Iris Barry. W. W. Norton Co., and The Museum of Modern Art (New York) 1938.

The Rise of the American Film, by Lewis Jacobs. Harcourt, Brace & Co. (New York) 1939.

History of the Film, by M. Bardèche and R. Brassilach. (London) 1945.
"The Necessity for Good Critics," in *The Spectator* (London) October 28, 1945.

"Ernst Lubitsch" in *L'Écran français*, No. 129 (Paris), 1947.
An Index to the Films of Ernst Lubitsch, by Theodore Huff. (Foreword by Herman G. Weinberg.) Index Series No. 9. The British Film Institute (London) January, 1947.
From Caligari to Hitler, by Siegfried Kracauer. Dennis Dobson Ltd. (London) 1947. (Also, Princeton University Press, 1947.)
"Twenty-five Years of the 'Lubitsch Touch' in Hollywood," by Mollie Merrick. *American Cinematographer* (Hollywood) July, 1947.

"Chez Ernst," by Jean-Georges Auriol. *La Revue du Cinéma* (Paris) September, 1948. *ibid.*, translated by Ingrid Burke. *Cahiers du Cinéma*, No. 9 (American Edition, New York) March, 1967.
"Les origines du 'style Lubitsch,'" by Lotte Eisner. *La Revue du Cinéma*, No. 17 (Paris) September, 1948.
Hollywood d'Hier et d'Aujourd'hui, by Robert Florey. Prisma Éditions (Paris) 1948.
"Liste des films d'Ernst Lubitsch," by Jean Mitry and Amable Jameson. *La Revue du Cinéma*, No. 17 (Paris) September, 1948.
"Parere su Lubitsch," by G. Pozzi. *La critica cinematografica* (Parma) May, 1948.
"Ernst Lubitsch—a Symposium," in *The Screen Writer*, Vol. 3, No. 8 (Hollywood) January, 1948.
"Il cielo può attendere," by Mario Verdone. *Bianco e Nero*, No. 17 (Rome) 1948.

"Lubitsch ou l'idéal de l'homme moyen," by Mario Verdone. *La Revue du Cinéma*, No. 17. (Paris) September, 1948.

"Ernst Lubitsch," by H. H. Wollenberg. *Films in Review* (New York) September, 1948.

"Ernst Lubitsch," by H. H. Wollenberg. *Penguin Film Review*, No. 7 (London) 1948.

Fifty Years of German Film, by H. H. Wollenberg. Falcon Press (London) 1948.

"Two Masters—Lubitsch and Eisenstein," by H. H. Wollenberg. *Sight and Sound* (London) Spring, 1948.

"Sophisticated comedy," by Giulio Cesare Castello. *Bianco e Nero*, No. 9 (Rome) 1949.

"Ernst Lubitsch," in *L'Écran français*, No. 195 (Paris) 1949.

"The American Film" in *The Film Till Now*, by Paul Rotha. Twayne Publishers, Inc. (New York) 1949. Subsequent editions 1951, 1960.

Histoire du Cinéma Mondial, by Georges Sadoul. Éditions Flammarion (Paris) 1959. (First edition: 1949). *ibid.*, revised and augmented, 1966.

"La porta si apri," by Mario Verdone. *Cinema*, No. 26 (Milan) 1949.

"Las grandes figuras de la pantalla," by Antonio Barbero. *Camara*, Nos. 198–205 (Madrid) 1951.

"A Tribute to Lubitsch," by Herman G. Weinberg. *Films in Review*, Vol. 2, No. 7 (New York) August–September, 1951.

Madame Dubarry, Sumurun, Anne de Boleyn, in *L'Écran Démoniaque*, by Lotte Eisner. Éditions André Bonne (Paris) 1952.

L'avventurosa storia del cinema americano, by Lewis Jacobs. (Turin) 1952.

Heimweh nach dem Kurfürstendamm: Aus Berlins glanzvollsten Tagen und Nächten, by Pem. Lothar Blanvalet Verlag 1952.

Histoire du Cinéma, by Maurice Bardèche and Robert Brassilach. André Martel (Paris) 1953–54.

Lo schermo demoniaco, by Lotte Eisner. Edizione di Bianco e Nero (Rome) 1955.

"Lubitsch und die Kostümefilme: *Madame Dubarry, Sumurun, Anna Boleyn*," in *Dämonische Leinwand: Die Blützeit des deutschen Films*, by Lotte Eisner. Verlag Feldt & Co. (Wiesbaden-Biebrich) 1955.

"Ernst Lubitsch," by Giulio Cesare Castello. *Enciclopedia dello Spettacolo*, Vol. 6. Edizione Maschere (Rome) 1956–1966.

Unsterblicher Film, by Heinrich Fraenkel. Kindler Verlag (Munich) 1956.

"Lubitsch Kann Alles," u.s.w. in *Das Gab's Nur Einmal*, by Curt Riess. Verlag der Sternbücher (Hamburg) 1956.

Der Weg des Films, by Friedrich von Zglinicki. Rembrandt Verlag (Berlin) 1956.

The Movies, by Richard Griffith and Arthur Mayer. Simon & Schuster (New York) 1957.

L'Amour-Erotisme et Cinéma, by Ado Kyrou. Le Terrain Vague (Paris) 1957.

"Cinémathèque," by Luc Moullet. *Cahiers du Cinéma*, No. 68 (Paris) February, 1957.

"An Open Letter to the Movie Magnates," in *The Seven Lively Arts*, by Gilbert Seldes. Sagamore Press (New York) 1957. (First published in 1924).

"Ernst Lubitsch," by Leonardo Autera, plus "Lubitsch Filmography," by Roberto Chiti. *Bianco e Nero* (Rome) January, 1958.

Von Reinhardt bis Brecht, by Herbert Mering. (Berlin) 1958.

"Lubitsch registra del tempo perduto," by Roberto Paolella. *Bianco e Nero* (Rome) January, 1958.

"A German Director in Hollywood" (with reference to *Lady Windemere's Fan*, originally published May 24, 1926) in the anthology, *The American Earthquake*, by Edmund Wilson. Doubleday & Co. (New York) 1958.

"Ernst Lubitsch," by Leonardo Autera. *Filmlexicon degli autori e delle opere*. Edizione di Bianco e Nero (Rome) 1959.

"Retrospetive: Le vedova allegra," by Giulio Cesare Castello. *Cinema*, No. 50 (Milan) November 15, 1960.

"Notes on Hollywood Directors: Ernst Lubitsch," by Dwight Macdonald. *An Introduction to the Art of the Movies*, edited by Lewis Jacobs. The Noonday Press (New York) 1960.

To Be or Not to Be and *Heaven Can Wait*, by Jean Douchet in *Cahiers du Cinéma*, No. 27 (Paris) 1962.

"Letter to Herman G. Weinberg," by Ernst Lubitsch. *Film Culture*, No. 25 (New York) Summer, 1962. (In special Lubitsch section.) *ibid.* In Premier Plan Series, No. 32, on Ernst Lubitsch by Mario Verdone. SERDOC (Lyon) March, 1964.

"TV: Lubitsch," by Adriano Aprà. *Film-critica*, No. 142 (Rome) February, 1964.

Histoire du Cinéma (Vol. 1—*Le Muet*), and (Vol. 2—*Le Parlant*), by M. Bardèche and R. Brassilach. Les Septs Couleurs (Paris) 1964.

Ernst Lubitsch, by Mario Verdone. Premier Plan Series, No. 32. SERDOC (Lyon) March, 1964.

"Lubitsch et les Films à Costumes: *Madama Dubarry, Sumurun, Anne de Boleyn*," in *L'Écran Démoniaque* by Lotte Eisner. Revised edition, Eric Losefeld—*Le Terrain Vague* (Paris) 1965.
Ernst Lubitsch: Credits and Synopses of *Die Austernprinzessin, Die Puppe, Kölheisel's Töchter, Die Bergkatze,* and *Sumurun.* Album-catalogue, 26a Mostra Internazionale d'Arte Cinematografico di Venezia (Venice) August, 1965.

"Four Times Lubitsch, Die Komödie als Zeitkritik," in *Action,* No. 1 (Vienna) 1966.
Dictionnaire du Cinéma. Foreword by Carl Dreyer. Éditions Universitaires (Paris) 1966.
"En regardent tourner Lubitsch," in *La Lanterne Magique,* by Robert Florey. Cinémathèque Suisse (Lausanne) 1966.
"Psychologie du Film," by Dr. Hanns Sachs, in *Positif,* No. 74 (Paris) March, 1966.
"Mary Pickford's Directors," by Jack Spears, in *Films in Review* (New York) February, 1966.

"A Tribute to Lubitsch," in *Action!* (Directors Guild of America) (Hollywood) November, 1967.
The Great Films: Fifty Golden Years ("Ninotchka"), by Bosley Crowther. G. P. Putnam & Sons (New York) 1967.
"Lubitsch," by Bernard Eisenschitz. *Anthologie du Cinéma,* No. 23. Supplement to *L'Avant-Scène,* No. 68 (Paris) March, 1967.

"Mary Pickford," in *The Parade's Gone By* . . ., by Kevin Brownlow. Alfred A. Knopf (New York) 1968.
Cahiers du Cinéma (Paris), Special Lubitsch Number, February, 1968.

Herman G. Weinberg was born in New York City in 1908. After attending the Institute of Musical Art where he studied the violin under Louis Svecenski, preparing for a concert career, he changed his mind and entered the field of motion pictures, first scoring foreign films at the Fifth Avenue Playhouse, then subtitling them when sound came in. Since then he has provided the screen captions for over 400 French, German, Italian, etc., pictures. Beginning with *Close-Up* in 1928, he has contributed articles on the aesthetics of the cinema to most of the leading film journals throughout the world, has lectured extensively on this subject in universities in the United States and Canada, inaugurated the Index Series on directors for the British Film Institute as well as a column, *Coffee, Brandy and Cigars*, now in its seventeenth year (and currently appearing in *Film Culture* magazine), comprising "notes for an as yet unwritten history of the cinema." In 1960–61 he served as a juror at the San Francisco and Vancouver International Film Festivals and in 1964 mounted an elaborate exhibition, "Homage to Erich von Stroheim," at the Montreal International Film Festival. The following year he delivered a memorial address on Stroheim at the New York Film Festival and in 1966 at the Canadian Film Institute. He translated and edited the American editions of *50 Years of Italian Cinema* and *50 Years of Ballet and Opera in Italy* and has contributed to many anthologies on the film here and abroad. He was for ten years American Correspondent for *Sight & Sound* (London) and served in a similar capacity for *Cahiers du Cinéma* (Paris), among other film periodicals. His short film, *Autumn Fire*, an early classic of the first American *avant-garde*, is now in the collections of most of the principal film museums here and abroad. He has been "profiled" in *The New Yorker's* "Talk of the Town" and in *Esquire* and has been working on a *"magnum opus," Sin and Cinema*, a moral history of the movies, off and on for the past decade. In 1967 he published a critical study of Josef von Sternberg. Since 1960 he has been teaching a course on the history of the motion pictures as an art at The City College in New York.